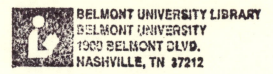

Using SOUNDTRACK

Soundtrack Version 1.2

Produce Original Music for Video, DVD, and Multimedia

CD-ROM INCLUDED

DV EXPERT SERIES

CMP Books

by Douglas Spotted Eagle

USING SOUNDTRACK

Produce Original Music for Video, DVD, and Multimedia

Douglas Spotted Eagle

CMP*Books*

San Francisco, CA • New York, NY • Lawrence, KS

Published by CMP Books
an imprint of CMP Media LLC

Main office: 600 Harrison Street, San Francisco, CA 94107 USA
Tel: 415-947-6615; fax: 415-947-6015

Editorial office:
4601 West 6th Street, Suite B, Lawrence, KS 66049 USA
www.cmpbooks.com
email: books@cmp.com

Managing Editor: Gail Saari
Cover Layout Design: Damien Castaneda

Distributed in the U.S. by: Distributed in Canada by:
Publishers Group West   Jaguar Book Group
1700 Fourth Street   100 Armstrong Avenue
Berkeley, CA 94710   Georgetown, Ontario M6K 3E7 Canada
1-800-788-3123   905-877-4483

For individual orders and for information on special discounts for quantity orders, please contact:
CMP Books Distribution Center, 6600 Silacci Way, Gilroy, CA 95020
Tel: 1-800-500-6875 or 408-848-3854; fax: 408-848-5784
email: cmp@rushorder.com; Web: www.cmpbooks.com

ISBN: 1-57820-229-9

CMPBooks

To Linda, Amanda, and Josh

Table of Contents

Foreword

Apple surprised the nonlinear software business at NAB 2003 by bundling in an entire suite of software applications with the upgrade to Final Cut Pro v4. The software in the suite that nobody expected is Soundtrack—an application for scoring pictures using audio loops as the basis.

Apple appeared to be building on the growth of the post-production market, veering into areas it never approached in the past. Traditionally, an editor was a visual storyteller who concentrated on visual flow, but as time has moved on editors are expected to have skills in compositing, typography, and, increasingly, audio. Along with the trend for multiple skills among editors, there is huge growth in the number of people participating in postproduction building due to the availability of high-quality, relatively low-cost tools. These people work on all aspects of their projects whenever they can, and Apple's Final Cut Pro v4 suite of tools is perfectly suited to their needs.

Soundtrack is an elegantly simple piece of software, in the Apple tradition. It is deceptively simple to use and much harder to use well. Ideally we'd all learn Soundtrack from someone who is a skilled musician and understands the structure of music: someone who has scored music and produced and edited video and is a skilled teacher.

Fortunately, CMP Books is fortunate to have Douglas Spotted Eagle to fit the bill. Douglas may be best known as a Grammy Award winner for his work in audio, but this is only one award among many he has received from the music industry. He's an accomplished performance musician who has scored soundtracks for productions as diverse as the *X-Files* and *Johnny Quest* cartoons and created music loops for Sony Pictures Digital Acid—loops that work well in Soundtrack. There's no doubt about his musical credentials.

Parallel to a successful musical career, Douglas has filmed, edited and produced media that's found its way into nine Emmy-nominated productions. He has also won film festival awards for personal projects and acclaim for his first music video project. His production and postproduction credentials are impeccable.

Anyone who has sat in on a class with him, or had to privilege to teach with him as I have, knows that he is no less talented in his ability to communicate his great joy helping people to access software tools, as well as personal creativity. Douglas is a proficient and popular teacher who is entertaining and informative.

Soundtrack is the nexus of picture and sound. I can't think of a better person to unlock its power for the rest of us than the very talented Douglas Spotted Eagle.

—Philip Hodgetts

Introduction

SOUNDTRACK IS A MUSICAL BULLDOZER

In one fell swoop, it levels the playing field for video editors held hostage waiting for music editors to create the "right" piece of music. It levels the playing field for creative people who "hear" music in their heads and want to express that music, but don't have a strong (if any) musical background. It levels the playing field for multimedia people who need a specific sound but can't find it in a music library, providing them the opportunity to create great sounds using great musicians they otherwise wouldn't have access to.

Imagine having Rudy Sarzo of Quiet Riot playing bass for you, Allen White of Beatles and Yes, or maybe Bunn E. Carlos on drums, Neil Schon of Journey, Reek Havoc, Phil Collen of Def Leppard on guitar, or perhaps you'd prefer André Mehitmo on classical guitar, Dave Trueblood on acoustic guitar? Denny Jaeger or Miroslav Vitous on strings, or perhaps even the Moscow Symphony driving your musical magic bus? Perhaps you need a nine-foot Bosendorfer grand piano sound, or even want the piano on which Paul McCartney recorded "Let It Be." With any number of well-known vocalists from Istanbul, Turkey, Mexico, Brazil, Ireland, Spain, Russia, or Native America singing for you, who needs singers?

While a private session with any of these musicians would cost thousands of dollars and involve all sorts of legal licensing hassles, these cats can now all come into your editing room via the loops that they've created. At no cost. With no royalties due. No needle-drop fees. No licensing. No hassle. With you in total and complete control at all times. All with a sound quality that you couldn't begin to approach recording or capturing them yourself unless you happen to own the best mics, preamps, monitors, control room, tracking room, and golden ears. You don't even have to pay for coffee breaks, deal with late musicians, or have anyone arguing with you about the quality of their performance.

Loops are composed and created, recorded and saved by some of the best musicians in the business. Sometimes loops are even extracted from recording sessions from greats like William Aura, James Brown, the Spinners, Moby, and other monster names. Loops have been used in music composition for years. Ricky Martin allegedly used loops for most of his hit "Livin' la Vida Loca." (I recognize many sounds on his album as ACID loops.) My own loops have been heard in hundreds if not thousands of broadcast projects as diverse as Jeep commercials and big screen films like "Open Range," "Murder by Numbers."

Even a person with no musical acumen can fairly easily create music for video beds, commercial spots, atmospheric and emotional expressions, while an editor with a slightly musical ear or possessing the most basic knowledge of music can create beautiful masterpieces. Of course any editor with musical skills and a concept of how emotion and picture come together can create a hit-level song if they really put their mind to it. Soundtrack makes all this and more possible.

This book is but one step in the creative process. It demonstrates how the application works; it cannot demonstrate the emotional palette although I've done my best to express some basic solutions to simple tricks to play on a listener's ear. Experience and time are the bigger part of the creative process. Maturing through involvement creates a true master of any craft, and creating music for film or video definitely requires a mature ear.

The main reason I wrote this book is that editors need audio libraries like bread needs butter. Without great sounds, no video production really carries the impact that it can otherwise carry. I submit that audio is 70% of the video experience. Our ears are far more sensitive than our eyes, hearing much of what is going on around us, and our eyes often receive cues from what we hear. Music libraries are either poor sounding or very expensive. You don't get "good" from a cheap library. In addition, many libraries require pay for use, and there are hassles with copyrights, royalties, and information access—just finding the copyright holder for a specific piece of music is often challenging, even with a clearinghouse like Harry Fox Agency. So what do editors do? Often, they use copyrighted music without permission. While they may get away with this for local and small productions, it's at tremendous risk to the editor and client. No editor with half a brain would ever attempt this with a national production whether it's for hire, for charity, for free, or for fun. It's a quick way to the poorhouse, as fines are incredibly stiff.

Sonic Foundry's ACID changed all this a few years back. Major television productions have been scored with ACID, including live shows like portions of the Academy Awards, scored by David Was. Most major musicians use loops at some point in their creative process, even if it's merely a sketchpad for the work. Quiet Riot still uses ACID to compose between the band members, e-mailing files back and forth until they've hit on a composition they like, and then they go into the studio to personally play the parts they've put together in the software. After adding their vocals they're done. This saves time, money, and often some of the hair-pulling frustration that comes with having four creative minds in the same room all at once. That alone is worth the price of admission to the Soundtrack world.

Loops now abound like rabbits in July, and at last attempted count, there were more than 200 websites offering loop downloads, and over eight million loops available. Having a terabyte drive filled with loops makes for difficult decisions when it comes time to work around a difficult sound, but at least I know the loop is there, I just gotta find it. Soundtrack's Loop Utility makes this much easier, but inserting the correct information about the loop is critical to useful searches. Having access to so many loops is the blessing and curse of a tool like Soundtrack. If you are a video editor, imagine having access to any kind of stock footage your heart could possibly desire, at a fixed price, and you know it was shot by the best camera men in the world in some of the most exotic locations in the world. This is what Soundtrack and loops bring to the table.

WHO DID I WRITE THIS BOOK FOR?

You.

This book is filled with opinion and personal experience that formed those opinions. I make no apology but also expect that you will form your own opinions from your own experience, which may well be different than mine. For instance, I find the Contour Shuttle Pro to be a useful tool, and a friend who had a lot of dialog with me while writing this book, finds it cumbersome. I guess that means he likes mice and key shortcuts: hence the number of shortcuts found in the book.

The book is not organized so that it's easy to skip through sections, as Soundtrack is a new tool, and so follows a fairly linear format. Beginning sections are at the front of the book, Advanced sections are in the middle of the book, with workflow tips and tricks towards the end. I've written it this way because as they say, "You need to crawl before you walk, walk before you run."

There are some tips and tricks related to Final Cut Pro, but you don't need FCP to make this application worthwhile. There are a couple tips for DVD authors and Flash animators as well, but this book is primarily about making music, and learning to make the music work for you and your client. Bottom line with Soundtrack is that you could blindly throw a bass line over any drum line, with a guitar thrown on top for fun, and have a song, zero thought required. But, to make it work with the scene, or to make it a musically compelling or interesting composition, this book will offer you the shortcuts, tips, and some tricks to make that happen for you.

WHAT IS ON THE CD IN THE BACK OF THE BOOK?

Loops, loops, and more loops. The folks from PowerFX, Sony, Peace/Love Productions, and Cheaploops, all made some additional loops available for you to use in hopes that your interest will be piqued and you'll want more. Loops are like a drug; they can be addictive. Available for download even more easily than iTunes, available in huge libraries or as single pieces. Even complete songs are purchasable as loops, you only need assemble them.

So, there are lots of loops on the CD.

There are also starter pieces of songs, plus songs related to specific tutorials. There are songs on the CD that are not mentioned in the book. You'll want to load all the loops on the CD to your hard drive for best results. These songs are for your use to complete, fade out, or use to your heart's content. There is no copyright on them, so have fun. You might find yourself tapping your feet to one or two of them.

There is also a lot of demo software on the CD. Not because I'm trying to help the vendors sell anything, but because these are tools that significantly improve Soundtrack (and Final Cut Pro, Peak if you have them).

Fade Out

Even though it's mentioned in the book a couple times, I strongly urge editors to think of music and musical components in terms of colors.

White colors equal bright, twinkle-like sounds.

Midrange colors, such as blues, reds, and greens, are solid, melodic or rhythmic sounds, without a lot of incidentals.

Dark colors are bass-oriented sounds, deeper sounds. Bass/deep sounds don't have to be equated with ominous but rather the texture of the sounds. Textures with lots of bass, and solidly moving, thick sounds illustrate darker colors well.

Composing with colors and how they play across the musical spectrum helps get the creative juices flowing. These aren't rules by any means. But everyone needs a place to start. And like these pages establish a good foundation, being aware of these small guidelines will smooth the field.

Acknowledgments

As with any written effort, the author assumes all responsibility for errors, but since I like to share responsibility, I'd like to thank several people for making this opportunity become a reality.

First and foremost, Linda and Amanda, the two stars in my sky. Thank you for supporting me throughout the work, and understanding why there were always two laptops laying around with wires poking all over the place. This book was done almost entirely on the road. As hotels are rarely good recording studios, I ended up writing a lot in my bedroom, where any spouse will tell you that wires don't belong. Amanda, thank you for keeping the Rocky Road ice cream coming and the cashew bowl filled. In all seriousness, I couldn't do what I do without the both of you. My life is so much better with you in it.

Huge thanks go out to Dorothy Cox, Paul Temme, and the entire group at CMP Media. What an awesome group. Thanks for putting up with various writings as the application changed over time. (Don'cha just hate new revs in the middle of writing?) Paul, thanks for the hand-holding during the conception of this book.

Stephen Schleicher, thank you for your amazing patience, inspirational input, and technical assistance not only as a tech editor, but a real help to the quality of information in the book and for pointing out the potholes I'd left in the road during the writing process. You are simply amazing in the breadth of your knowledge.

Alec, Chris, Xander, Mary, and Dmitri at Apple, thanks for your help in answering questions as various attributes revealed themselves. The use of the Apple graphics are much appreciated. Chris Molious, it's amazing that an ACID trip and a couple of libraries so long ago could lead to this project. Jason Long, you rock, dude. OS X is everything you said it was and more. Apple has a great advocate in you.

Phillip Hodgetts, thanks for spending the time and hours with me working on setting up my latest laptop. You and Rich Harrington have the patience of saints. I owe you both big. Tom Wolsky, thanks for your Final Cut Pro input. I'll do lunch with you anytime.

Jason and the crew at Bias, Bob, Gilad, Jay at WAVES, you guys have always been responsible for the great sounds I get from my machines and instruments. I wish everyone in the world knew how wonderful WAVES tools really are. (Or maybe I don't. I'd lose my edge.) Seriously, thanks for all the support, and for getting the AU shell done before this book was finished. It adds a lot to FCP and Soundtrack's capabilities.

Bil at PowerFX, Jason/DJ Puzzle at PeaceLove Productions, Dave Chaimson at Sony, Mike Schiebinger at Sony, Steve/Cheaploops, Guitarwav.com, thanks for the great loops.

As always, Milo and Bill at Echo Audio; you still make the best audio tools I've ever worked with. The Indigo I/O is a tool that every laptop shouldn't be without.

Mannie Frances, thanks for keeping the phone calls and emails at bay. Can't wait to do a Soundtrack/FCP VASST tour.

Rudy Sarzo, you're awesome—Quiet Riot, Ozzy Osbourne, and Whitesnake wouldn't be nearly as great without you. Thanks for the education, the inspiration, the shoulder, and your friendship. God bless, my friend. Looking forward to a wonderful future in digital media with you.

Keith Medley and Dan Moore, Mackie speakers make my studio as solid as a wall, and sounding like a symphony. Thank you for the tremendous support over the years. I hope Soundtrack brings you a bushel of new users.

Thanks to Angus at FXPansion, the adapter works wonderfully. VST in Soundtrack. Who'da thunk it!

I can't forget the terrific folks at Auralex, makers of sonic treatments, including the pyramids found in the voiceover/recording box in this book. Thanks Brian!

Steve at Audio Technica, makers of wonderful recording mics, all of my own loops found in this book are recorded with their amazing tools. I've been an AT endorsee for nearly 10 years, have won Grammys with their tools, and been nominated for several thanks in part to the AT tools.

Monster thanks to the team at Higher Octave Music/EMI, thanks for getting my music out there. Aura, you are one of the most amazing people I've ever known. Thanks for inspiring me to do this book. Craig Chaquico, you've always been an inspiration. Ozzy, one day I want to play like you do.

Thanks to the folks at Disney, HBO, Showtime, Sony Pictures, Capital Records, Windham Hill, and everyone else involved in my recording career. The tips in this book came about as a result of my career path.

Meade Steadman, thank you for living up to your last name. No one on earth is as steady or grounded as you. We've crossed the world a dozen times over, but it's always a fun adventure with you along. Thanks for guiding and directing the band.

Bill Bonifas, Eric Hervey, John Seydowitz, Stix, Sean Halley, Wil Grimshaw, Tracy Neilson; there is no better support band in the world. John Frazier, the Lakota Nation is much stronger for your spirit and percussion. Keep banging those hands and dancing for the People.

Lawrence Lim and Cindy Sheng, thanks for the time in Singapore. It was inspirational creating music in Asia, and the singing bowls are awesome. (Check out the loops on the CD in this book)

Special thanks to the DMN crew, www.dmnforums.com. Many of the posts inspired sections of this book. Thanks to David Nagel and Charlie White for all the great information and ideas.

Lou Wallace, Frank Molstad Steve Pitzel, Kim Allred, Steve Thomas, Lonnie Bates, Carl Jacobsen, Doug and Susan Morton/QUp, Mike Downey, Tim Kolb, Karl Penman, Jim Morrell, Hartley Peavey, Steven Seagal, Viggo Mortenson, Peter Buffett, Pete Hedrick, Ryan Lincoln, Kerri, Tom Bee, you are all tremendous inspirations. Thanks for all you do.

Finally, thanks to you, the reader, for being interested in the application and for reading this book. It's greatly appreciated.

Seriously, any and all errors in this book are entirely my own. I wish I could shift the blame, but it's my name on the cover, and therefore my responsibility.

Chapter 1

Soundtrack—
Music Creation by Nonmusicians, Too

Soundtrack, Apple's latest offering to the creative world, is a tool born and built for video editors who need music (soundtracks) for their video projects and loopable audio for a DVD menu, as well as for Flash™ animators, remixers of music, DJs, and the wannabe musician in most creative people.

Soundtrack isn't going to make anyone a Hans Zimmer or John Barry overnight, but it sure can go a long way towards creating good sound. Is it possible to make a hit song with Soundtrack? Absolutely. The loops available for Soundtrack have been recorded by some of today's most popular producers, musicians, and recording artists. These royalty-free, awesome musical puzzle pieces need only be assembled with an ear for good compositing and mixing. From the video editor's perspective, assembling a great mix is no different than assembling a deep composite of visual elements designed to excite the eye and transmit a specific message. Soundtrack works much the same way: you assemble various pieces of media to create an exciting musical message. The only difference is that the media has been created by the Spielbergs, Jaffes, Lucas', and Camerons of the music world.

Soundtrack is installed with the 4.0 version of Final Cut Pro (FCP) and is also sold as a standalone application. Whether or not FCP is part of your workflow, or Soundtrack is being used as a

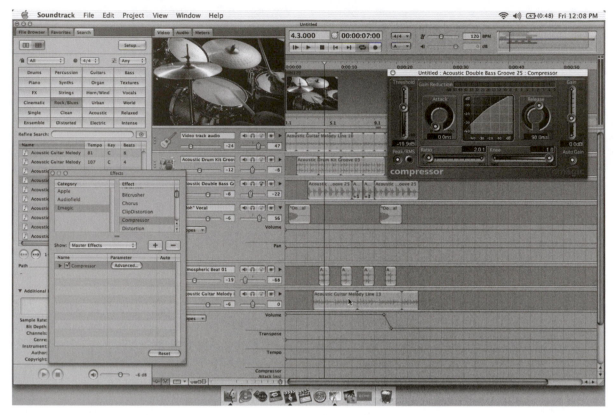

1.1   Soundtrack's workspace is much like a digital audio workstation (DAW) layout. Video clip from Artbeats.

scoring tool for another nonlinear editing (NLE) system won't be significant, since both formats are explained in this book.

HOW SOUNDTRACK WORKS

The audio bed used in a video or film project is often referred to as the "score." Actually, the original use of the term refers to the printed sheet music read by musicians during the recording or composing of the music used in the film or video soundtrack.

Music is built of repetitive mathematical values, most often based around groups known as "measures." A measure is a length of time, determined by the tempo of the music, typically broken

1.2   Place the Soundtrack icon on the docking bar for fast access.

1.3   Various beat counts in three different measures. Each measure is assigned a value of four beats per measure. In this illustration, one measure has a note on every beat, one measure has an eighth note on every beat allowing for two notes per beat, and the third measure has three notes per beat. The length of the measure does not change, only the number of fractions of a beat, or note value per beat.

down into a number of "beats." In most contemporary music there are four beats in a measure. Some music contains three or six beats in a measure. The time between beats in a measure is known as "tempo." If you can count to four, you can use Soundtrack easily, even if you can't always hear where the beats in music may occur. Of course, having a sense of rhythm and being able to hear musical beats is beneficial to you while using Soundtrack, but it is not critical.

Soundtrack uses a format of audio known as "looping." A loop is a number of beats, just like a measure in printed musical scores. The beats repeat after a determined length of time or a certain number of beats. The loop point allows the short section of audio to repeat without the listener being aware that a start/ end point has occurred. Think of a score as a long-form video project containing thousands of keyframes, potentially hundreds of scenes and a loop as a single scene or image that may be built upon in a composited project, possibly repeated for effect.

> **Compositions:** Songs are often referred to as compositions because they are often made of "composites" of blended musical phrases, instruments, and dynamics in layers of sound. Video is analogous to this because it too is composited by blending titles and multiple layers of imagery.

For a loop to be useful in most instances, the length is limited to four or eight beats in a measure. Occasionally loops are longer, but generally speaking, the longer a loop, the less control maintained over it during the musical composition process.

Using building blocks of loops, Soundtrack assembles the blocks and automatically matches tempo and pitch. This enables even the most tone-deaf editor to create an interesting score. In Figure 1.4, these blocks are seen in their various "moments" in the soundtrack of the video.

What makes Soundtrack unique is that loops are made to match up to each other, regardless of the tempo (speed) or key (pitch) in which the looped music was originally recorded. This is achieved through the inclusion of "metadata" or information related to the data in the sound file. Metadata informs Soundtrack of what tempo, pitch, musical style, and instrument content is in the loop, enabling Soundtrack to process intelligently.

This metadata, sometimes referred to as a "tag," is contained in both Apple Loops and ACIDized loops and inserted in various sound editing applications or in the Soundtrack Loop Util-

1.4   The beginning and ending points of the loop are usually easy to see when the loop has percussive elements. However, this particular loop is deceiving due to the placement of the downbeat.

ity tool. When authoring or converting loops, including these tags in the data of the file is important in order to search for the loop and ensure correct behavior on the Timeline. We'll look at authoring loops more deeply later in the book.

HOOKED UP

Soundtrack hogs system resources when a number of loops are used. Having the proper tools, system configuration, and high-quality equipment makes the experience with Soundtrack a good one.

Digital audio, while not as intensive and demanding as video files, shouldn't be taken lightly. Long projects, or projects that have a high number of loops, will eat RAM fast. While Soundtrack is able to run on only a 500Mhz processor and 384MB of RAM, having an 800Mhz processor with at least 768MB of RAM is recommended. To see how much RAM is installed in the system,

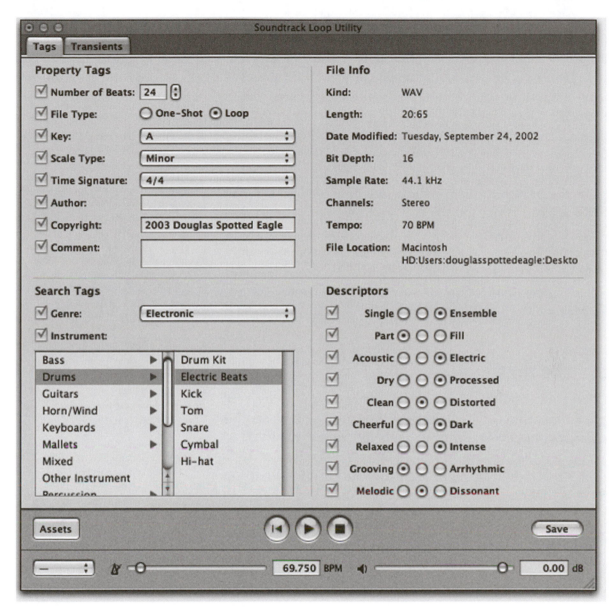

1.5   Metadata is defined in the Soundtrack Loop Utility. Notice that the metadata includes genre, tempo, pitch, and other information that aids in the search for the type of loop desired in a project.

click the Apple Menu icon in the upper left hand corner of the screen, and select About This Mac. Here you will find how much RAM is installed.

As with any application, the bigger, better, and faster the machine, the more pleasant the operation of the software. An iMac will run Soundtrack, though the number of tracks is limited and performance is thus diminished. A G4 Powerbook is quite capable of great performance. Of course, the ultimate setup is to have a loaded G5 with multiprocessors, lots of storage space, and lots of RAM. That setup is certainly not required, but if you are running other applications simultaneously, such as Final Cut Pro, the added expense of a top-end system will create a fast and efficient workflow. Soundtrack is capable of providing up to 126 tracks of playback, so if you are really adventurous and want to create monstrously deep projects, a fast machine fully loaded with RAM is required for this project. A Gigabyte (GB) of RAM is nowhere near overkill, and more than a GB is wonderful. Of course, if you are editing in FCP, you'll be happy for the extra RAM anyway.

Look for this logo which indicates Audio Unit compliance.

In the past, recording studios were often defined by their outboard equipment and by how each piece of gear complemented every other. Today's "outboard" gear in the form of processing tools, or "plug-ins," help define and control sounds, allowing every engineer, producer, or artist to create a unique sound. Apple's AU format uses fewer processor resources and RAM, yet plug-ins will rapidly eat up memory. It is best to have plenty available.

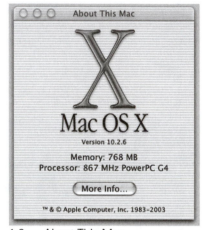

1.6   About This Mac

STORING FILES

Storage of audio, like video, is best done on a separate hard drive. Audio files will indeed stream from a CD-ROM, yet this is not efficient. Plan on copying audio files from a CD-ROM to a hard drive.

It's best to have audio files in a separate drive for maximum efficiency. Given the size of audio loops, though small as individual files, it takes little time to fill up a 180GB hard drive with loops. This is particularly true if you sign up for a loop-subscription service. Data tanks that use FireWire to connect to the computer are readily available for a nominal cost from ADS, Maxtor, Belkin, and other providers of FireWire enclosures.

1.7   AU Logo

These are great to use, particularly when using a laptop for ease of moving around. These drive kits are portable, so they may be taken from session to session, or even to remote recording locations. The drive enclosure mounts automatically when the drive is connected via the FireWire connection. To disconnect the drive, simply drag its icon to the trash/eject icon on the dock. This will dismount the drive and enable you to take it to the next recording event or editing session. *Make certain you do not disconnect the drive without first dragging it to the trash to disconnect it*. If by chance this happens, It's likely you'll need to run the First Aid/Repair Disk Permissions found in the Utilities folder on your hard drive. (Open the Disk Utilities to find the Disk Permissions tool.)

1.8   The ADS Data tank may be connected via FireWire or USB

Memory: Audio uses up a lot of memory quickly. A 44.1Khz/16 bit audio file will take up 10 meg a minute, and a 24 bit file will take up 15 meg or more a minute. While this is nowhere near as consuming as video, it must be considered when doing long or numerous compositions.

1.9   The Contour Shuttle Pro v2 gives users fingertip access to most common functions in Soundtrack.

For those using Panther, be aware that there are issues related to external FireWire drives that should be repaired by the time this book is available. You should be cognizant of the issue in the event Apple has not updated their OS.

MOUSIN' AROUND

Having a two or four-button mouse for tasks in Soundtrack is highly desirable. Soundtrack takes heavy advantage of right-click functionality and some users may find the Control+click to be cumbersome with the number of submenus in Soundtrack. Better still is the Contour Shuttle Pro, which not only allows fast function access in Soundtrack, but also provides a Human User Interface (HUI) for the user to control the stop/start and other common functions in Soundtrack. There is a set of Contour Shuttle Pro preferences on the CD-ROM contained in this book that may be loaded for immediate access to scrolling and controlling functions in Soundtrack and Peak.

Using a soundcard, such as the Echo Audio Layla or Indigo, will substantially improve the monitoring experience. It will also allow for higher sample rates to be used for non-video projects. (DV only allows for 8Khz/16Mb files to be printed back to the camera.) In due time, Soundtrack will most likely support multichannel interfaces for audio monitoring and output. So having the added channels now may not be immediately beneficial, but the quality of audio is worth the expense.

M-Audio (www.m-audio.com) has a solid product line of FireWire audio devices, as does Echo Audio (www.echoaudio.com). Also, Mark of the Unicorn (www.motu.com) manufactures audio interface devices in both PCI and FireWire units. Meanwhile, USB units at present are still too latent to be of serious use for monitoring and mixing audio with recording applications.

INSTALLING SOUNDTRACK

While installation of Soundtrack is fairly straightforward, there are some pitfalls that may be avoided.

1. First, be sure the computer has a fresh install of Final Cut Pro, and then update OS X prior to installation of Soundtrack or at the least run the Disk Utility. (Utilities in the Applications> Utilities folder.)

2. Soundtrack operates on OS X v10.2.5 or higher. To update the system, you'll need to be online, then go to System Preferences> System> Software Update. Select the Check Now button to update the operating system to the latest version. For the moment, only update the operating system.

3. Insert the Soundtrack or FCP disk and follow the installation instructions. If a separate disk is installed on the system, load the loops to that disk, while installing the application software to the C: drive. If any additional loop disks are available, now is a good time to copy those from CD to hard drive as well.

1.10   The Echo Indigo cardbus for iBook and Powerbook.

Master Volume: When working with audio in the NLE or DAW environment, place the master volume of the computer at the midway to three-quarter points. Access the Master Volume at upper right hand corner of your desktop or in System Preferences/Sound. Don't set it to maximum volume, although that may seem typical for most editing. Set system volume at mid-point or three-quarter volume Then let the NLE or Soundtrack set the volume in conjunction with the volume set on the monitors. Set a comfortable listening level with the NLEs output and Soundtrack's output controls, leaving the speaker monitors at the manufacturer's recommended level or 0dB.

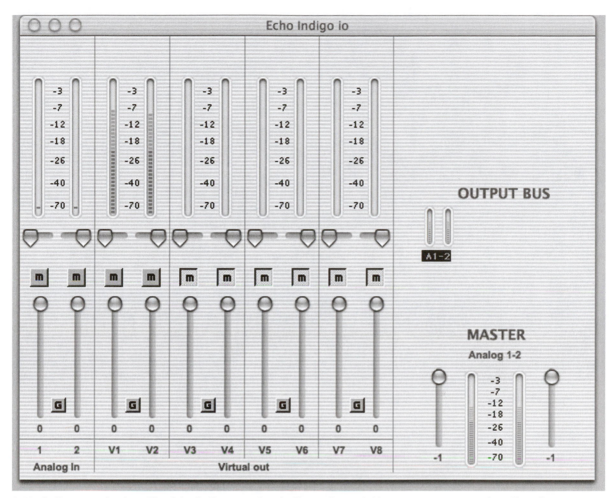

1.11 Indigo console shot. The Echo Indigo soundcard offers substantial improvement to sound quality when compared to the built-in sound card of the Apple Powerbook.

Again, It's important to store sounds on a hard drive rather than a CD-ROM for maximum playback capability and accessibility within Soundtrack.

While the OS X is fairly optimized for media authoring, there are a few tricks that may be employed to further optimize any system for video or audio editing/recording.

4. Click on the Apple menu icon in the upper left-hand corner of the screen and select System Preferences. This is the same place from which the Software Update was accessed. Return to the Software Update menu in that menu and uncheck the Automatically Check for Updates when you have a network connection dialog. This step prevents the Updater from checking for updates while you are in the middle of an editing/recording session and potentially causing a

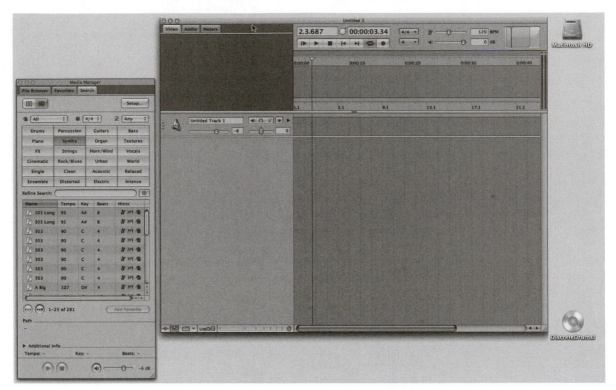

1.12   The Soundtrack work surface may be viewed as a single view or with separate windows.

1.13   The Disk Utility is
found in the
Applications
folder on the hard
drive.

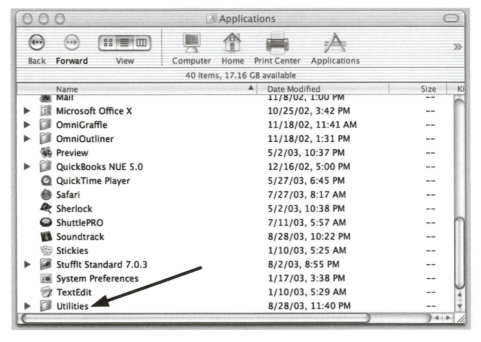

1.14 Run the Updates check often to be sure that the OS is up to date.

1.15 Uncheck any unwanted updates. Notice that the iPod update is not being accepted. *(left)*

1.16 The update manager will ask you to quit or cancel. Choose Quit if desired updates have been installed. *(below)*

Backup! Prior to installing Soundtrack, It's a good idea to copy everything on the system to a second hard drive as a backup. Unlike OS 9 where it is easy and fast to fully restore the system, OS X doesn't copy the OS. Also, there are hidden files, so simply copying the OS doesn't carry them over. You can create a disk image by using the Disk Copy utility, and then restore it by using the Apple Software Restore to rebuild the system/partition. Having a backup of the application and files is always a good idea when installing new software in the event that there is a problem.

1.17   The Application icon will appear on the OS X dock.

crash or unintentionally sharing system resources. Back out of the Software Update menu by selecting Show All in the upper left of the Software Update menu.

5. Now choose the General preferences and select '5' in the Application dropdown menu. Do the same for the Documents dropdown menu.

6. Select the Network icon by double-clicking it. The Network dialog will open. Select the Apple-Talk tab in this dialog and turn off AppleTalk. There should be no check in the Make Apple-Talk Active dialog box. Click back to the System Preferences menu by selecting the Show All button in the upper left corner of the Network dialog box.

7. This time, choose the Displays icon. Once again, double click it. Be sure that the display is showing Millions in the colors dropdown dialog box. Soundtrack requires a display size of at least 1152×768, but a minimum of 1280×854 is recommended.

> **Dock:** Any application, file, or drive alias may be placed on the dock for easy access, although It's quite easy to fill the dock, making it slow and unwieldy to manage and sort through. Keep only necessary tools on the dock for best results. Many users find keeping the dock small, hidden, and set up for high magnification works best for them.

8. Finally, return to the System Preferences by selecting the Show All button, and double-click the Energy Saver icon. Set this to the Highest Performance setting if you plan on long renders of multi-layer audio for video. This is less necessary for Soundtrack alone, but it is a good idea to set this preference when editing/creating video in FCP or any other editing application. This setting prevents the hard drive or system from going to sleep during long, slow renders. With the System Preferences menu open, select Command+Q to quit the application.

9. After Soundtrack installs, it will appear on the dock at the bottom of the screen (or another location where the dock may be specified to appear). Only the Soundtrack icon will appear. Users who create their own loops, or import loops, may find the Soundtrack Loop Utility is easiest to find if it also is on the dock. This is found in the Applications> Utilities folder. Drag it from the folder to the dock and place as desired, creating an alias for the Soundtrack Loop Utility. If only factory loops are being used, or other such loops purchased for use in Soundtrack, this tool will most likely not be used and is best left off the dock.

10. After installing Soundtrack, It's a good idea to check for updates to the application by visiting the Software Updates menu in the *System Preferences* folder. While updating Soundtrack, check for updates to QuickTime and any other audio- or video-related applications.

11. Also, when following installation of Soundtrack, whether as a standalone or with Final Cut Pro, don't forget to register. As a registered user, you are given notice of add-on tools, special offers, and other useful stuff.

DISCOVERING SOUNDTRACK'S INTERFACE

Opening Soundtrack for the first time may surprise users who are not familiar with the look of a digital audio workstation (DAW). Soundtrack's work surface is deceptively simple, but hidden inside the grid are all sorts of functions. The majority of the work is done in the two primary windows: the Timeline area and the Media Manager window. On first look, Soundtrack appears to be three work surfaces, but in reality, there are only two surfaces with which to be concerned.

Timeline

Found on the right side of the screen, the Timeline contains a window for video that is inserted and, when working with Final Cut Pro, scoring markers become visible complete with scoring marker names/tags. When working with the stand-alone version of Soundtrack, video may be imported, but no scoring markers/tags are available, as only FCP controls this interaction between the two applications. Creating music beds for video is only one of the uses of Soundtrack, other uses will be explored in other sections.

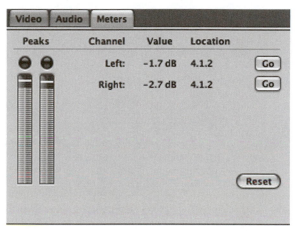

1.18 Output level is displayed in the Meters view

Media Manager

Moving to the left side of the screen, the Media Manager contains tools with which to browse for loops and video files, store favorite loops, locations of loops and video files, and search intelligently using metadata to locate loops based around personal preferences.

Above the track header area is the video preview window that indicates the location of the playhead in the video file. There are also tabs for audio and metering. The Audio tab will indicate files used thus far in the current project, this is much like a media pool or bin. The Meters tab, as shown in Figure 1.18, will display audio output levels.

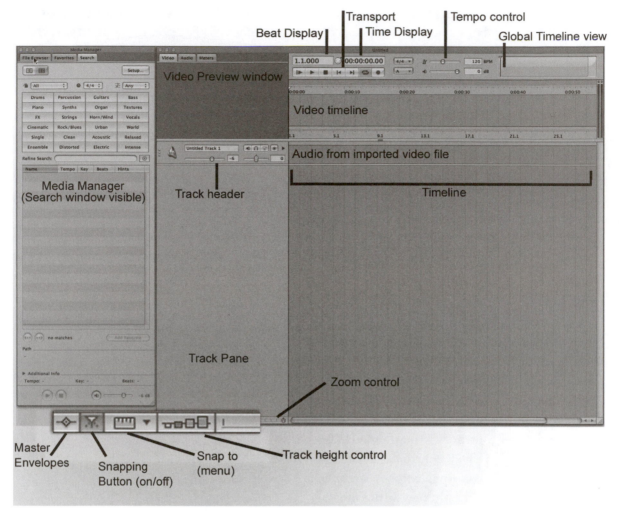

1.19   The primary tools in the Soundtrack workspace.

Layers of audio are created in the Timeline workspace and blended together, automatically controlled by Soundtrack's metadata. Volume, right to left/panning information, and effects are controlled at the track level. The name of a file is displayed in the track header in addition to the name of a file indicated in the waveform on the Timeline. Figure 1.19 points out the most-used tools in the Soundtrack workspace.

THE MENU BAR

Soundtrack can be set up to work with personal tastes. Find these settings under the Soundtrack Preferences menu. Preferences can be set to be more or less musically oriented, depending on the user's musical and technical capabilities.

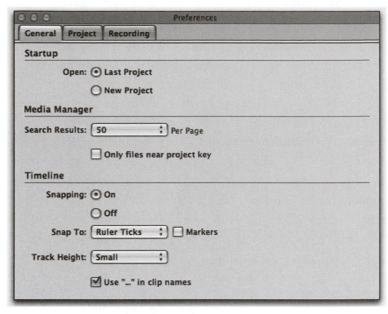

1.20 This menu allows users to specify how Soundtrack behaves in the editing and recording process.

In the General tab, users are asked to specify how projects open, how many search results should be displayed, and how the Timeline snaps. Users whose workflow might involve a lot of tweaking on a project will find the Open> Last Project to be of benefit. Soundtrack opens the last project modified. Checking the New Project box will open a clean slate (see Figure 1.20).

The Media Manager Search Results preference may be set here. Though logic might suggest viewing as many results as possible, most users will be happiest with fewer results. Setting this

1.21 For users who are not musically savvy, it is best to start snapping to either ruler ticks or markers.

does not reduce the number of possible loops that may be used in a project; this selection only reduces the number of loops viewed on a page. The more loops, the greater the potential to become overwhelmed with choices. At the time of this writing, there are over five million loops available for Soundtrack, so sorting them is a daunting task.

Timeline preferences allow users to specify whether the playhead/cursor will snap to musical time, ruler ticks, or markers. Newcomers to music composition and theory may find it most useful to snap to Ruler Ticks or Markers or both (see Figure 1.21). This assures that loops will snap to the most basic position and the most-used snap-to point in composing, regardless of the users' ability. Advanced users or users with a musical background desiring more precise placement of loops may wish to snap the cursor based around divisions of musical time, such as quarter notes or eighth notes. Generally, the Ruler Ticks and Markers are the most common snap-to points; however, edited loops, one shots, and split-loop sections may need more precise control and placement (see Figure 1.22).

1.22 Set the Search Results preference to suit individual needs. It's a good idea to set this for fewer, rather than greater, numbers of page views, simply for better organization.

Filenames may be viewed in three different locations: on the track header display (first file dragged/inserted to a new track), in the audio bin found beneath the video preview (all files used in project), and inside the waveform on the Timeline (references to locations of all files). These locations are particularly useful to know if more than one file is inserted on a track that already contains audio.

Track Height preferences may be set here as well. If the user is inserting large numbers of tracks, say greater than 10, it will probably be beneficial to set this preference at "small" while users who find themselves inserting fewer tracks may find that "medium" to "large" is optimal.

The Project tab creates preferences based on common musical practices. Setting the Length preference does not limit the project to only the length set in the dialog box, it merely creates a Timeline based on the preference. If the project is longer or shorter than the preference, Soundtrack will adjust the Timeline accordingly. While Soundtrack is certainly capable of long-form scoring, users will find individual scenes more appropriate for file management, tempo control, and efficiency from the perspective of viewing the screen. Truthfully, controlling the screen view is a one-button operation on the Timeline; so don't worry about this preference too much.

Tempo is also a set preference here. Loops are typically recorded at tempos between 85 and 140 beats per minute (BPM), with the largest number averaging around 125BPM. Setting a tempo preference won't dismiss loops at tempos other than the preferred speed; this is relevant to how fast the project itself will play. If fast-paced, high-action video is being scored, or if the typical project is fairly fast, this preference is best set at 130 or even 140BPM. At a maximum setting of 200BPM,

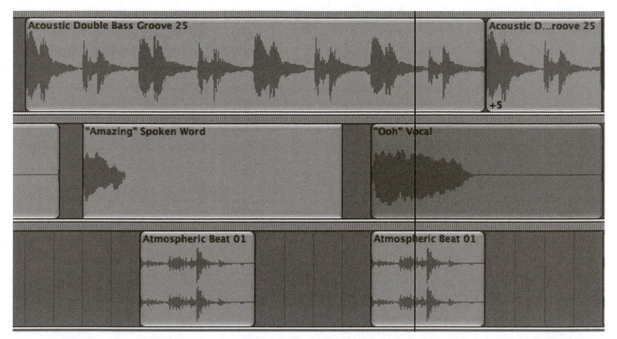

1.23 The Use _____ in Clip Names is very useful for identifying files on the Timeline, particularly when multiple files are used on the same line.

1.24 Checking the Use _____ in Clip Names allows files to display their full names providing a quick reference, particularly when using files from a library based around a single name.

Soundtrack has capabilities faster than even the most manic speed metal band. If longer romantic or artistic video or audio projects are the preference, setting this to a tempo of around 85BPM might be more useful. Keep in mind that this preference will have a minor effect on how audio is heard in the Media Manager preview, as the files will be played back at the project tempo. A loop recorded at 145BPM will sound a little strange when previewed at 80BPM, or nearly half of its recorded speed. This can be dealt with on the Timeline, but it's something to be aware of when setting preferences.

Setting the key signature at a point different than the default A major is best left to those who are musically inclined. The root note of A is used by nearly all looping creation tools, as A440 is the tuning pitch used as a reference point in all contemporary music. Many loop libraries are based around the key of A, or at least have references based around the A440 standard. However, if you find that your favorite libraries are based around a key standard that is lower or higher, then by all means change this preference.

The time signature is relevant to beats and measures, signifying how many beats are in a measure, and how many counts are given to each beat. Most contemporary music is founded around four beats, with four counts given to each beat, otherwise known as 4/4 music, indicated on a musical staff as shown in Figure 1.25.

Soundtrack supports the standard time signatures of 3/4, 4/4, 5/4, 6/8, and 7/8, though very few loops are available in any but the 3/4 and 4/4 time signatures. The musically inclined may find themselves recording their own loop signatures. The Total Spanish Guitar library is filled with 3/4-time guitar loops, so is the American Piano library. Both are available from Sony. The Apple Loops collection also includes a few of these time-signature files. If you will use library loops such as these, it is wise to leave this preference set at 4/4.

The Sample Rate preference is an oddity in current versions of Soundtrack. Most loops are recorded at 44.1KHz/16bit, but for use in DV they must be converted at the project level/export to 48Khz/16bit. Sampling rates not supported by internal soundcards visible in the dropdown menu and may confuse users. When Soundtrack is launched, setting this preference to any selection other than 44.1 will give an error message unless an audio card that is capable of supporting higher audio sampling rates/bit depths is present on the system. Some examples of these are Echo and M-Audio cards. If the project-sampling rate is output at 48KHz for matchback to a DV project/video project, it may be monitored at 44.1Khz and exported at the 48KHz sampling rate.

Soundtrack is capable of creating/monitoring audio files as high as 24 bit/96KHz, the same sampling rate as a DVD-Audio disk specification. Yet for video project export, the sample rate should never be different than 48KHz/16 bit. If this happens, the video application will either not be able to read the file or it will create additional work for the video editor since it will have to resample the audio during its final render of video and audio into the final video file.

1.25   Musical staff showing 4/4 time.

1.26   Sony's Total Spanish Guitar library has several odd-tempo times available.

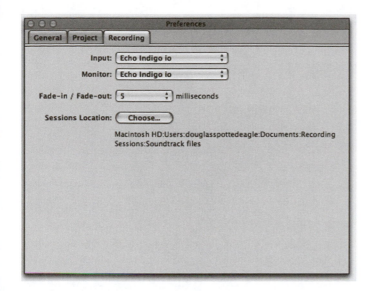

1.27 Specify where voiceover and other recorded files should be stored in the Recording preferences dialog.

The Recording Preferences tab offers choices for input of audio for recording, as well as what input source should be monitored. Additional choices offer locations where recorded files may be stored (see Figure 1.27)

The Input will typically be the Default setting, unless an external sound card has been connected to the system via Cardbus, PCI, USB, or FireWire connection. Input monitoring allows the user to hear himself as he is recorded. Often, this monitoring selection demonstrates some latency where a time lag is heard between the actual sound going into the computer via the microphone and coming back out of the computer via headphone or monitoring speakers. If a monitoring source is selected, in the event of feedback, be sure that a quick mute, software or hardware console selection, or another control is readily available.

The Fade-in/Fade-out menu choices allow a user to control popping sounds associated with the ending/beginning of audio files. This choice should never be less than two milliseconds (ms) and generally 5–8ms is sufficient. If set to None, the file will more than likely pop or snap at the beginning, end, or at both in an audio recording, depending on the sampling rate and bit depth. Newcomers to audio recording will find the default setting of 5ms to be satisfactory, and should only change this setting in the event that pops or snaps are heard in the file.

Feedback: Having a monitor's volume too high, and too close to a microphone can feed signal from the microphone to the monitoring speakers, and from the monitoring speakers back into the microphone, creating a sound loop known as feedback. Headphone monitoring is best, yet even this form of monitoring can generate feedback if the microphone is too loud or the headphone level is too loud. Be sure monitoring speakers are isolated from the microphone.

1.28 Open recent projects from the File>Open Recent menu option.

Audio files can be very large when in uncompressed formats, such as AIFF file formats. Having a default storage path that makes efficient access to audio files important. If a second drive is used for loop storage or other media storage, it's always a good idea to point audio files to this location. To direct file storage to a specific location, select the Choose button in the dialog. This will open up a dialog asking where the files should be located. If a folder was not created in the desired location previous to setting preferences, a new folder may be created in this preference. If a large number of voiceovers or lengthy files are anticipated, having a second hard drive is essential for efficient playback and recording of uncompressed sounds. If Session Locations are stored here, it's a simple matter to pick up the external drive and take it to a different computer. Glyph, ADS Technologies, Maxtor, LaCie, and other manufacturers all make external drive tanks/kits that function wonderfully not only for recording, but for storage of loops as well.

The File menu option is next on the Soundtrack menu bar. This is where new files are Created, Opened, Saved, Saved As, and Exported. Choosing the Command+N or New option in the file dropdown menu creates a new file. Multiple files may be open at the same time. This is advantageous as the same video file may be open in more than one Soundtrack file, allowing for various moods to be scored at one session and allowing a client to view a video clip while experimenting with various scores. This can be accomplished prior to exporting the audio file back to Final Cut

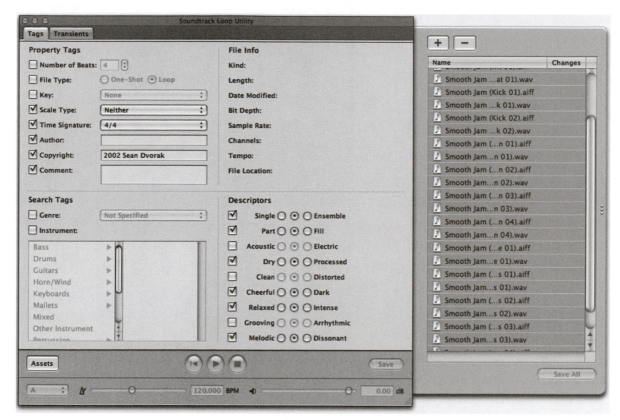

1.29 Soundtrack's Loop Utility will allow key information to be inserted as metadata.

Pro, or other applications. In creating a DVD menu for instance, having multiple choices to examine before proceeding with rendering is good. In the instance of having multiple files open, it is important to determine how one file might transition to another file. Musical selections may be previewed back to back in Soundtrack. This allows a user to determine if audio files for transitioning clips will go together appropriately prior to rendering the audio and experimenting on the NLE timeline.

Use the Command+O or Open choice to open files created in previous sessions. The Open Recent will display files recently opened in Soundtrack.

Audio files on the timeline may be opened directly in the Soundtrack Loop Utility, which will be examined in the Loop Utility chapter. This allows for files to be quickly modified and optimized for a specific speed or key.

Selecting the Close option will close the active file. A file not in a saved state will prompt for the file to be saved, not saved, or action cancelled. Command+W is the shortcut key for this choice.

Choosing File> Save will save the file to hard drive, saving only the project file, not copying or saving the audio files in the project, unless the Collect Audio Files checkbox is checked in the Save

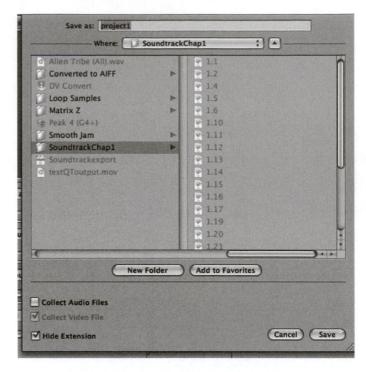

1.30 Selecting this checkbox will copy all audio files to one location, allowing for easy transport of the project to another computer.

dialog. Use the Collect Audio Files option to collect all related audio files for transferring files to a CD-ROM, external hard drive, or sending a project to another computer.

The Save As menu choice is used for saving an active project to a new file name. Use this to save various mixes under unique names for later recall. Shift+Command+S is the shortcut keystroke for this function.

The Export Mix option will render audio and video as a single stream for export as a single file. This is a good option for sending a finished file to a client or to Apple's Compressor application for upload to the Internet. This option may also be used to export a score in order to be reopened in Final Cut Pro once finished. The Export Mix option contains a checkbox that, by default, mutes the audio track from the video originally imported to Soundtrack. Uncheck this option if audio from the video clip should remain in the mix. If the audio stream associated with the video will be edited further in FCP, it may aurally conflict if the clip's audio is enabled as part of the exported mix from Soundtrack. Therefore, in most export-mix circumstances, leave the default checkbox filled. (If you don't have a project open, the Export Mix options will not be selectable. A project is required to use this function.)

The Export Tracks choice will export each individual track from Soundtrack as a separate audio file. For example, if the Soundtrack project contains 16 tracks, then 16 separate audio files will be created. In addition, any stereo tracks contained in the Soundtrack project may be exported as split mono tracks, thereby creating twice the number of audio tracks during the Export tracks

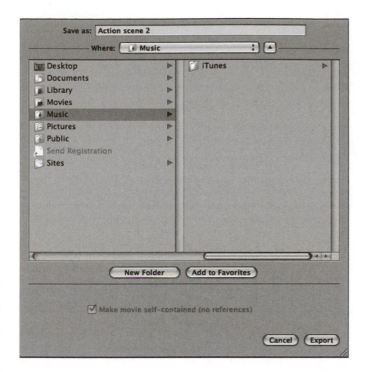

1.31 Exporting to QuickTime is a fast method in which a client can view and hear mixed tracks without sending a project back to the NLE application.

process. If the project contains 16 stereo tracks and the Output Dual Mono files checkbox is checked, then 32 mono tracks of audio will be created.

This feature is exceptionally useful for outputting pieces of a score that may require additional tweaking in the layback stage or post-production stage of a video project. It enables a user to make changes, such as individual instruments raised or lowered in volume, panned, or modified for specific emotion or atmosphere in the mix. In most Hollywood mix situations, the instruments or groups of instruments are sent to the post-production house instead of sending a finished stereo mix. This provides additional mix options to the director or sound director of the film project. Keeping options open until the final stages of the project is always a good idea and, of course, saved files may always be recalled and re-edited.

Finally, the Export to QuickTime menu option allows the entire project to be output as a mixed program. By default, the Make Movie Self-contained (no references) box is checked. This is great for outputting reference files to send to a client, outputting as a final project if working in tools other than FCP or on an audio-only project.

EDIT MENU

The Edit menu offers a large number of choices for editing media that have been placed on the Timeline. This is where cuts, ripples, duplicates, paste repeats, and other common editing functions are accessed. Regular users of Soundtrack may find it beneficial to use either the shortcut key

1.32   Create a selection in the Track Timeline Bar.

commands or a device such as the Contour Shuttle Pro to access these commands for an efficient workflow.

The Edit menu contains many shortcut keys to maximize efficiency in editing.

The Undo (Command+Z) function will undo the last edit function, restoring the project to its state before modification. The last action will display in this menu window. The counterpart to this action is the Shift+Command+Z, or Redo option. These two actions permit users to switch

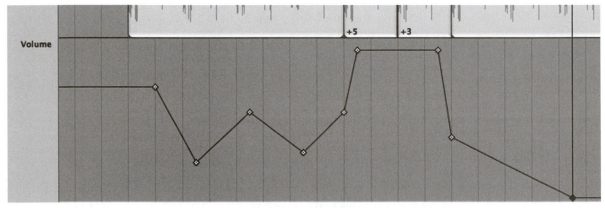

1.33   Audio envelopes may be compared using the Undo/Redo commands to compare levels.

back and forth between one edit and another, allowing for comparison of before/after edits to be heard. Using the Undo/Redo function is very practical when comparing, for instance, the sound of a reverb or compressor to a snare, or comparing an added guitar part or other instrument to the mix. It's also great for comparing the before/after of a piece of music that has been "ducked" to allow a voiceover to come through cleanly and clearly. (Ducking is where the volume of bed audio is reduced, or 'ducked' under the volume of the dialog or other featured audio.)

The Cut option (Command+X) does just that: it will cut the selected loop(s) from the Timeline, leaving a "hole" where the cut has been made. Loops that are cut may be pasted in other positions on the Timeline, as they are copied to the clipboard.

Ripple Cutting allows users to cut a specified section of a track while shifting all loops backward in time to replace the section removed during the ripple cut. This is great for removing entire sections of a track to place a chorus where a verse had previously been, shifting a series of sound effects to a new area, or simply removing extraneous audio while keeping audio that exists farther down the timeline.

To perform a ripple cut, select the bars to be removed in the Track Timeline bar. To select the bars in the Timeline, click and drag the cursor across the Track Timeline bar, highlighting them. The Edit> Ripple cut option (Shift+Command+X) is now available. Choose the option or use the shortcut to remove unwanted audio. Unselected audio on the timeline will shift to the left, filling in the selected area. To perform a project-wide ripple cut, select the audio in the videotrack audio timeline. All audio within that section will ripple to the left in accordance with the number of bars selected in the Timeline. This will also cut the audio related to the video's audio track, so be aware that the original audio will be replaced.

Copy/Paste functions are the same in Soundtrack as in other Macintosh applications: Command+C copies selected media to the clipboard; Command+V pastes copied media to the location of the cursor to a selected track. A unique Soundtrack feature is the Paste Repeat function Option+Command+V. This allows a loop or sections of loops to be copied and pasted in multiples. This is exceptionally useful if a single loop is to be used over and over, but pitch will change on several instances of the loop. For instance, a guitar loop is inserted on a track and copied to the clipboard. By using the Paste Repeat function, the single loop may be pasted as several individual loops, sparing the need to split the loop in order to change the key of the individual loop when it's called for in a composition. When Paste Repeat is selected it will open a dialog, asking the number of desired repeats. If several key changes are anticipated on an individual track, as opposed to a project-wide key change, this is a great way to insert separated loops. Otherwise, key changes on individual tracks will require splitting at the in/out points of the desired key changes.

A Paste Insert (Shift+Command+V) allows new loop information to be pasted in the middle of an existing series of loops, inserting bars for the length of the copied loop. The Paste Insert feature is project/timeline wide, so inserted audio will lengthen the entire project to the right. This is the opposite function of the Ripple Cut, allowing audio to be inserted, rather than cut. This will allow

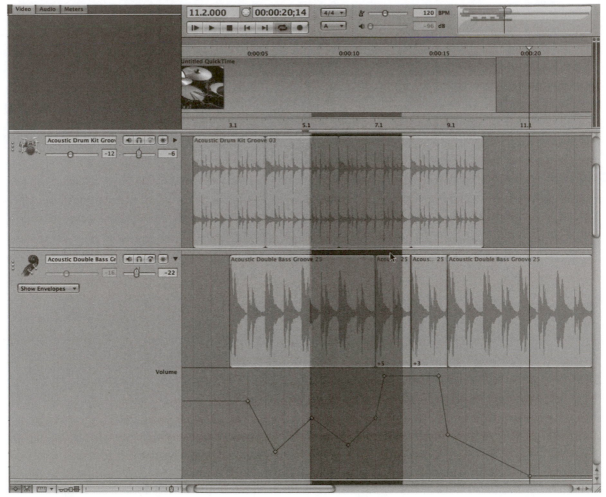

1.34 The highlighted section is removed and subsequent audio will move to the left, filling the hole left by the removed loop.

a series of tracks to be copied, such as a chorus section or other repeatable section, and inserted into the middle of a project. Selecting this option multiple times will allow for a fading chorus at the end of a song.

Deleting audio is as simple as selecting the loops to be deleted, either individually or as a group selected by holding the Control-key and pressing Delete. This will remove all selected loops from the Timeline, but not move any loop left on the Timeline. To delete and ripple audio on the time-line simultaneously, use the Ripple Delete function, or Shift+Delete. This works the same as a Rip-ple Cut, although a Ripple Cut copies loops to the clipboard and a Ripple Delete does not

Next on the Edit menu is the Duplicate Option command, or Option+D. Duplicating pastes a selected loop(s) to the ending point of the loop selected. Basically, it clones the loop being dupli-

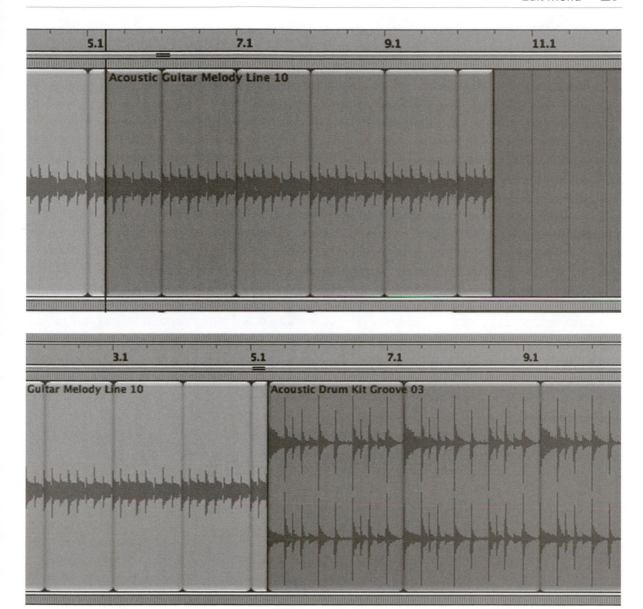

1.35 The Paste Insert option will insert copied media at the position of the cursor on the timeline. The Video Audio track must be the selected track to accomplish this task.

cated and inserts it following any selected loop. If a loop in the middle of other loops is duplicated, the In point of the next loop is truncated to the length of the duplicated loop. In other words, if a four-bar loop is next to an eight-bar loop and the four-bar loop is duplicated, the eight-bar loop becomes a four-bar loop, and the duplicated four-bar loop replaces the front portion/incoming portion of the eight-bar loop. Choosing Duplicate a second time will eradicate the eight-bar loop altogether. This is a great way to create an ending, repeat a phrase without the Copy/Paste, or duplicate a music bed loop such as an ambience. The Duplicate command is track only, and cannot be used as a project-wide duplicate. Use Copy/Paste Repeat to achieve a project-wide duplicate.

Pasting Key Changes:
Make desired key changes on one set/series of loops, then copy/paste that series containing key changes. If the music is oriented to sketchpad or music-only work, create the intro, verse, bridge, and chorus in the first bars. Then copy/paste the finished verses and choruses to a desired location. Inserting a bridge is as easy as using the Paste Insert function.

All loops on the Timeline may be selected by choosing the Select All or Command+A command. Highlighted loops may be copied and pasted as a group..

Splitting loops is a common task. This is accomplished by selecting a loop and choosing the Edit>Split command, or by selecting a loop and pressing the S-key. This task is a good one to assign to a key/button on the Contour Shuttle Pro, if one is available. Loops will need to be split if key changes are required on an individual track.

A loop that has been split may also be joined back together. Be aware that joined loops that are different in key take on the attributes of the first loop. If a loop section is at an original key is joined to a loop section that has had a key change, when the loops are joined the key change is deleted and the joined loop will be at original pitch. If a loop with a key change is joined with a loop next to it that doesn't have a key change, the second loop will take on the key-changed attributes of the first loop.

To join two loops, select a loop, hold the Apple (Command) key, and select the adjacent loop(s) on the Timeline. Press the J-key and all selected loops are joined. Loops may also be selected by selecting a loop on the Timeline while holding the Shift key and selecting a loop farther or earlier on the Timeline. All loops in between the two selected loops are selected with an option to join.

Volume Envelopes are used in Soundtrack to create a change in level or panning for each individual track. Envelope points, also called "variables," may be inserted by double clicking the envelope, or the line that appears in the track. This works in the same manner as FCP's volume and panning variables/envelope points. In addition to envelope points inserted at different points in a track, Soundtrack can change levels across an entire track, without changing the specific envelope points that may have been inserted earlier. This is a track-wide volume shift, used when the mix in the track is correct, but the overall volume of the track needs to be raised or lowered to help it sit more effectively in the mix.

Volume Envelopes are also accessible for a track-wide volume shift from the Edit menu. Select the envelope on a track by pressing the Show/Hide Envelopes button found on each track header. Selecting the Edit> Adjust Volume Envelope will open a dialog asking for the desired change in level, measured decibels (dB). Use this to raise or lower the overall track level. If the track contains variables in the track, having handles and adjusted levels, choosing this option in the Edit menu will shift the entire volume of the track by that amount. For instance, having a track with peak lev-

1.36   Splitting loops is a common function, accomplished with the S-key.

els of –6dB, then selecting the Adjust Volume Envelope command with input of 3dB upward adjustment, makes the peak level of the track –3dB rather than –6dB.

The Edit menu also provides options for nudging audio left or right by frames or bars and for controlling envelopes' handles with finite control. In order to do this, select the Edit> Adjust option and notice the various options. While the Nudge and Shift options are available via this menu, learning the shortcut keys will make this command much more efficient. Holding the Option key and pressing the Right or Left arrows will nudge selected audio to the right or left in one-pixel increments, while holding the Option key and pressing the Up or Down arrow keys will move a selected envelope point up or down one pixel, approximately 0.5 dB increments.

Shifting audio by measures , note values, or grid settings is accomplished by pressing the Shift+Option+Right/Left arrows. If the Snap-To settings are at Ruler Ticks, then the audio will shift to the right by a value of one ruler tick each time the command is executed. If the Snap-To setting is at a value of quarter notes, then the audio will shift right or left to the next/previous quarter note point. If snapping is disabled (G) then the audio will shift to the right or left by grid

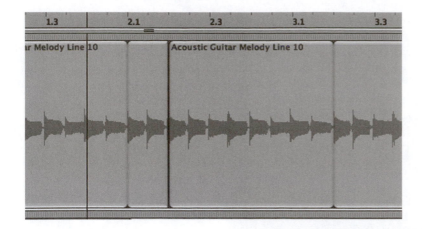

1.37 Loops may be joined together, removing splits in loops.

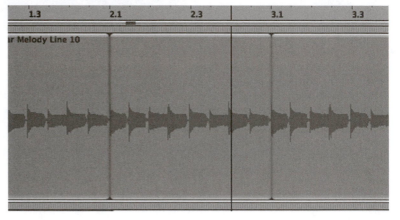

points. Holding the Shift+Option+Up/Down arrow keys will shift audio envelope points up or down by five pixels, approximately 3.5 dB.

Finite control of envelope points allows for extremely tight control of a mix where incremental volume changes are necessary. Use this control particularly on tight sections of audio that cannot be controlled by a dynamics controller, such as a compressor, to control the attack of a loop or oneshot. Nudge audio in pixel increments to perfectly line up a one shot or loop that allows for offset time. An instance when this is valuable is if a user duplicates a mono loop offsetting one track from the other by a pixel in one direction or the other. This action creates a larger sound overall. Building a drum loop from various elements such as a kick, snare, and hi-hat loop may occasionally call for offsetting the snare for a sense of reality or tension. The nudge tool is great for finding that just-right point of placement.

PROJECT MENU OPTIONS

The Project menu provides tools to efficiently add tracks, markers, and navigation around the Timeline.

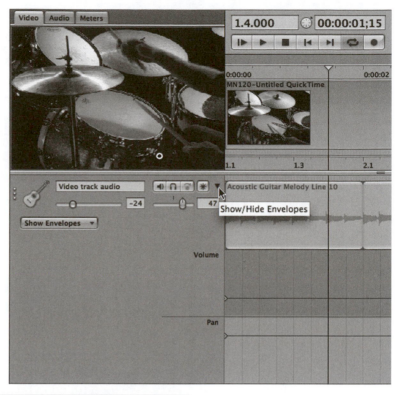

1.38   Access envelope views on a
       track by clicking this button.

1.39   Find the Nudge and Shift
       commands in the Edit>Adjust
       menu.

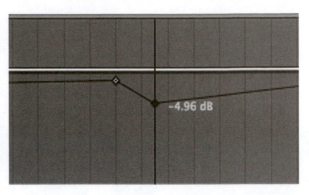

1.40 Use the Nudge command to shift a loop right or left to move audio into an offset to thicken a sound or to hit an exact mark in time.

1.41 Using the Shift+Option+Up/Down arrows provides very tight control over envelope points.

A project typically consists of several tracks of audio loops. When Soundtrack launches a new project, it provides a single audio track. Creating tracks prior to inserting loops is done via the Project>Add track (Command+T) selection. When audio is dragged to the Timeline and not dropped on an existing track, a new track is automatically created. One unique feature of Soundtrack is that a single track may contain multiple loops of a different nature, eliminating the need to have separate tracks for each unique loop found in the project.

Tracks may also be added by Control+clicking in the Project Window on a blank space. Using the Control+click view provides the option of adding a track below or above a selected track. Users of a two-button mouse can right click in a blank area and have access to these items as well.

Occasionally, tracks require removal. The Project>Remove Track (Shift+Command+T) will remove selected tracks whether they contain information or not. One such use is while creating a soundtrack to a video project. In this instance, it is valuable to create multiple scores in order to test the feeling of various musical composites. Tracks are muted or audible based on selection for preview. Once a track (or tracks) is determined, remaining tracks are deleted from the project. Tracks may also be deleted by Control+clicking in a track header and selecting Remove Track or by Control+clicking/Right clicking in the project window and selecting Remove Track.

Marker Handles

Beat Markers are indicated by Purple handles (B)

Time Markers are indicated by Green handles (T)

Final Cut Pro Scoring Markers are indicated by Orange handles (M in FCP)

Markers serve a critical function in Soundtrack and Final Cut Pro, assisting users in finding locations that require a scoring point, special effect, showing region/takes, change in score emotion (in record mode), or aural impact. Score Markers inserted in FCP

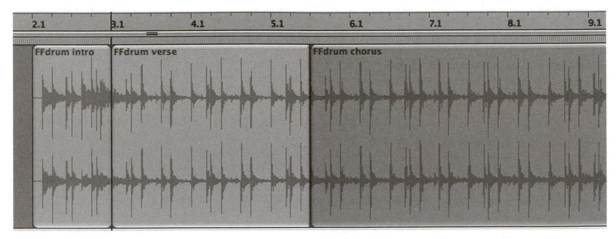

1.42 Many different loop sections may be put on a single track. This can create issues with loops that have effects assigned to the tracks; if loops are assigned an effect on the track, be certain that the effect works on all loops.

are visible in Soundtrack. Soundtrack enables users to create their own markers inside the Timeline as well. These can be set to video as Time Markers for non-FCP users, or created as Beat Markers to map out musical points. Markers appear vertically across the project, much like the playhead indicator.

Beat Markers are inserted by placing the playhead/playback cursor at the point that the marker should be placed, then choosing Insert Beat Marker from the Project dropdown menu. Beat Markers may also be inserted by pressing the B-key during playback or when the playhead is parked or by Control+clicking in the project window and choosing the Add Beat Marker at Playhead in the menu. Loops may be snapped to Beat Markers. Beat markers are linked to musical time, which

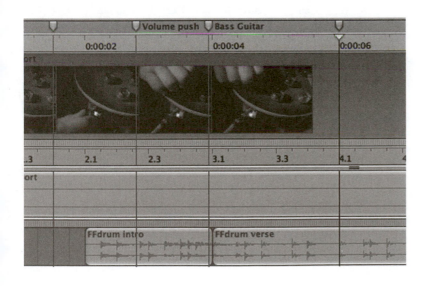

1.43 Notice that marker names from Final Cut Pro are visible in the Soundtrack Timeline.

does not change location with respect to sections when tempo changes (sections are bar:beat:tick). If the tempo changes, the frame of video will change at the location of the Beat Marker.

Time Markers are inserted by pressing the T-key or by choosing the Insert Time Markers from the Project dropdown menu. Inserting Time Markers will generate a new thumbnail in the Video Preview timeline, generated by the frame which the Time Marker falls on. Time Markers may also be inserted via Control+clicking in the project window and selecting Add a Time Marker at the Playhead. Time markers are in real time. These change location with respect to sections when tempo changes, but will remain on a constant frame of video because of the linkage to hr:min:sec.

Beat and Time Markers can be labeled by selecting the marker and pressing Control+click and selecting Edit from the pop-up menu. An edit window will open indicating the exact time and frame on which the marker lies, then provide the opportunity to name the marker with a unique name indicating what it represents in the project.

For the nonmusician, the Score Marker to Playhead can be confusing. This feature will decrease tempo from a marker point to the playhead, or increase tempo from the playhead to a marker, depending on whether the playhead is positioned after the next marker, or prior to the next marker. This feature is terrific for selecting a section in the video and having the tempo of a project lock up to work within that time space. However, if the distance is too great, then loops will either sound stilted and slow, requiring editing in the Soundtrack Loop Utility, (and even then there are some loops that this edit will not allow to be used at extremely slow or fast tempos) or the loop will require adjustment in playback rate on the track by Control+clicking the loop and adjusting its speed to another setting to properly fill the measure.

1.44 Insert Scoring Markers in Final Cut Pro, and give them a name for easy location.

1.45 Markers may be given a unique name relevant to what the marker indicates.

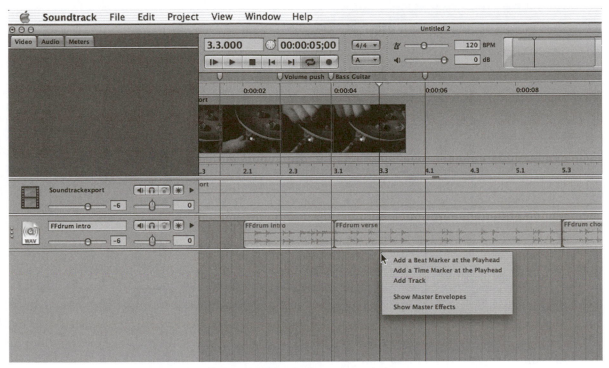

1.46   Markers may also be inserted by Control+clicking in the project window.

Score Markers to Playhead will create an envelope in the Master Tempo Envelope window. Envelope points created by the Score Markers to Playhead command will not be editable later on, but envelope points may be added prior to, or subsequent to, the locked envelope points allowing tempos to be ramped up or down. The primary use of the Score Markers to Playhead is to lock Soundtrack audio to the action/editing tempo of a video clip. While this will not synchronize the audio to events within the video, it will create a tempo that fits perfectly within the length of the video clip, allowing nonmusicians to score to tempo perfectly. (Musicians are challenged with the math of changing tempos in movie scores all the time.) This also assists in multiple tempos being used, such as multiple songs for a single clip, or if an entire video project is being scored. (Soundtrack allows a project of up to four hours in length to be loaded.)

Markers may be navigated via shortcuts or the Project dropdown menu. To jump the playhead to the next marker on the Timeline, press Shift+M-key, then to jump the playhead backwards to the previous marker, press Control+M. These functions work similarly to jumping from scene to scene on a DVD. The playhead may also be moved in frame-only increments by selecting the Command+Arrow keys. Use the right arrow key to move to the next frame and the left arrow key to move to the frame previous to the current playhead position. All of these shortcuts provide efficient and fast navigation of the entire Timeline and project.

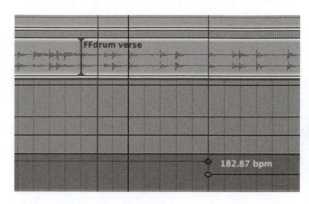

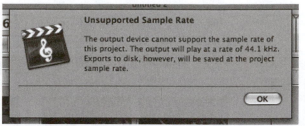

1.47 Score Markers to Playhead will automatically figure the tempo required between the playhead and previous or next marker.

1.48 Projects that do not match the output capabilities of the system soundcard will generate this message.

The Project dropdown is also where the sample rate of audio is selected. Sample rates available are 32KHz, 44.1KHz, 48KHz, and 96Khz. The 32KHz/12bit rate is most applicable when importing a video file imported from a DV camera that records audio at 32Khz. This is an inferior format for professional use because the resolution of the audio is very low. Use this sample rate as only a last resort.

CD audio is recorded at a sample rate of 44.1KHz/16bits. This is the quality at which most ACID® loops are recorded and is an acceptable quality. Loops are also available as 48KHz/24bits in some higher-quality libraries. Soundtrack can support loops of 48KHz/24bits as well as the standard 44.1KHz/16bit libraries.

The majority of digital video cameras record audio at 48KHz/16bits, with the exception of some offering those that offer optional four-channel recording at 32k/12bits, so for DV-based projects, 48KHz/16 bits should be the standard setting. Soundtrack will transcode loops recorded at 44.1KHz to match the 48KHz setting. Soundtrack also supports input devices that have capability up to 96KHz/24bits. Any sample rate setting not supported by Soundtrack or to the hardware connected to the computer will generate an error message. This message is with regard to the sample rate, requiring the project to be adjusted. For audio related to DV projects, be certain to render audio at 48KHz so that the audio matches up with audio in the NLE system.

VIEW MENU

Various windows and views are controlled and adjusted in the View menu. This menu also allows the user to show or hide specific functions found within Soundtrack.

Zooming in or out on the Timeline is a function accomplished by a couple of different keystrokes or commands. Zoom functions are another set of functions best learned as keystrokes or assigned to a button on a Contour Shuttle Pro, although these functions may be accessed in the View dropdown menu.

Zooming in on the Timeline is accomplished with Command+ = and zoom out is accomplished via the Command+−. Zoom in/out is also accomplished by selecting the Up or Down arrow keys, although this isn't found in the Soundtrack manual. If you are using a wheeled mouse, the wheel will also zoom views in/out. Zoomed views may be immediately restored to a normal view by selecting the Command+0. All tracks will fit to window by selecting the Shift+Z. Lengthy projects will appear quite squished if fit to windows.

Soundtrack works on a Timeline view, and the Timeline may be adjusted to view format for different workflows. The Timeline may be viewed in seconds increments, frames incre-

1.49 The View menu offers several choices for what is seen on the Timeline, and zooming actions on the Timeline

ments, non-drop frame, or drop-frame increments, depending on user's preferences. This view option is found under the dropdown menu when the Time Ruler Units choice is selected.

Locking tracks to specific grids or values other than Gridlines will often require zooming in reasonably deep, particularly when snapping has been disabled. To lock an audio loop to its exact location, use the zoom features to delve in deep to view the attack point of a sound and to lock it to other points, if necessary.

Like many other features found in Soundtrack, the height of tracks may be adjusted/modified in several different ways. The Track Height selection found under the View dropdown has four options:

Reduced	Command+6
Small	Command+7
Medium	Command+8
Large	Command+9

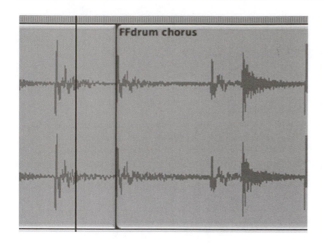

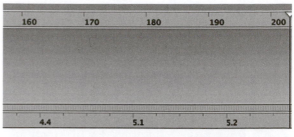

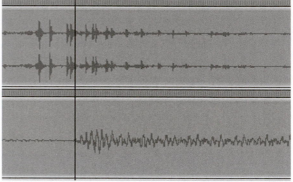

1.50 Zooming in with the Up or Down arrows accomplishes a quick zoom in/out. *(above)*

1.51 Timeline increment views are controlled with the Time Ruler Units menu. *(upper right)*

1.52 The attack point can be easily seen in transient sounds. Use this view to correctly line up audio with loops.

The Track Height views may be selected with shortcut keys for faster, more efficient workflows. Track height may also be adjusted/selected via the Track Height button found at the lower left area of the project window/workspace.

Keeping time tight and locked when dropping loops to the Timeline is critical. To keep loops locked to the time grid set up in the project window, Snapping should be enabled in most instances, yet there are instances when snapping should be disabled. Some such instances are during placement of frame-related sound effects and one shots and while locking inserted dialog. To disable Snapping, select the Snapping option found in the View dropdown menu. Snapping is also disabled by pressing the G-key or via the Snapping toggle button found in the lower left of the window/workspace (Enabling is activated this way too).

Soundtrack allows users to determine how tight loops will be snapped or at what point in the measure the loop should be snapped to. Nonmusical users of Soundtrack may find that snapping to Ruler Ticks is the best option. Musically-inclined users will find that snapping control allows for creative offsets for various loops.

To set the snapping point, select the Snap To menu choice in the View option. Choices under this menu are:

- Ruler Ticks (Default)
- Quarter notes

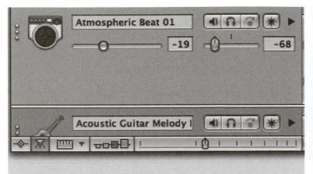

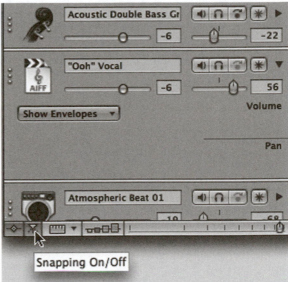

1.53   The track height may be adjusted with the track height control found at the lower left of the project window.

1.54   Snapping may be turned on or off via this toggle found in the lower left of the project workspace.

- Eighth notes
- Sixteenth notes
- Thirty-second notes
- Sixty-fourth notes
- Markers

Snap-To choices are also available on a button found in the lower left of the project window. Note that the Markers choice is not found in this pop-up menu.

Markers and Ruler Ticks are the safest snapping points for most users of Soundtrack, if a loop appears slightly out of time in the musical rhythm, this is one of the first places to look for what has happened. Therefore, if a loop is out of time, check this setting first. (Of course, this is after assuring that Snapping was enabled prior to dropping a loop on the Timeline.) If a loop is dropped on the Timeline while Snapping is turned off and appears to be out of sync or time with other musical selections, simply enable Snapping (G) and move the loop until it snaps to the nearest gridline. Loops can be snapped to any point on the grid at any time, allowing for maximum creativity. When working with musical selections, you may find that moving loops to unique positions with Snapping enabled or disabled creates interesting textures.

Moments of tension are often created in film work by using elements that are out of time, uncomfortable to listen to, or harsh in feeling and format. As an example, throughout the movie "Patriot Games" percussive elements are dropped in, aurally out of time, giving a sense of discomfort and impending danger. Occasional sounds placed in layers, with one layer out of sync/time

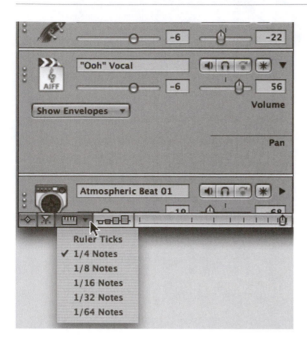

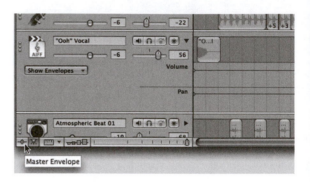

1.55 Snap To options are found in the lower left of the project window.

1.56 Master envelopes control the final output of the project; because envelopes can take a lot of space, toggle them on or off with the Master Envelopes option in the View menu.

with the rest of the project, can also create a deep sense of discomfort. Mix these sounds down low to create a hint of the sound rather than having the out-of-sync sound be loud. You might find it a very interesting and provocative moment in the mix. Sometimes experimenting with moving loops to uncommon in/out points can assist in finding dramatically emotional expression.

Show Marker Titles is an option in the View dropdown menu. This option enables or disables view of any naming/labels assigned to individual markers on the Timeline. If this view is turned off, marker names inserted in FCP will also be removed from view.

Show Marker Lines will remove vertical marker indicators from the project window view. Marker heads will remain visible above the Time Ruler, it is only the vertical indicators of the marker that disappear from the project window. This is helpful when working with many grid-lines, such as when a project is zoomed in deep.

Soundtrack enables users to create master envelopes to control project volume, panning, and any effects that might be assigned to the master system. Selecting the Show Master Envelopes will open Volume, Transpose, and Tempo Envelope views, allowing users to control both volume fade In/Out and transposition for the entire project, and tempo changes. Master Envelopes may also be viewed via Control+clicking in the project window and selecting Show Master Envelopes. This is found in the lower left hand corner and appears like a small diamond with a line drawn through it. When Show Master Envelopes is opened, any effects assigned to the master project will also be visible. Views of individual effect envelopes may be turned off by selecting various options in the Show Envelopes dropdown menu, shown when the Master Envelopes view is open. This is quite a practical option, since having a compressor and reverb added to a project means that the Master

Envelopes view will fill the entire screen with envelopes! A large number of envelope views can quickly become confusing even to the most knowledgeable user.

Show Master Effects opens a dialog that indicates which effects are assigned to the master system. Effects may be added in this view by selecting an effect in the dialog box, and clicking the + key. This adds an effect to the list of effects, in the order that they are added. Also, a selected effect in the effect menu may be dragged to the master list area. Effects may be deleted by selecting them in the master list and clicking the – button, or by clicking the Delete key.

Effects, particularly graphic EQ and compressor combinations, can be complicated in their use for a user not familiar with how these tools function. We'll examine the effects in a later chapter; though for the moment be aware that in most instances, a compressor should be the last effect in the chain. If a graphic EQ is inserted post-compressor for instance, then the compressor isn't really able to do its job and you may create a distorted file on output without knowing why. Typically, an EQ is inserted first and a compressor last. Sometimes it is desirable to have an EQ come after a reverb is inserted. Other times, it may be preferable to have the EQ in the chain prior to the reverb. But to reiterate, particularly for audio being exported to DV, it is best to have a compressor inserted in the chain at the last stage in the project, or as the final effect.

The final option in the View menus is the Layouts selection. Layouts may be controlled to suit individual users and, due to their importance, all layout views are assigned shortcut keys.

Users who don't find the Media Manager feature of value, for instance, might prefer to keep the Media Manager hidden. For some users, the Track Headers view might not bear value or use too much screen real estate. The headers may also be turned off. Most users will find the workflow of toggling between Command+2 and Command+5 to be quite useful, particularly when moving back and forth with FCP. This is another task well suited to assigning to a Contour Shuttle Pro, or other interface device that supports shortcuts assigned to keys. Soundtrack is also optimized to support dual monitors, allowing Soundtrack to be open in one view while FCP or other NLE is open on another monitor.

Shortcuts

The various layout views in Soundtrack can be toggled using shortcut keys.

Separate Windows	Command+1
Single Window	Command+2
Hide Media Manager	Command+3
Hide Track Headers	Command+4
Hide Both	Command+5

WINDOW MENU

The Window menu allows users to open and close views and toggle between open projects. Occasionally users need to toggle various windows to access other applications on the desktop.

To minimize the entire project window, select the Minimize option (Command+M). The current project will minimize, revealing either the desktop or any open Soundtrack project beneath it.

1.57   Projects that are currently open may be toggled via this menu and its shortcuts.

In OS X v1.3.1, a user can press F10 to show all projects currently in Soundtrack as tiled projects and select which project on which to work. This is a great tool for working between various mixes of the same project.

When using separate windows as a layout, if the media manager is closed, it may be opened from the Media Manager selection in the Window dropdown menu, or accessed with shortcut keys, Shift+Command+M. Also, open windows that are hidden beneath other project windows are brought to the front via the Bring All to Front menu selection found in the Window menu.

The Windows menu accesses projects that are currently open, allowing selectability via the dropdown menu. This provides a method by which to switch back and forth between various mixes of a score or check the flow from one mix to another.

Help Menu

Soundtrack's Help menu option opens the PDF files for the Soundtrack manual. The PDF file is searchable, but requires Adobe's Acrobat application to read the file. Check the Late Breaking News file, which is also a PDF file format. This contains additional information and a quick guide to common questions and known issues found in Soundtrack. The How to Search PDF file merely

1.58   Currently open projects may also be accessed from the docking bar.

demonstrates how to search within the bookmarks and various chapters of the Soundtrack Help file. While in Soundtrack's Help PDF, use Command+F to find key words or phrases.i

ACCESSING, PREVIEWING, AND CHOOSING LOOPS

Soundtrack's Media Manager is a powerful tool for locating and previewing loops prior to placing them on the Timeline for use in a project. The Media Manager can locate any/all loops that are compatible for use in Soundtrack. Also by searching the metadata found in the loops, Soundtrack can search with very defined parameters, saving time when looking for a specific style, tempo, or instrument. Although this is a smaller and easily dismissed aspect of Soundtrack, the Media Manager plays a huge role in the power and ease of use in Soundtrack. Used correctly, the Media Manager becomes a significant part of the composition process.

Not all loops installed during the Soundtrack installation will show up in the Search window. Some loops have no metadata associated with them, or the loop directory may not have been indexed by Soundtrack.

Opening the Media Manager (if Soundtrack did not load it), is accomplished by selecting View>Layouts>Single window or Command+2. There are three tabs: File Browser, Favorites, and Search. The File Browser works similarly to Apple's Find application, allowing users to locate files on the computer or external hard drive.

The File Browser directs the path to locate various files and also permits users to move from directory to directory fairly quickly. Pressing the Home button (located in the upper right corner of the Media Manager) will return the File Browser window to the local user profile, while selecting the Computer button will return to the root HD and CD-ROM directories. (If a CD-ROM is not inserted, the directory will not be listed.) The Path dropdown menu also allows quick navigation of the various directories in the browser.

The factory-installed loops should be found in the *HD:Documents:Soundtrack Loops:* directory. However, if you've specified a particular directory, you'll need to remember that location when indexing, searching, and locating loops.

When the loop is selected in the File Browser, it begins playing immediately at the key and tempo of the Soundtrack file that is currently open. Below the file name, the path of the file is displayed as well, letting users know where the file is coming from. Beneath the path display is an Additional Info option, indicated by a small arrow pointing to the right. Click this arrow.

This option displays not only the original tempo and key/pitch of a loop, it also displays the genre, instrument, file properties, length, beat count, and other relevant information to the file.

A window of information opens, displaying the waveform and pertinent information to the file. Most important in the window is the Scale Type field. Unless you are an experienced musician who is knowledgeable about scales, it's best never to combine minor scales with major scales, since this can lead to dissonant and uncomfortable musical scores.

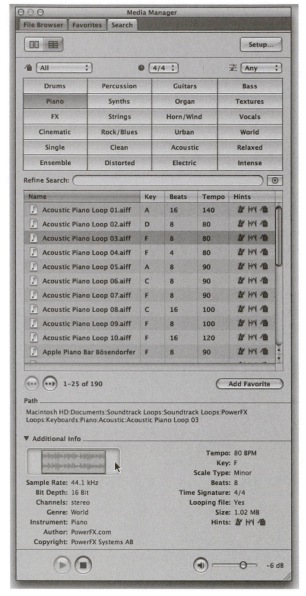

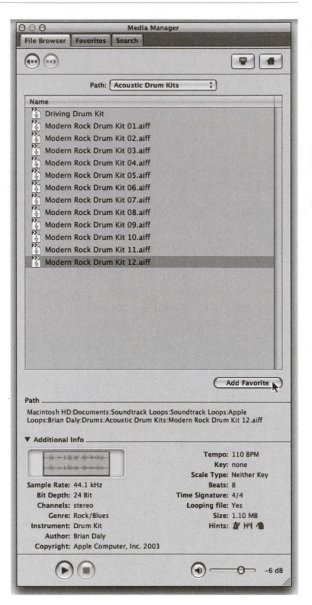

1.59 The Media Manager will autoplay loops when selected in the search window. *(above left)*

1.60 The File Browser window is where loops, directories, and video files may be located. Once located, they can be indexed or added to Favorites. Scrolling through the File Browser, go to; *Macintosh HD:Documents:Soundtrack Loops:Apple Loops:Brian Daly:Drums:Acoustic Drum Kits:Modern Rock Drum Kit 12.aif.* (if you've loaded your loops to anywhere but the default destination, you may need to browse or search for the file. After locating this file, click the Add Favorite button found at the lower right of the Media Manager window. This will add this kit to the Favorites folder. It can be removed later. *(above right)*

The waveform seen in this display may be dragged to the Timeline to indicate the bars that the loop will occupy. Also, video files will show a thumbnail only while audio from the video clip plays. A video thumbnail can be dragged from the Additional Information area to the Soundtrack Timeline.

The File Browser also has features not readily seen, accessible via the Control+click functions, or via the right click on a two-button mouse.

In the File Browser, Control+click a file. Notice that a number of options open in a menu. Files may be added to or removed from Favorites, replace loops currently on the Soundtrack Timeline, opened in the Loop Utility, or revealed in the Apple Finder application. The Replace option is much like selecting alternate media in FCP or adding media as takes in other NLE applications. A loop is selected on the Timeline in Soundtrack, with an alternative loop selected in the Media Manager. Using Control+click and Replace Selected Loops with _____ allows users to quickly substitute entire loop passages with replacement loops. Attributes of any selected loops on the Soundtrack Timeline will be applied to replacement loops as well. This is a great way to create similar-sounding files, yet with a different feel. For instance, a client wants several variations on a theme, each with a similar feeling. Using the Replace Media option in the Media Manager, alternative themes can rapidly be developed by replacing a piano with a guitar or replacing a heavy metal guitar with a harp.

While previewing files in the Media Manager, be certain that Snapping is enabled. This is enabled via the View>Snapping selection, using the shortcut key, (G), or by pressing the Snapping button found in the lower left hand corner of the Soundtrack workspace. If Snapping is disabled, files previewed in the Media Manager will not be locked to loops playing in the Soundtrack workspace.

FAVORITES

Soundtrack provides a location for favorite files to be immediately accessible within the Media Manager. Files may be added to Favorites from either the File Browser or from the Search utility/function.

SEARCHING FILES

Search is one of the most powerful attributes of Soundtrack. In the Search window, loops of a specific key or tempo are located quickly and easily. In the Search dialog, there are a variety of methods that may be employed to search for specific file types such as a specific instrument, instrument in a musical genre, or time signature.

Opening the Media Manager, via the Command+2 (if it's not already open as a window in Soundtrack), click on the View as Buttons button.

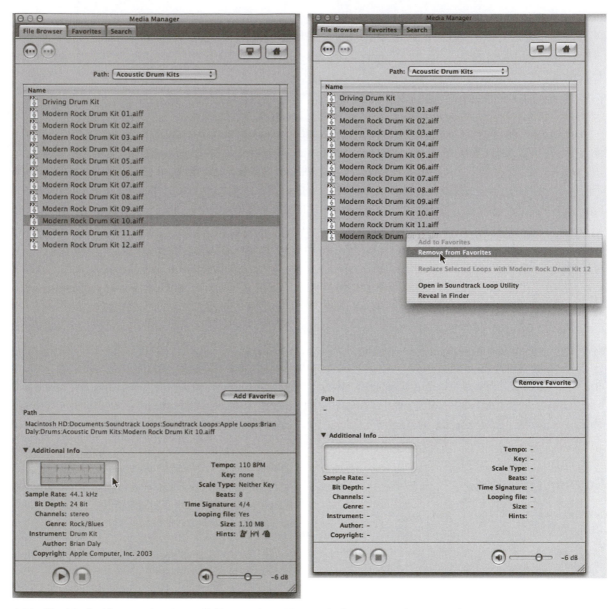

1.61   The Media Manager is where all files are found for use in Soundtrack. *(above left)*

1.62   Right-clicking on a two-button mouse or via Control+clicking in the Media Manager opens a number of additional options. *(above right)*

This puts the Search function as a single click, button-activated search of the indexed directories found on the computer. The default view of these search parameters is All, but this may be modified to suit individual users. Just below the View format button in the Media Manager is a

1.63 Files added as Favorites will be rapidly accessible for consistent use or similar project requirements, such as creating variations on a theme or use for chapter pages on a DVD menu. Reference commonly accessed loops or videos in the Favorites menu. This does not create a copy of the loops or videos, it merely creates a link to them. To remove files from the Favorites menu, select the file to be removed and click the Remove Favorites found on the lower right side of the Media Manager. Files may also be Control+clicked+Right click in the Favorites dialog and removed, opened in the Loop Utility, or revealed in Finder.

Search Refinement

Using the "*Limit search to loops that are within 2 semitones of project key*" (Keep Close) button found next to the Refine Search is a search-refinement tool that is valuable for nonmusical users of Soundtrack. This limits the search to loops that will not be stretched or speeded up too far to potentially create mixed loops that don't match up well. If a loop is tremendously dissimilar to the project key, it is very possible that not all loops will match up well to the project overall, particularly sounds containing a substantial amount of bass information, as the loop may well be stretched beyond a high quality sound. While this may be worked around, first time users of Soundtrack looking for the best loop matchup, this option assures that loops will match up without additional editing.

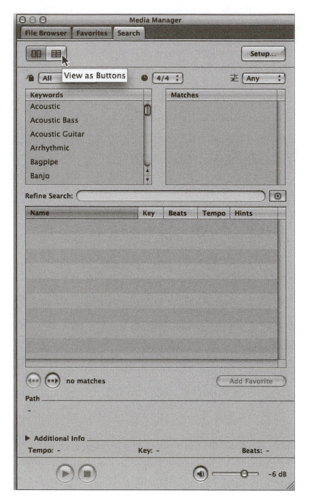

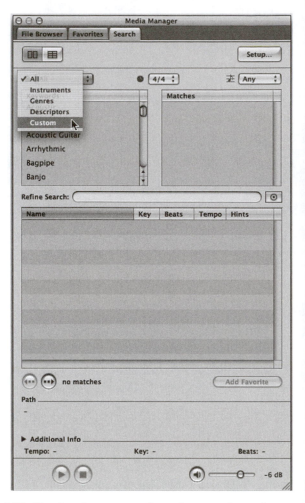

1.64 Search parameters may be viewed by individual buttons or as a list.

1.65 The dropdown menu allows for several search specifications.

dropdown menu that offers choices of viewing the buttons by Instruments, Genres (styles), Descriptors, or Custom viewing choices. Select Instruments from the dropdown menu and notice that the parameters for searching have changed. If no additional loop libraries have been added for Soundtrack, notice that there may be a couple of dimmed-out choices in the instrument parameter selections. Loading a new library from an Apple Loops provider that contains references to these instrument choices, or finding third party loops and creating references to these Loop Utility search parameters, will cause these loops to light up.

Next to the Instruments dropdown menu is a time signature dropdown menu that allows loops to be searched in 3/4, 4/4, 5/4, 6/8, and 7/8 time signatures. For nonmusical users, I recommend that this search parameter be left in the default 4/4 setting. For musically inclined users, the majority of loops available are in 4/4 time, however, there are a variety of loop libraries in unique time signatures. Also, any unique time signature loop created in Soundtrack, Peak, or another audio tool can be designated in the Soundtrack Loop Utility.

Next to the Time Signature Search menu is a dropdown menu that allows searches based around the scale of the loop: minor key, major key, any key, neither key, and good for both are all options. A more detailed discussion on key formats is found in later sections of this book, but suffice it to say that major and minor scales often do not work well together. The Neither option is good for finding spoken word or sound FX loops. The Good for Both loops are loops that will match up with either major or minor key loops. The default setting of Any is the best choice for nonmusical users of Soundtrack. Scale Type may be viewed in the bottom section of the Media Manager's Additional Info area.

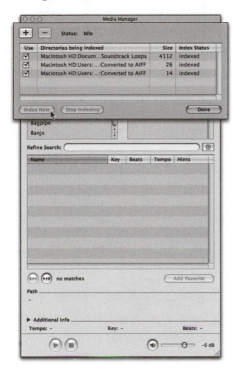

Using the Search function is a simple matter of selecting a button relevant to the desired instrument, genre, or descriptor. Setting the Time Signature and Scale options will further narrow the search. If there is a specific loop or series of loops desired, the search can be refined by using additional descriptor words. Comments inserted in the Soundtrack Loop Utility will also be searched in the search function if the Refine Search option is utilized. Sounds that meet the descriptors, instruments, genre, or all of the above are displayed in the Search Results window.

Custom searches can be set up within Soundtrack's search utility as well. While these buttons are not user definable, they are user determined. This means that a specific set of buttons relevant to a particular workflow or house standard is allowed.

1.66 The index feature instructs Soundtrack to look at specific folders and directories for files that may be used on the Timeline.

INDEXING LOOPS

Loops that are not part of the Soundtrack loops directory must be indexed in order to be part of any loop search. Indexing allows Soundtrack's Search function to access the loops for quick location. Of course, files may also be copied directly into the Soundtrack Loops folder as well. However, if the default *HD:Documents: Soundtrack Loops* directory is used, it may quickly fill the hard drive and slow the entire computer system. As previously suggested, if use of a large number of loops is anticipated, a second or external hard drive is highly recommended.

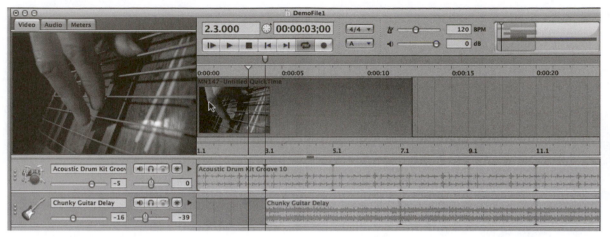

1.67 The video preview will display the first frame across the Timeline. The preview window will update as the project is played or scrolled through, while the Timeline display will remain as a static thumbnail.

To access the Indexing dialog, click on the Search Tab in the Media Manager and select the Setup button. This will open a dialog that allows the addition of specific directories containing loops. Click the + symbol in the upper left of the dialog and browse to the desired directory or folder that you wish to include in the Search operation. After adding all desired directories/folders, select the Index Now button on the bottom left corner of the dialog. Depending on the number of directories and quantity of loops in those directories, this operation might take a few minutes while Soundtrack looks at the files.

TIMELINE FUNCTIONS

The Timeline provides many options for controlling the workflow in Soundtrack. These options, found at the top of the Soundtrack interface, permit efficient navigation in Soundtrack. Also, they allow a master view of the number of loops and position of the playhead in relation to the master program.

Video Tab

In the upper left section of the Timeline, there are three tabs: Video, Audio, and Meters. The Video Tab is where any video being scored will appear as a preview monitor, indicating by frame, the location of the playhead. Video can be dragged from the Favorites, Browser, or Search location and dropped in the Video Preview area. If video is dropped in the Preview window, a video timeline will be filled with the first frame of the video for the length of the project or longest loop section.

Audio Tab

The Audio Tab will display the name of all loops currently in use in the project, acting somewhat like a bin in most NLE applications or a file folder display in a digital audio workstation.

Meters Tab

The Meters Tab will display a detailed meter reading of the audio mix coming off the Timeline. Soundtrack is capable of displaying two meters, since there is always a meter active on the far right hand side of the Timeline. The full time meter found on the right side of Soundtrack is good for getting an idea of levels, but it is not a specific meter and does not give a dB-scale reading. On the other hand, the Meter pane does provide specific values. The meter pane also includes a Go button for each channel. Selecting this button causes Soundtrack to seek the loudest point in the track and move the playhead to that point in the Timeline. If audio in the project is too loud at any point, it will clip (distort) and the meters will display a clipping indicator at the top of the offending channel, or on both channels if the level is too loud on both the right

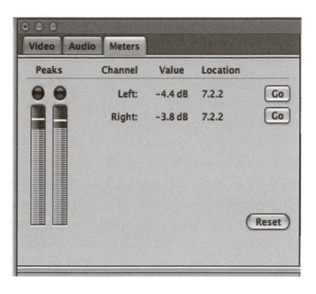

1.68   Selecting the Go buttons will locate the loudest point in the Timeline and move the playhead to that location.

and left channels. Selecting the Reset button will reset the meters to a zeroed state. Resetting the meters does not affect audio in any manner.

Master Control

The Master Control section of Soundtrack offers several navigation options. The Beat Display in the master window indicates the location of the playhead by measures. The Time Display shows the location of the playhead by hours, minutes, seconds, frames. Clicking in either window allows specific measures/time designations to which the playhead will be moved. So if a user is working from a cue sheet or EDL generated by an application other than FCP, this provides an efficient means of navigating the playhead through various points in the project.

The time signature of the song can also be modified in the master control section of the application. Time signatures supported are 3/4, 4/4, 5/4, 6/8, and 7/8. Nonmusical users will find the default 4/4 to be the most commonly desired time signature. 3/4 time signatures are used for waltz

---

> ### *Tonality*
>
> There are 12 keys in the Western/conventional scale; A, A#, B, C, C#, D, D#, E, F, F#, G, G# are keys used in the creation of loops. Soundtrack transposes loops to the project key regardless of the key at which they are recorded. A loop recorded in the key of F and a loop recorded in the key of B will sonically match, even if the project key is set to G. This is one of the powerful capabilities of Soundtrack: the automatic matching of key and tempo. This is one of the primary reasons that users of Soundtrack need no musical ability to create great music with the tool. Shifting a project key during the experimental stages of composing a score may yield unique effects on a song. Raising the key of a song by a value or two might create a happier feeling, while lowering the key might create a darker feeling. This is entirely dependent on the loops used in the project. Don't be afraid of playing with this control, it will shift the entire project key up or down, regardless of the loops on the Timeline.

songs, not commonly found in today's pop music. The time signature of the project should nearly always match the time signature of the loops being used in the project. Rarely will loops of a 3/4 time signature be used in a 4/4 project. If the first number in the time signature isn't the same as the first number in the project, then the first number must be a multiple of the first number of the project. In other words, a 3/4 project would lock nicely with loops that are 6/8 in time, but not 7/8 in time. A 4/4 time signature project will play loops recorded as 2/4 loops, but would generally not match up with a 5/4 loop properly.

The key signature plays a significant role in Soundtrack projects. While a large majority of loops are recorded in the key of A or key signatures near the A pitch and the key of A is the default key in Soundtrack, this does not mean that songs are required to be in the key of A. Users may specify any key within the 12-tone scale. The Project Key dropdown menu will shift the entire project key signature rather than requiring users to shift the project one loop at a time. The key of the project can also shift via keyframes or handles on the Timeline. However, if the score does not contain key shifts, the key signature menu is the appropriate method of shifting the project key.

The key of A major is often used as a benchmark in musical tools, since the A tone above middle C on the piano is a perfect harmonic of 440Hz. This is the tone used by musicians around the world as a tuning reference.

Tempo Slider

The speed or tempo of the score is determined by the Tempo slider in the Master Control. Tempo is measured by Beats Per Minute, or BPM. Tempo can be controlled for the overall project via this slider or the tempo can be shifted at various points on the Timeline using keyframes or envelope points. This is similar to how filters might be controlled in an NLE system. Soundtrack has the ability to automatically create a tempo based on space between markers, giving users the ability to define a length of time and having Soundtrack automatically determine the tempo of the music in that defined length of time. The default setting in Soundtrack is 120BPM. The tempo value is displayed next to the Tempo slider. Specific tempo may be directly entered in this window by clicking in the window and typing the desired value.

Master Volume

Beneath the Tempo slider is a Master Volume for the entire Soundtrack project. Volume level is indicated by decibels, or dB, in the window next to the Master Volume. Specific volume levels can be entered by clicking in this window and entering the desired value.

Master Control Buttons

The Master Control section of Soundtrack also provides buttons for navigating and controlling the playhead that are similar to a tape machine's control. Play From Start, Play from Current Position, Stop, Rewind, Fast Forward, Loop, and Record are all accessed via the Master Control. Pressing the spacebar will cause Soundtrack to start/stop from the playhead position, while pressing the Enter key (on the keyboard, not the 10 keypad) causes Soundtrack to rewind and play from the beginning. If the looping option is enabled, Soundtrack will play to the end of the last loop on the Timeline before returning to either the beginning of the project or returning to a defined loop beginning point. These actions are handy to have programmed on a HUI device such as the Contour Shuttle Pro device, as they are commonly and consistently accessed in Soundtrack.

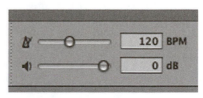

1.69 The Tempo slider controls the overall speed or tempo of the project.

Next to the Go To End button in the transport bar is a Looping button. This enables/disables looping in the playback of files on the Timeline. When this is disabled, the playhead will continue to move down the Timeline regardless of any loops existing post-playhead or not. Enabled, the looping button will cause the playhead to either return to the beginning of the project, or to the beginning of any created looping region.

The Lock To Incoming Sync button instructs Soundtrack to look for any incoming MIDI Time Code (MTC) and lock to it. This allows Soundtrack to be controlled by external hardware or software. In version 1.2 or higher, Soundtrack also sends MTC so that Soundtrack may also be the master in a studio project.

Master View

Finally, Soundtrack offers a Master View of the project, displaying a composite of track layout, complete with a mini-view of clips and their locations relative to each other in the project.

The playhead is animated within the Master View window, indicating the position of the playhead relative to the entire Timeline.

1.71 The Master View allows all clips to be viewed in their relative placement within the entire project.

Inside the Master View is a semitransparent rectangle that indicates the specific area that is visible in the project window. Any clips outside this semitransparent area in the Master Preview area will not be visible in the Timeline project area. Clicking on and moving this semitransparent area to the right or left allows users to specify the working area of the project's Timeline. This is particularly useful when working with long-form video, where condensing the Timeline is counterproductive to editing/authoring music scores.

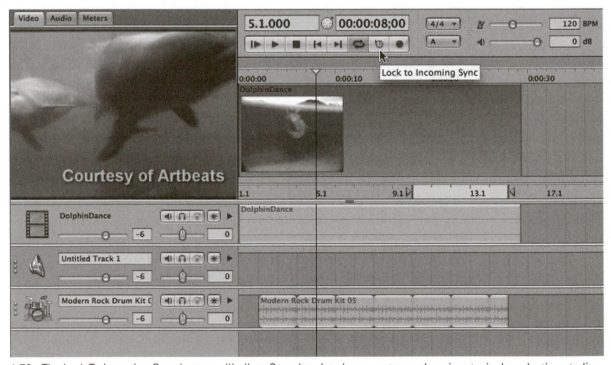

1.70 The Lock To Incoming Sync button will allow Soundtrack to be a master or slave in a typical production studio workflow.

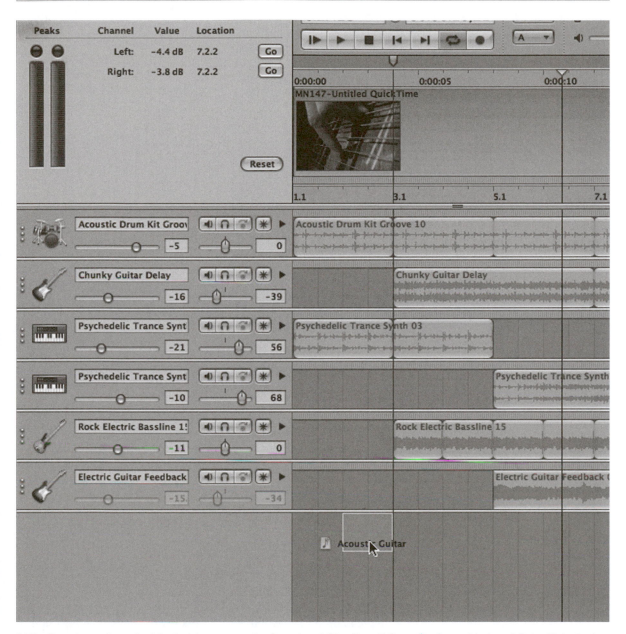

1.72 Drag loops from the Media Manager to the Soundtrack Timeline. If Snapping is enabled, and Ruler Ticks is the designated snap-to in the grid, loops will automatically lock to each other.

Getting Loops on the Timeline

Placing loops on the Timeline is as simple as dragging from the Search, Browser, or Favorites window to the desired location on the Timeline. If Snapping is enabled and the snapping format is set

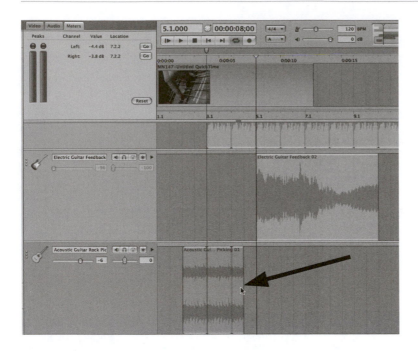

1.73 A loop is dragged out to as many measures as are necessary for the project.

to the Grid (View>Snap to>Ruler Ticks), loops placed on the Timeline will automatically lock in time to any other loops placed on the timeline.

Once a loop is on the Timeline, it may be dragged/stretched in length to fit within a determined timespace. An inserted loop will repeat for as many measures that the loop is dragged out. Holding Option while clicking on and dragging a loop creates a copy of a loop. At times, using copies of loops is infinitely more useful than using a single loop dragged out, particularly when key changes, pitch shifts, and certain mix tasks are to be accomplished.

As mentioned earlier, loops will always match with other loops regardless of tempo or key. There is no effective limit to how many loops may be placed on the Timeline, dictated only by processor speed and available RAM. Up to 126 tracks containing multiple loops are enabled. Nonmusical users will find that keeping Soundtrack's Snap function set to Snap to the Ruler Ticks prevents loops from accidentally becoming disrhythmic. Soundtrack will always lock loops to the time grid properly if snapping is enabled, but if options other than the Ruler Ticks are chosen, the downbeat of a loop may occur in a displeasing location. However, this is an area for experimentation.

Moving loops on the Timeline is also a simple task. When the cursor is hovered over the left or right edge of a loop, the cursor changes appearance to an indicator of an In or Out point.

Clicking on the edge of a loop allows the loop to be dragged out in length in order to fill a desired length of time. When a loop is dragged out, the loop will repeat upon hitting its end. The repeat point is indicated by a small divot or carrot at the top and bottom of the loop.

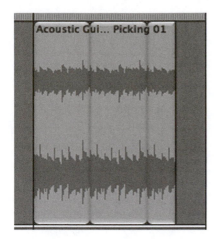

1.74 A divot/carrot indicates the ending/beginning point of a loop.

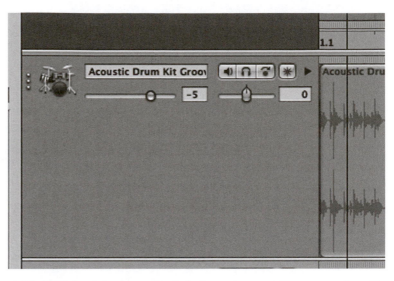

1.75 Track headers automatically indicate the type of instrument found in the loops. If metadata indicating the instrument is absent from the loop file, no icon will be created.

Notice that each time a loop was put on the Timeline, a new track header appeared. This track header is where each set of loops is controlled. The first loop dropped on a new track, or any track created as the result of dropping a loop on a blank area of the workspace will be named with the same name as the first loop dropped. An icon related to the type of loop instrument or style is created on the track header as well. This icon is created based on tags in the metadata found in the loop. For instance, if a drum loop is dropped on an empty area of the workspace, Soundtrack will

- Create a new track and track header
- Generate an icon indicating the track type
- Name the track
- Set the volume and pan to default levels

If the loop does not contain metadata indicating the loop instrument, then there will be no icon on the track header. The icon may be changed by Right clicking or Control+clicking the left side of the track header and a new icon selected from the menu that opens.

Each track has its own level/volume control, a Mute button, a Solo button, Effects Bypass button, Show Effects button, and Show/Hide Envelopes button.

SAVING YOUR WORK

Soundtrack projects are saved with reference indicators only. In other words, loops aren't copied as part of the project, unless Soundtrack is instructed to do so. The saved file will reference the

Timeline Project

Here is a quick project to get started with on the Soundtrack Timeline:

1. Open a new project in Soundtrack, using the default setting of 120 BPM and key of A.

2. Locate Acoustic Drum Kit Groove 10 *(HD:Documents:Soundtrack Loops:PowerFX Loops:Drums:Acoustic Drum Kits:Acoustic Drum Kit Groove 10)*

3. Place this groove on track 1 beginning at bar 1. It will occupy two measures on the Timeline. Grabbing the right edge of the loop, drag it out to fill 12 measures, or a total of six repetitions.

4. Play the project from the beginning and listen to the drum loop.

5. Locate Chunky Guitar Delay (*HD:Documents:Soundtrack Loops:Apple Loops: Xander Soren:Guitar:Electric Guitar: Chunky Guitar Delay)*

6. Place the Chunky Guitar Delay on Track 2 at the four-measure mark. By default it will occupy four measures on the Timeline. Drag this loop out to fill 8.5 measures, or 2.5 repetitions.

1.76   This short project should end at bar 13.

7. Play back the project thus far, and notice that the drums and Chunky Guitar Delay are perfectly locked in sync.

8. Locate Psychadelic Trance Synth 03 (*HD:Documents:Soundtrack Loops:Apple Loops:Alan Cannistraro:Keyboards:Synthesizer:Psychadelic Trance Synth 03*)

9. Place this synth on the Timeline on track 3 beginning at bar 1. This loop will occupy two measures, drag it to fill a total of four measures, ending at bar 8.

10. Play the loop, and notice that the synth is in perfect sync with the drums and guitar.

11. Finally, locate the Psychadelic Trance Synth 02 in the Soundtrack library. (*HD:Documents:Soundtrack:Loops:Apple:Loops:AlanCannistraro:Keyboards:Synthesizer:Psychadelic Trance Synth 02*)

12. Place it on track 4, beginning at bar 8. This loop will occupy four bars, drag it to fill a total of 16 bars so that it ends at bar 13.

13. Once again, play the project.

Everything is totally in sync and you have just created your first Soundtrack project. We'll be working with this project more in later chapters.

1.77   This is how the first project should appear.

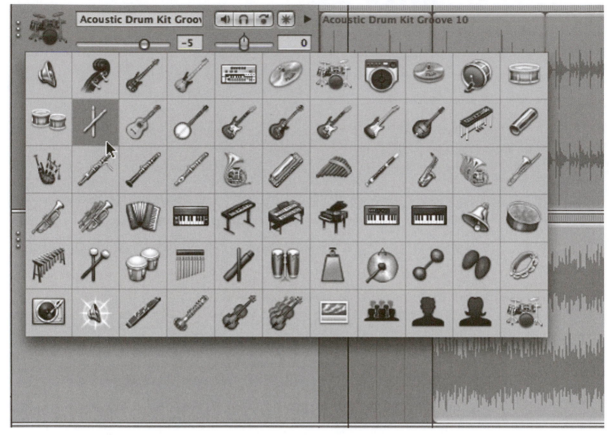

1.78 Track icons may be changed to suit personal preferences.

location of loops used in the project. All project parameters such as volume/pan envelope points, effect settings, video references, and markers, are saved as part of the project, including any effects and settings used.

Save the project by selecting File>Save or pressing the Command+S as a shortcut. The new name of the file is displayed at the top of the Soundtrack project window.

If the Collect Audio Files check box is selected, then all audio loops will be packaged with the project. This can create huge files, as it copies loops used to the directory/folder on which the Soundtrack project was saved. This is useful for keeping on a separate, mobile hard drive, sharing the project with other users, or for archiving a project on a CD-ROM.

Video files are automatically collected with the project by default. To save a project with a different name, use the Save As dialog. Saving various versions or mixes of the same project is a fast way to compare progress or approaches to a file. For example, a fast version of a score containing a heavy metal guitar as the featured background instrument might be called "scene1heavymix1" and a similar version of the same project featuring a fast table mix conveying a similar sense of

1.79 The track header is where all attributes of the track are controlled.

1.80 Storing various mixes is an efficient method of comparing mixes for a scene.

urgency might be called "scene1tablamix1." Mixes can be individually saved as well. An example of various mixes can be saved as "Scene1bassmix" and a less bass-heavy mix might be labeled as "Scene1lessbassmix."

In the next chapter, we'll begin identifying advanced tools and their uses, including plugins, FX, and navigation tools. Before moving on, open the various files included on the disk, and practice with the tools outlined in this chapter. Get familiar with the interface, and the next chapters will make more sense and be more readily absorbed.

Chapter 2

Moving Past the Basics

PREFERENCES

Setting preferences should be the first step in learning to work with Soundtrack. If Soundtrack Preferences are set for an efficient workflow before starting a project, many frustrations are avoided.

General Tab

Open the Preferences dialog by selecting Soundtrack>Soundtrack Preferences. This opens a three-tab dialog. In the General Tab, Startup, Media Manager, and Timeline preferences are determined.

The Startup offers Last Project, which means that Soundtrack will open the last project created. New Project launches a blank workspace, allowing for the immediate start of a project.

Selecting Search Result numbers from the dropdown menu determines how many loops are displayed in the search window during the auditioning process. Soundtrack displays 25 loops per search by default; this may be decreased to 10 loops or increased to 50, 75, 100, 250, or 500 loops per search page. Note that higher resolutions/large screen displays can display greater numbers of loops by default.

In the Timeline preference, Snapping can be enabled or disabled by default. I recommend leaving this to the On preference, as Snapping can be temporarily disabled by pressing the G-key as a shortcut. Re-enable Snapping by pressing the G-key again. An indicator displays the status of Snapping in the lower left corner of the Soundtrack workspace.

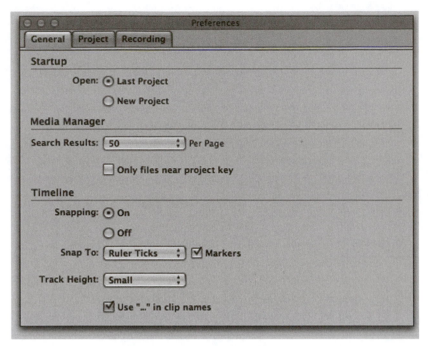

2.1   The Soundtrack Preferences dialog enables a user to set default behaviors for a project.

Snap-to defines what value loops snap to when dragged to the workspace. For newcomers to composition, it's a good idea to leave this set to the Ruler Ticks setting, with the Marker's checkbox checked. Otherwise, loops could potentially be snapped to a value that is offset from the beginning of a measure. Of course, this value may be reset at any time. If any other value for starting users is selected, I'd suggest the Quarter (1/4th) note value, allowing rhythms to be offset by a half count. More refined settings, such as an Eighth (1/8th) note value, work best for users creating fairly complex loop sections one note at a time.

The use of "____" in clip names places a tag in the upper left corner of each loop, indicating the loop's entire name. This is exceptionally useful in working with large projects, helping to determine quickly if a loop has been used earlier in the project. (Loops used in the project will also be displayed in the Audio bin, found beneath the Video Preview window).

2.2   Snapping status is indicated in the window found in the lower left corner of Soundtrack.

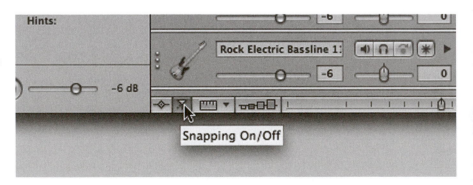

Project Tab

The Project tab allows preferences to be set for how each project opens up. The default length of time in the project is determined here, as well as time signature, tempo, and key. By default, this is set to 120BPM, key of A, time signature of 4/4. I recommend leaving the default properties. Time, tempo and key may all be adjusted in the Master Control or via envelopes in the project; default preference settings are a great starting point.

Sample rate by default is 44.1KB/16bit. This does not match the default audio settings of DV media.Be certain an export to Final Cut Pro (FCP) or other nonlinear editor (NLE) is set to 48KB/16bit. Note that Soundtrack has 96KB/24bit capability. Also, special or external hardware-based soundcards, such as the Indigo and Layla, are required for accurate playback of high-resolution files.

Recording Tab

The Recording Tab specifies where audio will be input from, whether it's a default audio card built into the system, or an external card such as the Layla or Indigo. Recording may be monitored as well, allowing the audio to be heard as it's being recorded. Latency may be a factor here, depending on the card used.

Fade-in/Fade out is also selectable. If not set by default, set this to 5ms as a starting point. If no fade point is selected, loops recorded in Soundtrack may pop or click due to transient differences in the in/out point of the recorded loops.

Choose a session location where recorded audio will be stored/recorded on the hard drive. This is usually best if it's a secondary hard drive and not the system drive, however, the system drive is capable of recording loops as well. System efficiency is always better when the system drive used for the OS and application data and video/audio are recorded to and stored on a second hard drive.

Editing Techniques

Soundtrack provides tools for complete control over the musical score. Having a workflow that takes advantage of these tools will not only make the composition of musical scores more efficient, but will also inspire a more creative environment.

Arrangements of loops are what make the difference in the overall emotional quality of a composition. Most musical forms are repetitive at some point; Soundtrack's tools can be put to use to take advantage of repetition without the music sounding stagnated and repetitive.

While scores may be composed by merely throwing loops on the Timeline and locking them together, this only scratches the surface of what can be done in Soundtrack. Changing keys, shifting melodies, arranging loops in aurally appealing sequences, mixing techniques, using FX are all

To select a clip in the Timeline, simply click on it. Selected clips are darker than the rest.

Multiple clips can be selected by holding Command while clicking on desired clips. Also, multiple clips can be selected by clicking slightly ahead of a clip, then dragging the cursor across several clips.

If two clips are next to each other on the Timeline, hold Shift while clicking the two clips.

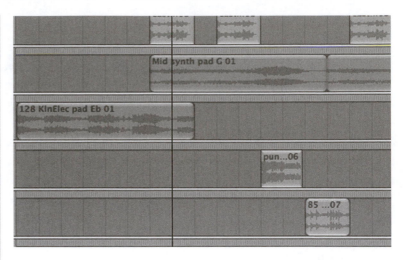

2.3   Selected clips are darker than their unselected counterparts.

part of making the score speak to the ear. If coupled with video, this is can be even more compelling and interesting, too.

Loops that are key-based can be shifted on the Timeline, allowing loops to be moved up or down in pitch. This function allows a user to grab and use melodies, interesting chord changes, musical turnarounds, and other arrangements that make the score enticing and attention grabbing. While the creation of in-depth melodies by way of splitting and shifting loop points may prove challenging to the nonmusical user, Soundtrack provides the tools for these users to create musical expressions that are provoking and moving. Soundtrack is capable of pitchshifting individual loops only or shifting an entire project via an envelope point in the Timeline. This will be discussed later in this chapter.

Music Basics for Soundtrack Users

This next section could easily turn into a discussion of music basics. I'll attempt to keep it simple and stick to music concepts that relate to Soundtrack only.

Creating a pitch change is as simple as Right+clicking/Control+clicking a clip and selecting Transpose from the menu. A submenu opens with choices for shifting audio up or down as many as 12 steps.

In the Transpose menu, increments of a half-step are available; this is where a basic knowledge of music is beneficial, but not required. A great deal of modern music follows various formulas based around chord intervals. An interval is the relative difference between two notes. These differences are measured in "steps." Intervals may apply to individual notes in a melody or apply to chords and the distance between the chords. The two types of steps are measured in full steps or half steps. Half steps are also referred to as "semitones." For example, if the root note is the key of

Do Re Mi: The western scale consists of octaves. Remember the song from the *Sound of Music?... Do, a deer, a female deer, Ray, a drop of golden sun, Mi, a name, I call myself*, etc. That song contains eight notes, just as most school children are taught. Do, Re, Mi, Fa, So, La, Ti, Do is the scale we all were taught in fourth-grade music. However, that scale does not take into account the black keys found on a piano. These are known as "accidentals" and they are a half step, or semitone, above or below the adjacent white key on the piano. Accidentals are counted as sharps and flats on the musical scale. Therefore, a note such as A can be stepped up a semitone, creating the note A-sharp or stepped down a semitone as A-flat. To add more confusion, A-flat is the same as G-sharp, also A-sharp is the same note as B-flat. There is no B-sharp or C-flat or E-sharp or F-flat. An octave includes all of the 12 notes between the first note and the last note of the same name. While a strong understanding of music is not at all required in order to use Soundtrack, having an elementary knowledge of music scales can help while creating melodies, whether this is the endeavor of the video editor, DVD menu author, or Flash music bed author.

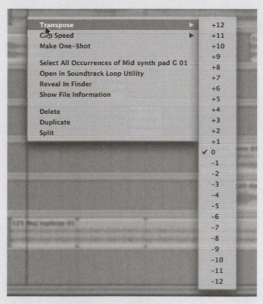

2.4   To transpose audio up or down in pitch, Right+click or Control+click the loop to be transposed.

A (default in Soundtrack), then a full-step interval would be up to B, while a half-step interval or a semitone would be the A-sharp note.

If you don't recognize how important intervals are in a song, here are a couple hints that might help a user to discover intervals by humming to yourself. Warning: this does take a minimal amount of musical acumen.

- To recognize the interval of a third, hum the first notes of "Michael, Row the Boat Ashore."

2.5   Intervals are measured between notes.(This is easiest seen on a keyboard.) An octave is made up of eight full steps or 12 half-steps.

Transposition

While understanding chord progressions at an elementary level is very helpful in composing music for video or other projects, it's not necessary. This chart shows the most common intervals and their transposition tables. The intervals are not listed in musical order, but rather in the order that they are most commonly used in loop-based music.

Interval[a]	Semitone (upward)	Semitone (downward)
Perfect 5th	+7	−5
Perfect 4th	+5	−7
Major 6th	+9	−3
Major 3rd	+4	−8
Major 2nd	+2	−10
Octave	+12	−12
Minor 3rd	+3	−9
Tritone/Diminished 5th	+6	−6
Minor 6th	−6	+6
Major 7th	+11	−1
Minor 7th	+10	−2
Minor 2nd	+1	−11

a   In order of most common use, not in order according to scale

- To recognize the interval of a fourth, hum the opening notes of "O Christmas Tree."
- To recognize the interval of a fifth, hum the first notes of the "Star Wars" theme.
- To recognize the interval of a sixth, hum the first notes of "My Bonnie Lies Over the Ocean."

Two very popular chord formulas are based on what is known as 1–4–5. In other words, the tonic, or base chord, is the foundation and the secondary chords in the structure are the fourth and fifth chords. To create this sort of chord structure in Soundtrack can be confusing at first. For

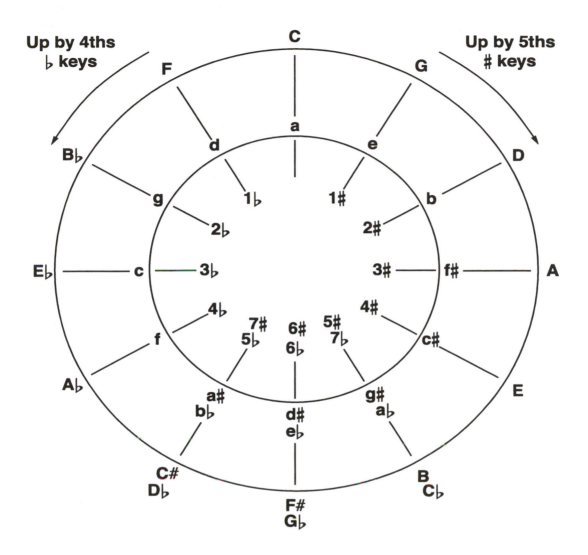

Up by 4ths
♭ keys

Up by 5ths
keys

:.6   Use the Circle of fifths to find the relative minor of any key in the Western scale. This is useful when trying to find the relative minor of a major key. Since A is the default key in Soundtrack, the relative minor for instance is F-sharp minor.

instance, while creating a 1–4–5 structure, it might make sense to shift audio up +4, then in +5 increments. Also, it's important to remember that increments are half-steps in the Soundtrack menu, meaning that a 4 full-steps is really +5 and a 5 full-steps is really +7. Another way to think of this is as −5 full-steps down for a fifth and a −7 full-steps down for a fourth.

This same pattern may be reversed, or inverted, so the pattern of chordal structure might be either 5–4–1 or 4–5–1.

Another common interval pattern, particularly in a minor key, is to drop a minor key by –4, then move to the next note up, which would be dropping the original note by –2 before returning to the original note. This is known as a VI–IV–V pattern. For example, an A-minor chord is the sixth note from the tonic of the key of C. This is also known as the "relative minor." Therefore, a 6–4–5 chord progression can be A minor, F major, and G major. This is a very common pattern and is created easily in Soundtrack because of the number of minor loops available in loop libraries. In the Media Manager, a user finds whether a loop is a major or minor key displayed. Also displayed are any clips imported from another loop library that can be designated as major or minor.

Working with Loops

Open the Minor Pitch Shift project on the CD-ROM. This project shows how clips can be split and pitch shifted, then used in a project. Feel free to change the instruments/replace the instruments to experiment with various sounds.

Loops may be placed on the Timeline as they are, with no shifts in pitch whatsoever. Over a period of time, loops that merely repeat may become dull and lifeless, and actually detract from any video associated with the music.

The easiest method of making the music breathe with a little life is to count in bars, not being repetitive for more than eight bars at a time. Even a simple one-shot added to a point in the Timeline can be used to punctuate a specific moment and add life to an otherwise redundant series of loops.

Nontransposing: Instruments that do not contain key information do not transpose, such as drums and percussion. One-shots and some spoken word pieces do not contain key information, nor do most sound effects such as traffic, industrial, or nature sounds. Therefore, transposing these sounds will not affect their pitch.

Open the punctuation file on the CD-ROM found in the back of this book. Notice that various moments in the file are punctuated with one-shots on the Timeline, saving an otherwise less-than-interesting video score from being redundant.

Melodies can also be created in Soundtrack by slicing loops note by note and shifting the slices up or down in pitch. Depending on the loop, this can be a pleasing sound or a displeasing noise. Slicing a loop into individual notes is best accomplished by snapping to 32nd or 64th notes, then zooming deep on the Timeline, placing the Playhead at the desired note, and splitting using the S key. While zoomed, Right-click/Control+click the split note and transpose to the desired key.

If the music being composed is for purposes of underlying video, particularly video that contains dialog, a melody is rarely desirable, as melodies may detract from the dialog, or interfere with the dialog. Therefore, creating a score known as a "bed," or music that doesn't contain a melodic line, is usually desirable in this circumstance. Creating a bed is far less complex than creating a melody-directed score, as a bed contains predominantly rhythmic elements.

The entire project may be transposed in pitch as well, excluding loops containing no pitch information, such as drum loops, percussion loops, and one-shots that have not had key metadata inserted. To transpose the entire project, Control+click/Right-click in an empty area beneath the track headers and select Show Master Envelopes. Selecting View>Show Master Envelopes will also open the Master Envelopes view.

In the Master Envelopes view is an envelope labeled Transpose. There are no envelope points on this envelope by default.

Double-click the envelope at the point that a transposition or shift in pitch should occur. It's normally best that Snapping is enabled when inserting a Transpose envelope point. If snapping is not enabled, it's easy to insert an envelope point one or two note values ahead or behind where a pitch shift should occur. This creates strange artifacts in the decay of a sound that has already begun or an odd effect, depending on the contents of the loop(s) being shifted.

Shifting pitches at the project level is a great method of getting familiar with how pitches shift for the nonmusical user. Shifting pitch alone can make a tremendous difference in the attitude of the composition.

When shifting pitches, some loops will shift better than others depending on the frequency range of the instruments in the loops. Low frequencies do not shift as well as higher frequencies, so expect bass guitar and low piano sounds to take on some less-than satisfactory attributes if shifted down farther than the frequencies allow. If this turns out to be the case, tempo may be increased or decreased to lessen the effect of shifted pitch.

Artifacts: With some loops that prove to be difficult to shift in pitch, shifting tempo will compensate for any artifacts introduced in the shifting of a pitch. The same holds true for loops that sound odd at a tempo that is tremendously faster than the loop's recording. Shifting the pitch down will often "repair" the quality of the loop, particularly when masked by other loops in the project.

In addition, loops may be imported to the Timeline that haven't been transposed and might be stretched beyond the loop's capabilities or natural sound. Most often, transposing these clips up or down an octave and changing playback speed to double or half-speed will bring the loop to an acceptable quality.

CLIP SPEED

For loops that cannot be shifted or tempo-changed, try shifting the speed of the individual loop by Right-clicking/Control+clicking on the problem loop. The dialog that opens offers a Clip Speed selection. In many cases, doubling the speed of a clip will correct artifacts resulting from a pitch shift.

Clips may be sped up or slowed down by a factor of four, allowing quadruple speed, or one-quarter the original speed. This can be used as an effect in a piece of music to give it a sense of heightened movement or tension.

Another technique employed to fatten up or create a "larger" sound is duplicating a track and, on one or the other track, doubling or halving the speed of a loop.

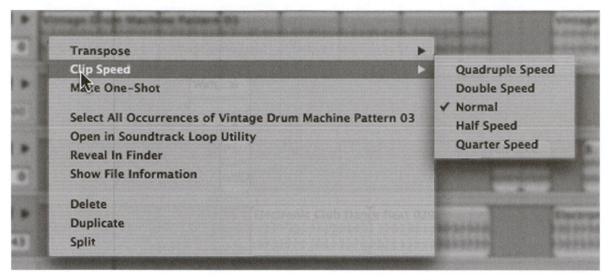

2.7 Right+click or Control+click to access the submenu that accesses clip speed change.

Open the *Global Pitch Shift* project found on the CD-ROM in this book to hear two tracks doubled against each other, one at normal speed and the other at double speed.

This plays the same loop against itself with one copy playing at double or half-speed from the original. Pan the original to –50 and the copy playing at double or half speed to 55. This typically gives a lush and fat sound. Similar techniques account for the famous "Wall of Sound" from Phil Specter in the day of the Beatles' later recordings.

This technique may be employed on any loop/track with the exception of one-shots. For those who are really daring, use three or more copies of the original loop, slowing one to half speed while doubling the speed of another, or experimenting with various clip speeds varying from the original clip speed. On a recent video project that required simplicity, I created a composition that used only two guitar loops, but doubled, effected, and shifted clip speed on them over a span of eight tracks. The audio was effective: simple, yet deep and filled with emotion, while not detracting from the video shown.

Open the *Lush* project file from the CD-ROM in this book.

A loop may also be converted to a one-shot, nullifying the ability to loop the clip. If the loop is converted to a one-shot in the project, it does not convert all instances of the loop to a one-shot and only affects the selected loop. To convert a loop to a one shot, Right+click/Control+click the loop on the Timeline and select Convert to One-Shot from the submenu. This will disable the loop's ability to be drag repeated and may cause a loop to go out of sync after the initial attack of the loop.

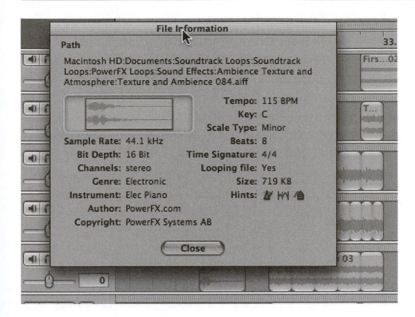

2.8 Viewing the File Information reveals metadata inserted in the loop, providing quick reference to a clip's properties.

Occasionally, a loop's beginning point may not be desirable in a project, but the ending point of the loop is. For example, a drum loop that has a drum roll at the end of the loop that would serve as a perfect introduction to the drum's appearance in the composition. This can be accomplished by one of three methods.

The first and most obvious method is to place the loop so that the end of the loop is in the correct position. Audio not desired in the earlier part of the loop is split out and deleted.

The second method is to do the same, placing the loop at its correct point and inserting a volume envelope. The envelope controlling the incoming audio removes the beginning point of the audio.

The third method, while not as obvious, is the most efficient and useful for most applications. The clip may be offset so that the loop doesn't include the incoming audio at all by using Command+Option+Drag to the left.

This allows the audio at the end of the clip to be used at any point in the loop. The loop length will not change. The clip's loop point will shift, indicated by the divot moving to the left of the loop. The loop offset cannot be set past the beginning point of the loop.

CLIP PROPERTIES

When a clip is dragged to the Timeline, its properties may still be viewed. Control+clicking on a file provides a choice of properties in the menu that opens. Selecting this choice displays the start point of the loop, length, type (loop or one-shot), metadata information (tags), offset (how many beats from the start of the clip till the audio begins playing), and transposition information (if the clip has been transposed up or down).

Any changes made to the properties of the original clip are displayed in the edited clip, as well as the original clip. Editing a clip on the Timeline does not effect the properties of a clip. If a clip does not contain metadata or other relevant information in the properties, the clip may be opened in the Soundtrack Loop Utility and metadata can be added. Open the clip in the Soundtrack Loop Utility by Control+clicking on the clip and selecting Open in Soundtrack Loop Utility. The Loop Utility will then offer choices on adding metadata to the clip's properties. For more information on using the Soundtrack Loop Utility, please see Chapter 3 and the section on the Soundtrack Loop Utility.

WORKFLOW

There are a variety of methods in choosing and using loops to create a soundtrack, whether for video, DVD menus, or Flash applications. Workflows may be different depending on the desired result. Musical users may find that selecting a rhythmic, polytonal instrument first inspires a score, while nonmusical users may find a percussion or drum-oriented loop drives the video piece. In this next section, we'll examine some methods of getting loops on the Timeline in an efficient manner.

When working with video, there are usually points in the video project that require musical punctuations, expressions, or indications of changing scenes or emotion. Finding, identifying, and marking these locations is known as "spotting." Soundtrack makes it very easy to spot a video project by allowing playback, dropping a marker (press M at the desired points), then creating a score that hits those points. If the video project is lengthy, a large number of tracks and loops are sure to be used because the musical expressions, tempo, and instrumentation are unique to each scene, section, or point in the video project. Soundtrack is capable of importing video files of up to four hours in length, although performance is significantly reduced with projects of such lengths if many loops are used in the project.

1. Begin by importing video to the Timeline. Use the Media Manager to locate and import the QuickTime or MPEG-2 video.

2. Drag the video from the Media Manager to the preview window and drop it. An audio track is automatically created for audio contained in the video stream.

3. Press the spacebar to begin playback of the video file.

   Video will contain motion/continuous update in the preview window, although the frame in the Timeline remains static. In other words, as the Playhead moves across the Timeline, video has full motion in the preview window, though the thumbnails of the video won't reflect the differences from one frame of video to the next.

4. While viewing the video playback, press the M or B key to insert markers on the Timeline to indicate key points for musical changes, sound FX, or any other aural indicator that's desired. Playback, too, may be paused at key points, allowing frame-accurate marker insertion. Press the spacebar to pause play-

 Pressing the B key drops Beat Markers on the Timeline while pressing the M key drops a Standard Time Marker on the Timeline. See Chapter 1 for information on the differences between Beat Markers and Time Markers.

back at key points. Then press the M or B key to drop a marker.

5. Position the Playhead at either the start of the Timeline, or on a marker placed where the score should begin.

6. Set a loop space that is the length of the project or of the scene being composed.

    A specified area to loop may be assigned/created by Click+dragging across the bar indicator in the Timeline. This creates a light blue triangle at both the In and Out points of the looping section. Setting a loop section keeps the Playhead in a localized and specified area so that a particular area may have loops auditioned against it. This is of tremendous benefit in a long-form project where only a small section is scored.

7. Open the Media Manager if it's not already open.

8. In the Media Manager, click on one of the search parameters, such as an instrument.

    The type of video being scored is the determining factor in selecting a starting instrument or genre. Fast paced, driving video often scores most efficiently when it begins with an energetic drum track and/or bass track, while slower-paced video might call for a string section or guitar track. Using fast attack sounds, such as percussives, plucked sounds, aggressive sounds, and drums, helps to create the sense of being driven or pushed. Look to sounds of gentle piano grooves, finger-picked acoustic guitar, ethereal pads, or slow-attack sounds to provide the backdrop for "sensitive" or slow-edited video or video action.

    Whenever a loop is clicked on in the Media Manager, playback of that loop will begin whether the Timeline is moving or not. This is known as "auditioning" or previewing the loop.

9. Once a loop is selected, drag it to the Timeline and drop it in the desired position.

    If snapping is disabled and the loop does not snap to the marker position, enable snapping by pressing G, or using the View>Snapping menu to enable snapping. Make certain the Snap-to setting is set to Ruler Ticks and Markers.

    Snapping may be temporarily disabled or enabled by holding the Command key while dragging a loop. If snapping is enabled and Command is held during the drag, the loop will not snap to its normal snapping point. If snapping has been disabled, holding Command will force the dragged loop to its nearest snap-to point.

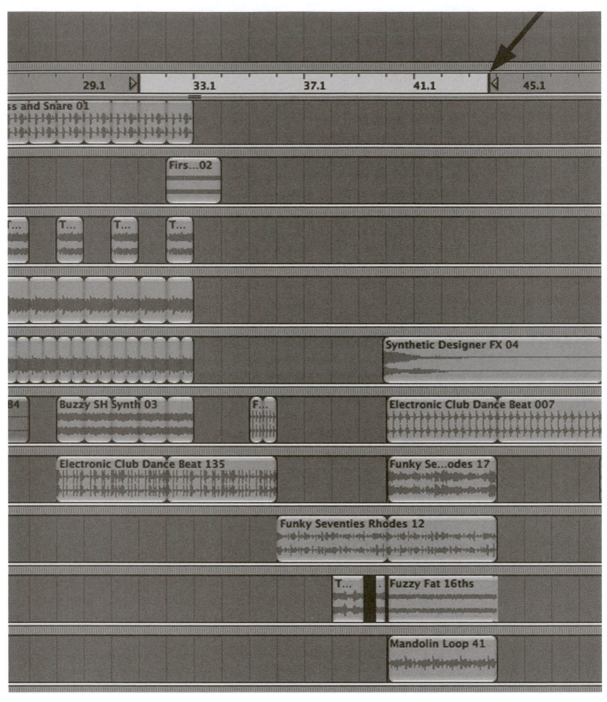

2.9   Loop playback area can be specified for looping in a given area. This is exceptionally useful when working with long-form video projects or auditioning loops against a particular section of a composition

Adding Tracks

Files may be added to the Timeline from the Media Manager by:

- Dragging a file from the Additional Info waveform display.
- Dragging a file from the Media Manager file list.
- Dragging a file from the Favorites list.
- Dragging a file from the Finder to a new or existing track.

Tracks are added whenever a file is dragged to a new area on the workspace, unless Master Envelopes are visible. Only if Master Loops are visible, loops may be dragged to existing tracks. When dragging a file from the Preview window to a track or lower portion of the Timeline, the volume level of the Preview window accompanies the loop. As a result, if an auditioning or previewing loop is mixed in the preview area, it will retain that volume setting when dragged to a new track.

10. Drag the loop out in length to fit the desired timespace. Press Enter to locate the Playhead at the beginning of the project and press spacebar to start playback.

The video may "feel" different with the beginnings of an underlying score; This is common. A score placed under a video clip typically causes a video to seem different and since the ear is a great deal more sensitive than the eye, the ear often fools the eye into "hearing" something different than is really there. This phenomenon can work two ways. Either the score drives home the action on the screen, or it creates a mood different than what the images on the screen portray. The result depends on what the editor or director prefers to do. As an example, a slow moving scene of a boy and a girl kissing can be romantic by using slow loops, strings, piano, light guitar, pads, and no percussion. Taking the same scene and using hard rock guitars, drums, driving bass, or other assertive sounds will give the video image a feeling of rebellion or new beginning. Playing a solo instrument that is sparse and very airy, or lacking many notes between passages, gives a melancholy feeling, perhaps a feeling of the relationship ending.

 Open the *Emotions* file on the CD-ROM contained in this book. Solo the various audio tracks to get an idea of how emotions may be created on the same video file. Some sections are sorrowful, while others assert machismo. The video takes on very different roles depending on the audio found beneath it.

Auditioning

Now audition other loops. If a drum loop is selected to start the project audio, then perhaps a bass or rhythm instrument like a piano or guitar would suit the next track. Typically, the best way

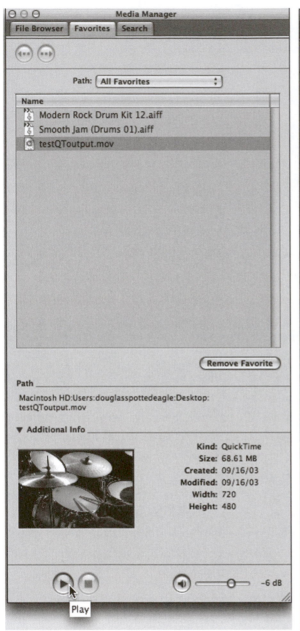

2.10 Double-click video files in the Media Manager to begin playback of the video in the Media Manager's preview window.

2.11 When the Timeline is playing, any loop chosen in the Media Manager will begin playback at the downbeat of the next measure. Any loop playing from the Media Manager can be muted by selecting this button.

to audition a loop is to start playback on the Timeline and allow the playback to run while auditioning loops from the Media Manager. This allows the loop being auditioned to be heard while listening to already-existing audio, permitting the loop to be heard in the context of other loops on the Timeline.

Volume of the current auditioning loop is controlled at the bottom of the Media Manager by reducing or increasing the slider position. Default volume setting is 0dB. If there is a lot happening on the Timeline, the level may need to be increased during auditioning to get the best idea of what's happening with the loop being auditioned. The loop playback can be stopped during audition by pressing the Stop button in the lower left corner of the Media Manager. Playback is resumed by pressing the Play button in the lower left corner of the Media Manager.

Auditioning files are soloed by stopping playback of the Timeline. If the Timeline is stopped/paused, files playing in the Media Manager will play back in solo mode.

Starting an auditioning loop's playback during playback of the workspace timeline results in the loop waiting for a downbeat in the next measure before the auditioning/previewing loop will begin. Auditioning loops can be muted during their playback by pressing the Mute button, found in the lower left of the Media Manager. Muting a loop doesn't stop playback of the auditioning loop. Adjust the volume of the auditioning loop with the slider found next to the Mute button.

One-shot loops will not loop in auditioning/preview playback or on the workspace timeline because one-shots don't contain looping data.

Drag satisfactory loops onto the Timeline. Don't be afraid of dragging a large number of loops to many tracks; The Delete key is always close by. Sometimes great combinations are found by accident. Other times the loops simply won't complement each other. Picking and choosing loops, how long and when they should be heard, and in what key they should be heard, is the process of arranging the score. Arranging loops is much like choosing words that belong in sentences and choosing which sentences are part of a paragraph.

1. One method of working that is simple and powerful is dragging loops on the Timeline as individual loops and using Option+drag to copy the loop next to itself, perhaps creating a series of copies. Loops are split easily at any point in time, you can do this by using the S key. Loops across an entire project may also be split by positioning the Playhead at the point that all loops are to be split and selecting the Edit>Split option. All loops covered by the Playhead will be split. This feature is great in order to end a project with all

> On occasion, when dragging clips to the Timeline, clips are accidentally overlapped. Soundtrack truncates the beginning or end of any overlapping clips, which may cause a pop or click. If a clip is accidentally overlapped on another clip, either undo the action Command+Z, or slide the overlapping/new clip to the right or left so there is no overlap. Afterwards, drag out the clip to the desired length. Overlapping clips does not damage the clips involved because of how Soundtrack nondestructively manages files, so don't worry if you accidentally overlap clips.

Additional information regarding files being auditioned/previewed may be accessed by clicking on the Additional Info button found in the lower third of the Media Manager. Selecting this option displays the location of the file, path to the file, original tempo, key, major or minor scale, number of beats, size of the file, author/copyright information, sample rate/bit depth, stereo/mono, genre, loop or one-shot, and a visual display of the file. Clicking and dragging the displayed waveform allows the wave to be placed on the workspace Timeline. This information is not only helpful in identifying loops for use in the project, but also good for learning to identify key and scale structures. The amount of additional information shown is dependent on the amount of metadata placed in the loop by the author or in the Soundtrack Loop Utility during the recording or conversion process.

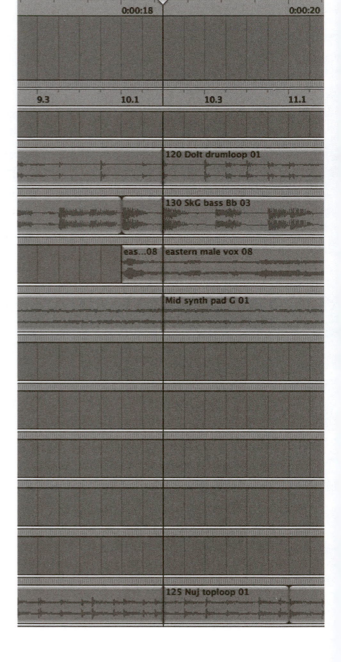

2.12 Split all clips on the Timeline by placing the Playhead, selecting All (Command+A), and pressing the S-key.

loops ending at one point. If a project contains a number of copied loops that don't end at the same point in time in the project, simply place the Playhead at the end point of the project and press S. Then drag/select all remaining clips and delete them or use Control+clips selected after the split point and Delete.

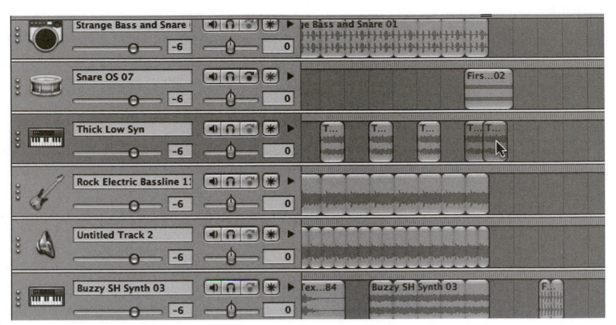

2.13   Using the *Option*+drag function or copy/pasting loops is slower than dragging loops onto the Timeline, but has benefits for the new user.

2. Loops that have been split or are copies of the same loop next to each other may be joined as a single clip by selecting the two clips to join and pressing the J-key.

3. Later on in the editing of the project, some of the loops placed on the Timeline are transposed for the purpose of creating some aural movement. Though for now, locate loops that sound good to your ear and place them on the Timeline with other tracks.

4. Loops can be copy/pasted as single loops or entire tracks on the Timeline. Simply select a loop or loops that should be copied and select the Edit>Copy or press Command+C to copy the loops to the clipboard. Place the cursor where the loops will be copied and select Edit>Paste or press Command+V to paste the loops. If multiple loops across multiple tracks have been copied and need to be pasted, Soundtrack will paste the loop from the topmost track into the currently selected track. If, for example, loops from four individual tracks are copied and the third-lowest track is selected for the paste location, then Soundtrack asks if you'd like to create new tracks for the additional two tracks that won't have a location to paste to if new tracks are ignored. If the New Tracks option is ignored in this instance, then only two tracks of audio will be pasted. Soundtrack always pastes loops to the selected track. If no track is selected after the loop has been copied, Soundtrack pastes the loop to the same track from which it was copied.

5. If multiple copies of a loop should be pasted to the Timeline, copy a selected loop, then position the cursor where the first copy of the loop will be pasted. The copy of the loop appears at the

2.14 Pasting several loop copies permits normal loop activity while providing separated loops for easy transposing or movement on the Timeline.

Playhead position. If loops will be copied to a new track, create the new track. Choose Edit>Paste Repeat or Option+Command+V. A dialog box opens and asks the number of repeats desired. Input the number and choose OK in the dialog box. The loops are pasted for that number of repeats.

6. Occasionally, as a project matures, an instrument or loop that sounded great at the onset of the project may not be particularly fitting and yet the whole thing is successfully arranged. Perhaps the loop has been edited in an audio editor and given a new name. In any event, all instances of a particular loop may be selected and replaced with all attributes assigned to the loop kept intact. To perform this function, Control+click/Right-click the loop to be replaced and choose Select All Occurrences of "(*Filename*)" from the submenu that opens. Next, select a replacement loop in the Media Manager, Control+click/Right-click the replacement file, and choose Replace Selected Loops with "(*Filename*)" from the submenu. This replaces all loops of a unique filename with the newly selected loop. Another way to consider this feature is like having access to audio "takes" that can be selectively switched out. This is valuable when the loop is edited in an editing tool such as Peak™ or a new loop has been recorded. See Chapter 3 for more information on recording loops.

7. Play back the Timeline and pay particular attention to the action of the video and its interaction with the music in the score.

At this point, if more than three or four tracks of audio are part of the project, it may easily sound cluttered. Therefore, it's a good idea to start setting the blend or mix of the project.

MIXING TRACKS

Mixing audio is an art form in itself; this is why in the film, broadcast, and corporate video industry, traditionally, there have been video engineers and audio engineers, post houses, and mixing engineers. Now, desktop video is changing this and enabling video engineers/editors to do audio and audio engineers/editors to do video.

Mixing is a task that requires a good set of ears. Mixing audio is much like creating a deep composite of images: too much of anything can diminish the message and too little may prevent the image from being seen/heard. Just as many compositors learn the art of compositing from watching film, editors can learn the basics of mixing by listening to music in similar genres as the music being mixed for a project. In this section, I'll attempt to demonstrate some of the fundamentals of mixing dialog, music, sound effects, and stingers to create a great audio track for a video, DVD menu, or Flash animation.

Mixing audio is a practice based entirely on personal preference, but there are some standards and techniques used by most engineers and producers to achieve mixes that meet industry expectations. Each person's ears are different. This is what makes one producer more popular for certain kinds of music than another. Mutt Lange, a very well known producer of heavy metal and pop rock, is one of the few to jump from one musical style to another. (Based on the string of country hit songs he's produced, marrying country legend Shania Twain sure didn't hurt his career.) Peter Gabriel is renowned for his production of world pop music, just as William Aura is known for his adult contemporary work. Alan Parsons, Tom Lord-Alge, Ross Collum, Danial Langios, are all well-known producers/mix engineers, each reflecting a unique style. Each of them credits their years working with the equipment and producers in the studios where they cut their teeth as third engineers, janitors, or receptionists. Each of these producers got to where they are not only because of their inspired sense of what people want to hear and how to bring artistic talent to the fore, but also because they understand the basic principles and practices of mixing audio. Knowledge and a practiced ear are the two most important things to create a great mix. Knowledge is easily acquired, but a practiced ear can take years to develop. The basic principles of understanding a mix are fairly simple, thereafter it simply becomes a matter of expanding experience.

Setting up a mix is entirely dependent on the content of the tracks, whether it's straight instrumentation, bed music with a voice over, Foley, sound design, or all of these. Bass frequencies tend to be more centered in a mix than high frequencies. Bass drums and bass guitar/synthesizers are generally mixed to the center, and higher frequency sounds are spaced throughout the right to left areas. In the past, drum and bass tracks were mixed dead center when mastering for vinyl, as the bass/kick drum tracks could cause the record player needle to either jump the groove or carve out a groove in the vinyl that removed the higher frequencies. One or two plays of a record with bass frequencies hard panned and the record would be nothing more than thump.

Mix engineers typically start a mix at one end of a mix or another. This means they either start with the bass or the bottom of a mix as a foundation, then mix up to the vocals/dialog. Another possibility is that they start with the most important elements of a mix, such as dialog, and mix down multiple tracks to stereo tracks (Right/Left) from there. For working with a dialog-based mix for film or video, this is a good way to start by getting the voice to a level that is comfortable. It should be loud, but never cross the −3dB mark, so there is room for other elements to maintain their dynamic expression. Adding a compressor to the primary element is a fairly standard prac-

---

Simple Mix

A simple method of conceiving a mix is to look at a photo of a beautiful mountain vista. The mountains form the base of the image and the eye is drawn to the bugling elk in the forefront, slightly off center. Notice the green trees and the stream or brook flowing through the picture. The primary subject of the picture is the elk in the foreground, but without the surrounding beauty, the elk image is stark. Creating a good mix is just like that: several individual elements draw the ear to a primary element. In the instance of using Soundtrack to set up a mix for video, the elk is the dialog in the video and the other elements of the "picture" are the instruments in the track. Picturing the mix visually with the soundtrack in your mind's eye helps achieve the end goal.

---

tice, but this should be done in FCP or another NLE, if possible. However, for purposes of setting up the mix in Soundtrack, it's a good idea to apply a similar compression setting to the video's audio track while previewing the mix in Soundtrack.

If the primary track is a voice, start with light compression settings of 1.5:1 or 2:1, working with the threshold to suit the mix. Be cautious of squashing the sound too much, as this is the most out-front element of the mix. (Compressors are discussed more in depth on page 97.)

Next, begin to place the foundation elements, such as static walla, traffic, or background noise. In a musical context, these elements are the kick drum and bass guitar or other bottom-end elements. If the bottom sound is muddy or tubby, remove some of the frequencies in the 300Hz region. In a musical mix, insert an equalizer (EQ) and add a little 1.5k for some snap in the kick drum and bass guitar tracks. In a mix for video with dialog, it's a good idea to insert an EQ and leave some of the upper frequencies out of the background/bed audio, perhaps even dampen or reduce them a bit, so there's no fight with the frequencies in the primary element/front voice. Use a compressor, starting with a basic setting of 3:1 or 4:1, and work with the settings from there in order to keep the mix from becoming too dynamic in the low frequencies.

One of the dangers of not having dialog or primary audio present when performing a mix is that elements of the mix may overshadow or compete with the video's audio at various points in the mix. If the dialog/primary audio isn't present to make qualified comparisons, key elements of the mix can be compromised and may require remixing once the score is imported to FCP or another NLE system. One of the benefits of Soundtrack is that multiple tracks can be individually exported as separate tracks to the NLE, allowing for a mix to be created in the NLE instead of mixing in Soundtrack only, leaving mix decisions as a possibility until the final render.

Next, sound design comes into the mix with motion and depth filling the speakers with moving elements that may be musical or not. Either way, the sound should be a filling sound that underlies the other pieces of the mix. In a music-oriented mix, this would be the rhythmic element. Try to avoid panning this sound hard right/left, if possible. More of a nine o'clock and three o'clock is the standard, washed wide rather than being too loud and taking away focus from the aural subject.

Basic Instrumental Settings

Various instruments respond well starting with basic settings. Try these EQ points when beginning to set the tone for various instruments:

Vocals (sung): Slight boost at 4KHz. Pan slightly right or left.

Vocals (spoken): Slight boost at 1.5–3KHz, then slight boost at 150Hz. Potentially a slight cut at 500Hz, depending on where recorded and the mic used. Pan marginally right or left if overpowering at center.

Acoustic Guitar: Slight boost at 3–6KHz, then slight boost from 250–400Hz. Be cautious of muddying the mix if the guitar is blended with many instruments in the same frequency range. Pan slightly to one side, as much as ±50.

Electric Guitar: Cut at 150Hz, slight boost at 800Hz to 3KHz, depending on where in the mix the instrument sits. Pan slightly to one side, as much as ±50.

Synth: Generally need little EQ, perhaps a slight boost at 2KHz. Leave centered unless multiple synth sounds are used. In the event of multiple synths, pan to unique locations for each.

Bass Guitar: Boost around 1KHz for definition and attack with slight boost around 100Hz for fullness and width. Little or no pan is best in most mixes.

Kick Drum/Bass drum: Boost at 3–4KHz for definition and attack, match the low end EQ of a bass guitar if any is used. Little or no pan is best with most mixes.

Snare Drum: Boost or cut around 4–5KHz to add/remove snap, build thickness/fullness around 300Hz. Pan to approximately –20 in most mixes.

Cymbals: Boost or cut around 6–10KHz to add or remove sizzle. Be cautious not to create harshness or distortion. Pan according to desired location.

Strings: Boost at 7KHz to increase bow attack. Too much and the strings will become brittle and painful to the ear. Pan to desired location.

Guitars, synths, and background vocals all fit into this space, too. Be cautious of wanting too much sparkle or bottom end in these elements in order to leave room for the primary and foundation sounds. Use reverbs or delays to wash these sounds across the sonic canvas, rather than increasing the volume of an individual instrument. (We'll discuss reverb and other FX on page 87.) These sounds contribute a sense of color or timbre of the musical element. If everything was taken away except this element and the lead element, there would still be something worth a listen. If

2.15 This is a rough overhead view of a mix starting point placing various sounds in the stereo field and depth of focus field. Obviously, there is no hard and fast rule for setting up a mix, but this provides a visual starting point.

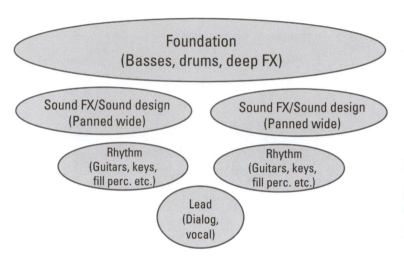

there are inconsistent sounds in this element, try to bring them in and out gently rather than with surprise. Otherwise, they'll detract from the front elements.

Finally, the special FX, or signature sounds of a piece, are placed. In the musical context, this is the moving sound of a synth that has a signature to mark the song or scene, rather than a synth that is emulating a traditional keyboard. In a video context, this is the cannon fire, bullets flying, spaceships, aircraft swoops, or another action sound. This element should be placed to move right to left/left to right, as the exciting elements of a stereo video mix. This movement may also be done within the NLE system, but it's a good idea to place the element even temporarily in Soundtrack for purposes of setting the musical mix and getting familiar with audio happening at specific points in the mix. Another benefit is that the sound effect may also be enhanced with musical or even nonmusical loops timed to coincide with them.

Simple Mix

Recently, while working on an advertisement, a tennis player became the subject. My assignment was to make the impact of the tennis ball seem immense and surreal. To achieve this goal, a cannon shot was reversed in the audio editor, so that the initial attack of the cannon was at the end of the file. Audio slowly ramped up to match the motion of the ball approaching the racket, when the ball hit the racket strings, the impact of the cannon in reverse was heard alongside the sound of the ball/racket connecting. This created intensity in the moment; the goal was achieved. Illustrated in film, in the opening of the movie *JFK*, a similar effect was created using gunshots timed to match flashbulbs going off, raising slowly in volume until the gunshots were nearly as loud as the flashbulb audio. This not only gave the flashbulbs intensity, but it also successfully set the stage for an ominous incident later in the film.

Remember, these tips are mere rudiments. From here, the mix can be tweaked according to the individual ear. Mixing has no right or wrong approach, just trials that are more or less pleasing to your ear and mixes that add or detract from a video scene.

Each track used in the project has a volume slider. When setting up the first mix, or *pre-mix* settings in Soundtrack, this volume slider should be used. When the time arrives for automated volume changes, envelopes are inserted to control those automatic changes. The volume control has a range of +6dB (very loud) to –96dB (silent).

Soundtrack also provides a panning control on each track. This panning control shifts audio found on the track to the right or left channels of a stereo mix. Set up rough placement of each track's audio using this control. To do this, start by placing bass-oriented instruments to the center, or slightly off center, along with drum or percussion tracks. (Most often drum and percussion loops are in-stereo, while bass loops are in-mono.) Be cautious panning a stereo drum or percussion loop too far to the right or left, this may cause an imbalance in instrumentation. This is in instance when having a good set of audio monitors is critical. See Chapter 3 for more information on setting up a monitoring system.

Inserting volume or panning envelope points effectively disables the sliders found in the track headers as the volume or pan position defaults to the envelope setting. If no envelope points are inserted, the slider controls the volume or pan of a track.

> **FX Load:** Placing many effects on a project at either the track or project level is weighty on the processor. Performance varies depending on the processor speed and amount of RAM found in the system.

INSERTING EFFECTS IN THE SOUNDTRACK PROJECT

Soundtrack offers the opportunity to insert FX at two points in the audio chain: inserted to each individual track, effecting only the individual track's audio, or inserted to the master output, effecting all aspects of the mix. This gives a Soundtrack user a powerful control over audio in the project.

Track-based FX will typically differ from FX placed on the project output. For instance, a compressor might be found on a track and also found on the project bus, while a flanger or chorus would be typically found only on a track. A reverb might be applied to a project as well as an individual track, but this is somewhat uncommon. The same holds true for a distortion effect; it is typically found on a track and not on a master output.

Some FX are automatable, allowing for level changes, time changes, mix parameters, and other functions to be performed as the Playhead passes specified time markers.

Also, FX may be inserted in multiples; this is known as "chaining" FX together.

There are many different types of effects that can be inserted into the Soundtrack project or tracks. Effects are based in time, frequency, or the modulation of one or the other, even both. Other effect types control dynamics of audio. For instance, an EQ is a set of filters that effect specific frequencies. A delay is a time-based effect, allowing the original signal to have a delayed repeat, while a chorus or flanger effect uses a combination of filters and time shift. Compressors control the level or dynamic range of audio, while distortion may use a combination of filtration and dynamic range control.

Soundtrack installs the following effects plugins:

- Bandpass
- Chorus
- Compressor
- Delay
- Ensemble
- Fat EQ
- Flanger
- Graphic EQ
- HiPass
- Low Pass
- Low Shelf Filter
- Matrix Reverb
- Modulation Delay
- Noise Gate

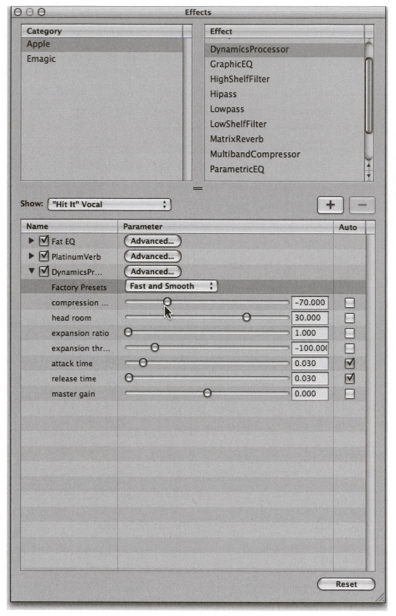

2.16 Wet versus Dry Settings

- Peak Limiter
- Platinum Verb
- Soundtrack Reverb
- Stereo Delay
- Sub Bass
- Tape Delay

In addition, Soundtrack installs the following Logic effects plugins:

- Auto Filter
- Bitcrusher
- Clip Distortion
- Distortion
- Overdrive
- Phase Distortion
- Phaser
- Tremolo

Additional effects plugins are installed from software produced by companies such as WAVES, as long as the plugins meet the Apple Audio Units specification (AU).

To insert FX to a track, press the Show Effects button found on the Track Header.

The dialog that opens shows two FX folders: Apple and Logic. (If the VST-AU adapter has been loaded, then VST plugins may be seen.) There are unique effects in each folder. Browse through the various FX available, choosing which effect will provide the desired sound on the track. Double-click the desired effect and it is inserted on the track, displaying itself in the FX dialog as an inserted effect. Select the effect and press + to add the effect to the track.

Effects are added in a hierarchy; the last effect inserted is the lowest effect on the list of effects added to the dialog. Therefore, if a compressor is first in a chain of FX and an equalizer is last, the compressor is not able to function properly and the equalizer affects the output of the compressor

VST to AU plug-in

Using the FXPansion VST to AU adapter, some VST plug-ins work correctly in Soundtrack and FCP. The released version of the VST to AU plug-in was not available at the time of this writing, yet Beta versions did function with most plug-ins inside Soundtrack. However, some plug-ins would cripple FCP and prevent it from fully loading. This is an issue based around the various plug-ins and not around the FXPansion adapter. The AU protocol is a recent shift in plug-in architecture for Apple. Third-party plug-in development will continue to provide more tools for Soundtrack and FCP.

and any other FX in the chain. The order of effects may be changed by dragging effects in the Effects Parameter dialog to the desired position in the hierarchy.

Now, playback the track with the inserted effect. It's often a good practice to solo the effected track in order to get a better idea of how the effect is manipulating the sound on the track.

Adding FX to the Master Output is accomplished by Control+clicking/Right+clicking an empty area beneath the lowest track header on the workspace and selecting Show Master Effects. Also, Master Effects can be inserted by selecting View>Show Master Effects.

Control+clicking/Right-clicking in an empty area of the header area of the workspace and selecting Show Master Effects opens the Master Effects dialog.

Select effects to be dropped on the Master Effects output and either double-click or select the effect and press + to insert it.

Some effects will have an Advanced button next to them. This denotes that the effect has a graphic user interface (GUI). Clicking the Advanced button in the Effects dialog opens the GUI of the effect. Insert the Emagic Platinum Reverb on a track and press the Advanced button. The reverb opens, providing an interface that can be controlled/adjusted in real time.

> **Dynamics:** When inserting dynamics to a track or master project, the dynamic controller, such as a compressor, should nearly always be last in a chain. Otherwise, the compressor won't see the entire signal chain and may not receive enough information to do its job properly. Adding an EQ to the chain after a compressor, for example, can create a problem that leads to distortion of the audio output and may be difficult to track down.

Depending on the plugin, EQ levels may be set, wet or dry mixes controlled, dynamic thresholds managed, and other critical parameters adjusted using the knobs and sliders provided in the GUI.

These same parameters are also controllable via envelopes in the Envelopes views.

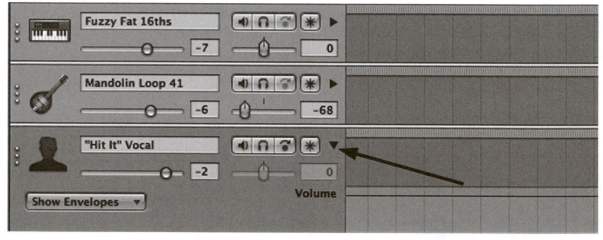

2.17   Pressing this button will open the Insert FX dialog that allows FX to be inserted and chains to be created.

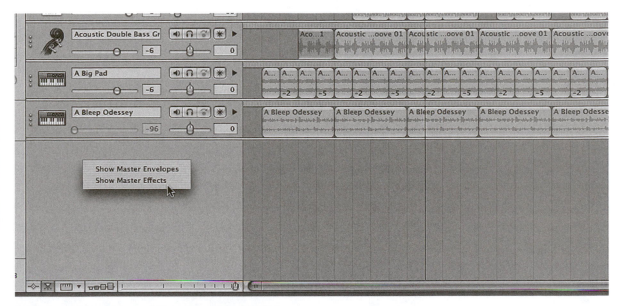

2.18   Insert Show Master Effects from Control+click

Some effects may be automated, meaning that the parameters are controlled over time. For example, the wet/dry ratio of a reverb could change over time in a composition with more reverb heard at the end of a song instead of being loud during the composition, which could create a mushy and muddy sound. To automate an effect, select the horizontal triangle at the left edge of any effect in the Effects Parameter dialog. This opens the adjustable parameters and displays an Auto checkbox to the right side of any automatable parameters. An envelope is then created in

VST to AU plug-in

A "Wet" signal is a signal that is completely-processed audio with none of the original sound heard. A "Dry" signal is audio that is completely original and contains no processing. Blending or mixing the wet and dry signals determines how the sound is heard. Sometimes a completely wet signal is desired for a total effect. Many pop songs use a totally wet signal that encompasses the entire mix as a means of creating a bridge or short moment in a song to shift focus from an otherwise repetitive groove. As an example, open the *Reverb* project on the CD-ROM. By default, the Wet setting is at 30%. Begin playback of the project and while it's playing, increase the wetness to 70%. Notice the depth in the reverb shifting. The volume of the conga appears to lessen due to its attack being washed out by the amount of reverb applied to the mix. Adjust the Reverb time to 10 seconds. Notice how the congas appear even more washed out. Too much reverb is far less desirable than too little reverb. While it's always tempting to make reverb time very large and long, this has a tendency to muddy the overall sound of the audio, though sometimes this is desirable for effect. Use caution and prudence to set this effect. Experiment with various times, densities, room shapes, and spreads on this file to get a good idea of how the various controls effect the quality of the sound.

2.19   The Emagic Platinum Reverb is an excellent plugin and can be used to add a smooth and sweet reverb to a mix.

either the Master Envelopes or Track Envelopes view, depending on where the effect has been inserted.

To view the envelopes' related automation tasks on a single track, select the horizontal arrow found on the Track Header. This opens the Envelopes view. By default, the Volume and Pan envelopes are visible. If the Effect Parameter envelope is not visible, select the down arrow in the Show Envelopes menu. This opens a dropdown menu that allows users to select which envelopes are shown in the Envelopes view. This same function also allows envelopes that don't need to be controlled to be hidden, saving screen real estate and reducing any potential confusion when quickly viewing track envelopes.

To view envelopes on the Master Output, Control+click/Right+click in an empty header area beneath any tracks found in the workspace or select View>Show Master Envelopes. This view also

2.20   Some FX parameters may be adjusted over time. These are controllable by envelopes found in the Track or Master Envelopes view, depending on where the FX have been inserted.

Auto FX

If a vocal line reaches a break just before a chorus, or a space in time needs to be filled and a long delay is needed, automated FX can change the length of the delay time. Instead of using another FX, only send for the vocal breaks. Perhaps an EQ sweeps just as a car passes from right to left, creating the illusion of a Doppler Effect will make the sound more believable. Frequency sweeps added to drum mixes, or to a main instrument sound, become part of the instrument itself, creating an unmatchable identity. Remember "Axel F," the theme song from "Beverly Hills Cop"? The sweeps heard on the bass lines in that song were created by synthesis, but the sound itself was a huge part of the song. Techno music is nearly always automation dependent due to the repetitive nature of the music.

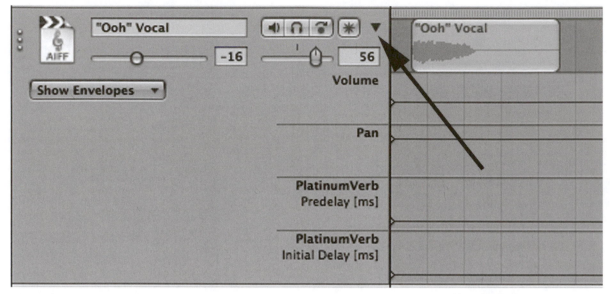

2.21   Click this button to view envelopes available to control FX parameters.

provides a Show Envelopes menu that permits users to determine which envelopes are viewed or hidden.

Envelopes in either Track or Master Output in Envelope Views are controllable over time. Double-clicking the envelope allows users to set the value of each parameter/envelope by placing a node/envelope point and adjusting to the desired position. Envelope points may be moved with the mouse cursor or moved by clicking on the envelope point and holding Option while pressing the Up or Down arrows. This moves the envelope point by one pixel. Holding Option+Shift while pressing Up or Down shifts the selected envelope point by five pixels. Envelope points may be shifted right or left by holding Option+Right/Left arrows. If Ripple editing is used, envelope points shift to the right or left with inserted or deleted audio.

Envelope points may also be copy/pasted anywhere in the project. Simply drag-select over several envelope points/shape in the envelope row to create a selection, then copy.

Position the Playhead to the location where the envelope is to be pasted, then paste. Envelope points can be pasted into envelopes of the same type. For example, Volume envelope shapes and points may not be pasted into a Pan or FX Parameter envelope.

Be aware that if Snapping is enabled, it may get in the way of setting envelope parameters. Disable snapping (G) if an envelope parameter must be set in between a note value or grid spacing. Another option is to set Snapping to its finest value of a 64th note. This will keep Snapping enabled, locking an envelope parameter to a grid, but also allow fairly specific placement of the envelope handle. If snapping is set to Ruler Ticks during work on the project, be certain to set it back to Ruler Ticks so no problems are created when placing loops on the Timeline after envelope points have been set and created.

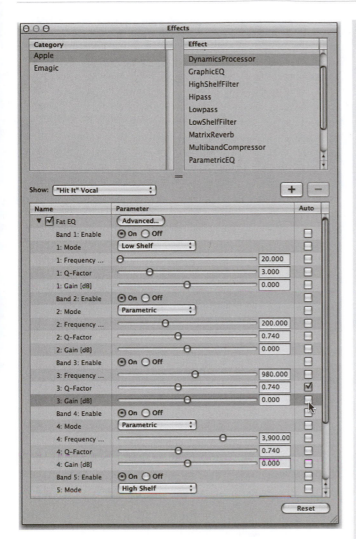

2.22 In the Effects manager, parameters to be automated are selected by checking the Auto checkbox. Only check the boxes that require automation, as checking all boxes creates many envelopes, which might lead to confusion.

FX Controls

While sometimes useful, certain parameters of effects are not controlled over time, but instead are set to the audio of the project and not changed until a new project or audio section is "seen" by the FX processor. Some of these parameters are Attack, Release, and Threshold, among other compressor settings, or perhaps time parameters of a reverb or a delay. In Soundtrack, delay times are automatically determined based on the tempo of the project. If the project increases or decreases in tempo, inserted Apple or Logic delays automatically adjust to time. Removing these parameters from the Master Output view cleans up the view, removes the opportunity to accidentally create a setting in error, and inadvertently shift a system-set parameter to an incorrect setting.

Where these parameters are of most value is when a long project containing many different Soundtrack compositions with output levels and controls that need to be unique at different moments. For instance, if a long-form video project is scored with various tempos and levels of project amplitude, having control of compression settings (volume) is beneficial. The same would hold true of some reverb, delay, chorus, and other settings applied to tracks or master output settings.

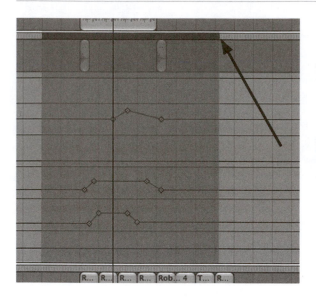

2.23 Drag-Select over envelope points, allowing them to be copy/pasted.

2.24 Grab the track here to drag the track to a new location in the Soundtrack workspace.

TRACK ORDER

To aid in the mix process, tracks can be moved into any order in the project. This feature is useful when doing a mix, as the track being focused on may be dragged to the top position in the project without effecting audio playback, levels, or effects in any way. For example, in a 12-track project, much of the audio is not visible in the project as it scrolls beyond the computer screen. While working on the mix, it comes time to have easy access to tracks beyond the screen. When this happens, grab the lower tracks at the left edge of the track and drag them higher into visibility to any convenient position.

In the analog tape world, this is the same as moving audio from track 12 to track 1; this is very difficult to do. Regardless of the arrangement of tracks, the audio sounds the same. This also

2.25 Use this button to disable Snapping, or press the G key. If snapping is enabled, any file dragged to the Timeline or moved on the Timeline will snap to the value determined in the Snapping preference.

allows all tracks of a similar nature to be grouped together: all drums, percussion, and rhythmic instruments next to each other as tracks; all guitars, keyboards together; all bass and low-frequency instruments viewed as a group; and all vocals viewed together at once. While Soundtrack does not have grouping capability, this track reordering feature serves to function in much the same capacity.

As indicated in Chapter 1, new tracks may be inserted at any time by pressing the Command+T key. This inserts a new track below any existing tracks in the project.

EFFECTS AND FILTERS

Understanding how effects, filters, and dynamic controllers function is important when choosing effect plugins for tracks or main outputs. Some FX are critical to creating a good mix, other plugins are merely enhancements sometimes used to create the "personality" of a mix, imbue a sense of spaciousness, or create a unique signature. Let's take a look at how some of the effects, filters, and dynamic controllers function.

Compression

While digital audio has an extreme dynamic range, it is also less forgiving than its analog counterpart because the "zero point" in the digital world is harsh.and limiting. In the analog world, the dynamic range is also fairly limited, ranging in the upper 60dB area, depending on the quality of equipment used. A 24bit digital recording, however, may have a dynamic range of 138dB. Dynamic range plugins help reduce dynamic range while maintaining most of the nuances of a fairly dynamic performance. They could be considered automatic volume controls. By limiting, or subtly compressing, the exceptionally loud portions of a performance, the performance still maintains its soft-to-loud moments, but at the same time cannot exceed the preset point.

One might say that it's nearly impossible to do a quality digital mix without compression. Yet compression is one of the most misunderstood parts of the mix and audio process. First, it's important to understand the difference between a compressor and a limiter.

A limiter prevents audio from passing at a predetermined volume. Any audio that attempts to pass the preset level is squashed to fit the preset level. Limiters are generally not good for music or audio for video mixes, but are suited for situations where all elements of the media cannot be controlled.

There are hard-limiters and soft-limiters; the difference is how much of a dynamic the limiter is set at prior to the hard-limit point. In other words, a limiter can be preset to assure that nothing greater than −3dB is allowed to pass, but the majority of the audio information is at −5dB with lots of dynamic and an ability to be much louder than the −3dB maximum. Using a setting that instructs the limiter to start reducing levels at −9dB allows some dynamic feel to remain in the audio track. Often limiters squeeze the high end out of a mix, making it dull and boring. Television

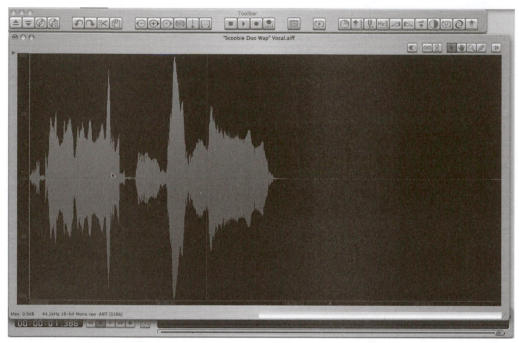

2.26   Audio before being limited *(above)*

2.27   Audio after being hard-limited *(below)*

2.28   Threshold set at –27.5dB and variable compression ratio: Notice the compression curve following the dialed-in settings. (Image courtesy of WAVES)

commercials are often hard-limited and compressed to give maximum volume. (One of the annoying things about the overall volume of a television commercial is when they are improperly compressed; they sound like they're screaming at the viewer.)

Most compressors also have built-in limiting ability. Compressors can make audio louder while at the same time ensuring the dynamic range is reduced. Generally, a compressor is used to keep dynamics as accurate as possible, while at the same time preventing audio from crossing a chosen threshold or making it easier to get an event/signal louder while maintaining control over the apparent signal.

As an example of compression as it is required is when a singer or voiceover artist in the studio moves towards and away from the microphone. Levels recorded are not consistent. Perhaps the

How a Compressor Works

Comprehending the Ratio, threshold, attack, and release are the most important pieces to understanding compression.

Vocals generally won't be heard correctly with compression of greater than 6:1. All dynamics of the voice are squashed to the point of having no performance or nuance left in the audio.

Typically in the video realm, vocals and voiceovers are compressed as a means of keeping the dynamic range of a voice to a minimum while raising the level of the voiceover to its loudest possible level before distortion.

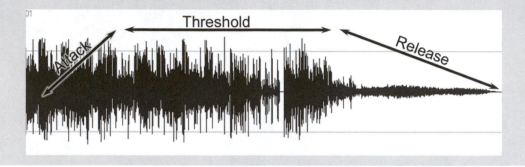

same vocal artist performs various passages from very quiet to very loud. A compressor can even out these differences.

A compressor is also used by guitar and bass players to sustain the notes of a plucked or strummed chord. It will smooth down the attack on the strings and open up/release, gradually allowing the note or chord to appear as though it is longer.

 Practice using compression on the Compression Techniques file on the CD-ROM found in the back of this book.

Using Equalization

Equalizers, also known as EQ (not to be confused with E.Q., or Emotional Quality), are one of the most oft turned-to tools in the plugin arsenal. EQs are used to cut frequencies of fat sounds that occupy space in the audio spectrum that other sounds may also occupy. Too many sounds can create confusion. EQ may also be used to "fatten up" thin sounds in order to occupy a greater space in a mix than a sound might be able to fill if left alone. Also, EQ is used to correct problems with a tracking room or poor frequency balance in a microphone, or to enhance a performance or characteristic of an audio event. While invented initially to "flatten" out sound over the telephone, today EQs are predominantly used to "unflatten" sound; in jest, some engineers call these tools

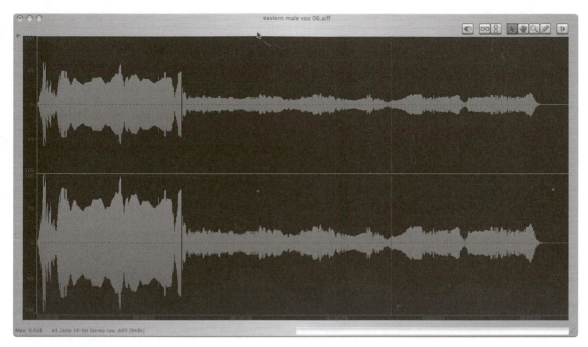

2.29 Light compression at 2:1, threshold at −8dB allows the signal to be louder overall due to the reduced dynamic range.

2.30 Beginning the attack earlier in the signal with a lower threshold makes a huge difference in the behavior of the compressor.

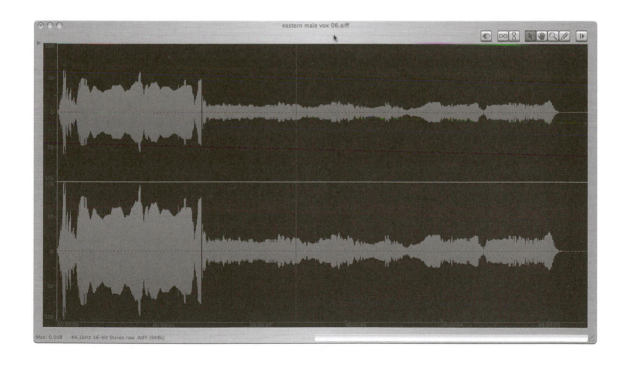

"unequalizers." Equalizers originally were designed to repair audio. Now they are used as much if not more for effect than for repair.

The use of an EQ must be judicious. Too much boost of any frequency may cause overload of the outputs. This may cause a compressor to work harder than it needs to because of excess volume boost or can create distortion.

EQs typically come in two types:

- Graphic: Frequencies are preset and only the gain of specific frequencies may be increased or reduced. Found in octave, half-octave, and one-third octave in most instances. The octave of 125Hz is 250Hz. The half-octave of 125Hz is 176Hz.
- Parametric: Parametric Equalizers can select a specific frequency center, select the amount of bandwidth that frequency has control over, and control the gain or reduction of that same frequency band. Usually Parametric EQs allow for several frequencies to be specified and controlled.

Tight Q is very useful for cutting out a specific frequency that may be a hum, distortion, or simply a problem frequency. Tight Q is also valuable for enhancing specific frequencies, such as boosting presence in a vocal to give it an airy quality in order to reach the pop vocal sound that is popular today. Figure 2.32 demonstrates a tight Q, while Figure 2.33 displays a wide Q.

Bandpass Filters

Bandpass Filters are very simple equalizers, allowing audio to "pass" above or below the specified frequencies or not. For example, a high-pass filter set at 150Hz will pass audio above 150Hz, while audio below 150Hz is cut off from the signal flow. Soundtrack approaches this a little differently, allowing users to operate the filter like a single-band parametric equalizer with no Q control, passing frequencies above or below a set frequency, but still having a resonance control.

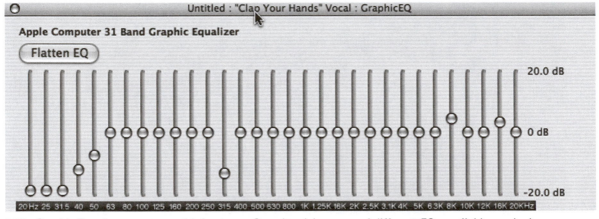

2.31 Graphic Equalizer set at one-third octaves. Soundtrack has several different EQs available as plugins.

Open the High-pass Effect project for a demonstration of this tool in use.

Time Delay Effects

Time-based plugin FX are based on just that: time. Delays, reverb, chorus, and flangers are all based on delaying, recombining, and/or reflecting a moment in time. When a sound originates, some of it is perceived as reflected within a given space, the percentage depending on the specific acoustic environment. Some types of music are predominantly based on reverbs and delays, which can be used to create emotional expression and fill holes in a song. Without long delays and reverbs, many of the ballads and arena anthem rock songs would sound empty and powerless because the lead vocal and chorus vocals would lose their presence and power. Time-based effects are used more than any other effect to create emotional responses. Dripping water combined with huge reverb setting is part and parcel of nearly every horror movie made, just as the familiar simulated sounds of space (space has no air, therefore sound cannot pass through it) include reverbs and delays.

A delay may be used to fatten a sound, allowing it to occupy more space in a mix than it otherwise might. Delays are also used to split audio to right/left channels, widening the sound and potentially clearing the center for a dialog. Time delays are quite often used on sounds to give them a sense of depth, as in sound effects. In order to do this, use a delay that is predominantly dry at the top of a sound effect with increasing wetness towards the end of the original sound all the while reducing the volume of the original sound. This will give the sense of the sound moving away. Use a modulation device to further enhance effect.

2.32 Tight Q

2.33 Wide Q

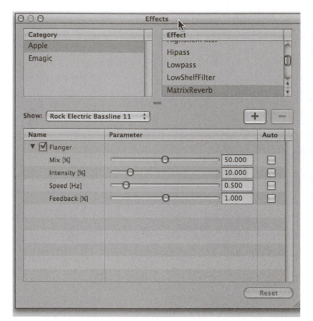

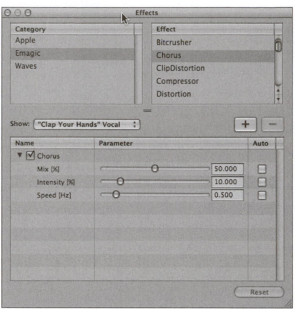

2.34 Flangers get their name from the way that tape engineers in the early days of tape recording took a pair of tape machines, fed the same sound to both machines, and using their thumbs against the flanges of the tape reel would cause a slight modulation and delay when the reels slowed down. The two recorded signals became mixed. The resulting combination was known as a "flanged" sound.

2.35 Soundtrack has several great plugins, such as this chorus, to benefit the overall sound. Chorus does just as its name implies; it causes a single instrument to sound like a chorus of the same instrument by delaying and modulating the original sound. Notice that this Chorus is automatable.

Other time delay effects include Flangers, Chorus, and Phase shifters. These effects are created from varying time delay. The delay time varies over time, creating the effect of multiple voices. In the case of a flanger, time moves more quickly than in a chorus, while changing the pitch of the wet sound in small increments. Flangers get their name from recording engineers who, holding their thumbs on the flanges of a tape reel in the old days, slowed the tape from one direction and caused changes in speed of the tape machine, thus creating this effect. Flangers may be used on any instrument to fatten or create a unique sound.

Chorus effects are traditionally used on just about every instrument excepting drums. Actually, for a period of time, chorusing was even used on drums in the Phil Collins and Hugh Padgham mixes. Choruses, just as their name implies, make a single instrument sound like a multitude of the same instrument. Horns, vocals, guitars, and particularly basses benefit tremendously from this effect. The effect is particularly effective on sparse mixes where there is only one guitar and one bass plus a drum track. Inserting a chorus on both guitar and bass, panning one instrument slightly to the right and the other slightly to the left, creates a fat sound in most instances. An overdone chorus sounds metallic and false, but is easily heard with even low-quality monitoring systems, allowing a producer to reduce the mix to a more pleasing ratio. To really fatten up a sound, duplicate a track three times. Then apply slightly different chorus settings to two of the tracks, panning each to opposite sides of the stereo spectrum, thus leaving one of the tracks dry or processed with another tone. Use prudence in the application of this effect, as it will quickly overpower the other tracks in the mix.

Finally, Phase Shifting works in much the same manner as Flangers and Chorus, except that wet audio is returned to the mix with the wet sound slightly out of phase from the original audio. As the audio shifts from phase position to phase position, the two audio channels collide, creating holes or notches in the equalization of the audio; this gives the feeling of movement. Jimi Hendrix was one of the musicians to popularize the Phaser, later used by many guitarists of the late 60s and early 70s. The Pink Floyd song "Money" uses a phaser heavily in the overall guitar sound, also flangers are used throughout the song to tie other instruments to the sound of the guitar. However, phasers aren't limited only to guitars. When composing a soundtrack for a video project, the sky is the limit. Adding a phaser can add a layer of excitement to an otherwise dull track. Another idea is using Automation, slowly adding in a phaser as a transition occurs, will heighten tension to introduce a new scene.

Using Reverb

Reverb, short for reverberation, can be used for any kind of audio mix, whether for video, audio, spoken word, or music; it is also one of the most overused effects in the palette of tools available. Reverb is used to reproduce various room environments. In the past, music had to be recorded in large chambers or rooms with large, reflective areas. The reverb created in such large rooms helped to blend sounds together, creating a cohesive yet individual expression of instruments or vocal authority. Ever notice how the voice of God in film or recording is nearly always accompanied by a large reverb?

Reverb simulates the sound of audio waves bouncing around a space. The walls, ceiling, and floor of the space all have characteristics that effect how sound reflects or reverberates. The surface composition itself has a tremendous effect on how the audio will sound. For instance, a room made of concrete produces a different sound characteristic than a room with wooden walls. A room of wooden walls with a carpeted floor has a different sound characteristic than a room with no carpet on the floor. Small rooms have a different reverberation characteristic than large rooms. Rooms that have squared walls have a different sound than rooms without square walls.

As technology and creativity grew in the audio industry, reverberation was emulated in tubes, springs, complex room systems, then in electronics, and now in software. Reverb can express a vastness and spatial distance or an intimate communication made up of certain consonants, syllables, and instrumentation, of attack or inflection, sounded within a reverberant space. Musicians,

2.36 Reverbs can be fairly simple or very complex. While the controls may appear to be intimidating, they are actually quick to master. Knowing when to apply reverb is more challenging than learning how to apply reverb.

engineers, and producers will often notice the personality of a room, commenting on how "sweet" the room is. Singing in the shower makes even a poor voice sound rich, while that same voice singing in a closet sounds dull and lifeless. This is because the shower is full of hard surfaces and the closet is full of soft surfaces. The hard surfaces effectively create a "doubled voice"-sound that the ear hears immediately, whereas the soft surfaces absorb nearly all sounds, preventing almost all reflections. This makes the voice in the closet harder to hear. Large rooms with reflective surfaces, such as cathedrals, auditoriums, and long hallways, not only reflect the sound, but reflect it repeatedly, expanding and elongating sound, while softening the sound and giving an illusion of infinity.

Somewhere between the sound of a closet and cathedral, there are reverb settings useful to nearly every situation. Soundtrack has many great reverbs built in and there are incredible software reverbs available from several third-party manufacturers, such as software, WAVES, and Logic. (Demo versions of AU Reverbs are found on the disk in the back of this book.)

Overusing or overly-loud reverb can wash over too much of the audio spectrum, making audio sound muddy and without clarity. Again, use reverb carefully.

Consider using reverb at short, quiet settings for interviews, which might be too dry from being in a small, quiet room or may have some ambience that probably won't wash with other sounds or beds. Reverb is useful for making a mono audio signal appear to be stereo by creating artificial reflections that reach the ear at different times. Try to feed a mono voice or instrument into a bus or FX send that's only the reverb, then route it back to the Master output. Make sure the reverb is fairly short, and has very little predelay. Panning the reverb or sending the reverb to the same location as the dry sound is also a great technique for keeping the sound large, but located. Before adding reverb, pan the original signal to where it sounds right in the mix, then use an FX send to route the dry sound. Pan the reverb to the same space. This technique works well with vocals mixed into a music bed and with single instrument sounds, such as guitars, snare drums, keyboards, and other single-point source instruments.

Be very cautious of reverb sounds that are too bright. While they will usually warm up a voice, bright reverbs also tend to elaborate sibilance and can easily create distortion in the high end. Use a de-esser, or EQ, before the reverb in the FX chain if this occurs.

A final word about using FX and processors: if used properly, they become part of a mix or sound; if used improperly, they stand out and appear artificial. For the most part, FX are for enhancement, not for identification. FX are somewhat like makeup in film or video production; if you can "see" the FX, then they are probably laid on too heavily. This is one of the pitfalls that many starting-out musicians get caught. Video editors who are just starting out in the business often use odd and inappropriate transitions, also, audio engineers and composers can fall into the same pattern. Use prudence when applying FX to an overall mix or a track. Listen to the mix at low audio levels, in mono if possible, and at loud levels to see if any instrument or track jumps out more than others. If the final mix is destined for video with dialog, test the mix frequently against the dialog. It could be that a snare or cymbal interferes with a consonant or sibilant in the main dialog and needs to be corrected with an automated volume, pan, or filter.

Media Manager's Advanced Search Features

Media Manager has basic and advanced search features to help locate specific files or styles. Clicking on a genre or instrument initiates a search for instruments in that genre, based on metadata inserted into the loop. Soundtrack also enables advanced searching based on keywords in the loop's metadata. In the Refine Search window dialog, input keywords to refine the search to specific instruments. For example, clicking on the Drums search button calls up many drum loops, but not nearly all of the drum loops in the library. Refine the search by inputting the word "Cymbal" in the Refine Search box and select "Enter." Only cymbals show up in the Search Results window, also instruments that have the word "cymbal" in descriptor tags. This is useful for all loops, but one instance in which this is particularly useful is for Acid™ libraries that have been converted for use in Soundtrack. When Acid™ loops are converted using the Soundtrack Loop Utility, loop tags are created from the original file names that may be specifically searched in the Media Manager.

If a loop has been previously auditioned, but the name, genre, or instrument is forgotten, put the first letter of the loop's name, genre, or instrument in the refined search field. Soundtrack then displays all loops beginning with that letter.

2.37 The Refine Search field assists in the location of specific genres, descriptors, or instruments in the loop database.

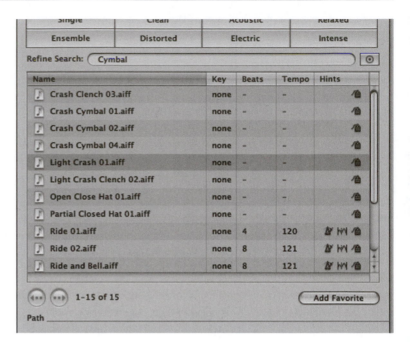

By default, on most systems, Soundtrack displays 25 loops in a search. (Larger monitors with higher resolutions may display greater numbers of loops.) This number of displayed loops may be increased or decreased in the Soundtrack /General preferences. In the Preferences dialog, select a higher or lower value for Search Results per page. This can be increased as high as 500 loops, or decreased to as few as 10 loops per page. As mentioned earlier, there is also a checkbox for selecting files tuned near the project key. My recommendation is to leave this box unchecked and do limited searches from within the Media Manager, so as not to disallow potentially usable loops from wide searches.

Making the Match

Loop files, particularly bass loops and other low frequency files, do not always hold up well when being pitch shifted farther than seven semitones from the original pitch. Therefore, finding files

ACID® Efficiency: Sony's ACID® loops do not require conversion from .wav to .aif file formatting. Soundtrack will playback the .wav files from ACID® libraries with no issue, correctly reading metadata and naming conventions. However, for most efficient use, use the Soundtrack Loop Utility to convert files and store them on the hard drive. Loops always play back more smoothly from the hard drive instead of playing from the library CD, particularly when several loops are called for from multiple libraries.

whose original pitch is as close to the project pitch is always best. Soundtrack provides a search function that will only locate loops within two semitones of the project key.

To the right of the Refine Search dialog is a small button that resembles a target: one circle within another. Clicking this button limits searches to loops within two semitones of the project key. Therefore, if the project key is the default key of A, then the search is limited to loops in the keys of G, G-sharp, A, A-sharp, or B. This is a good way to search and be assured that no matter what the instrument is, the key will not have odd artifacts due to pitch shifting. For newcomers to loop-based composing, this tool is a great feature. It does have one minor drawback, it may preclude loops from being located in the search that will work within a project. A good practice might be to most often use this feature for bass and other low-frequency loops, so there's no missed opportunity to audition great loops.

Most loop libraries have a variety of keys used to create the loops. Some focus heavily on one or two keys, often using the farthest spreads to accommodate pitch-shifting loops. Many loop libraries are in A, D, C, and G; this span is wide enough that it's easy to find loops that match.

Loop searches may be further restricted by using the Major/Minor/Any/Neither/Good for both dropdown menus. Whatever is selected in the dropdown menu restricts the search. For instance, if Minor is selected in the dropdown menu, only loops in minor keys are located in the search.

Finally, loop searches may be restricted by time signature. In the dropdown menu labeled 4/4, other time signatures may be chosen. For example, if the dropdown menu designates a time signature of 6/8, the search function ignores any loops that are not in the 6/8 time signature.

Searches of multiple keywords are possible in Soundtrack, too. Holding down Command while clicking several genres, instruments, or descriptors, will enable multiple selection of buttons to further refine a search. While there is no limit to how many buttons may be Command selected, there certainly is a point of diminishing returns where various loops may be ignored by the search function as a result of cross matching. However, by selecting an instrument and genre, or instrument and descriptor, locating desired loops is faster and more accurate.

Search categories can be customized in the search window to meet individual workflow requirements. In order to set up search categories for customized buttons, choose Custom from the dropdown menu in the upper left of the Search window.

A submenu appears, indicating choices of Instruments, Genre, or Descriptors. Selecting any of the three opens a secondary submenu, offering selectable tags that appear in the custom window. The Custom Search window may be filled with tags based on user choices. Refinements and search limiters will function identically in all search windows.

Import/Export to Final Cut Pro

One of the primary benefits to Soundtrack is its integration with FCP v4.0. Scoring marker points can be dropped in FCP that may be read in Soundtrack, complete with marker identifiers indicat-

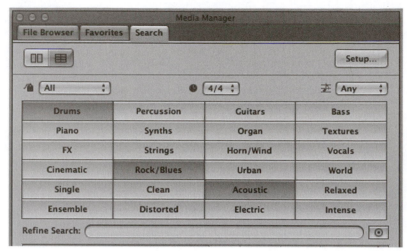

2.38 Holding Command while clicking on various instruments, genres, or descriptors will enable narrowed loop searches.

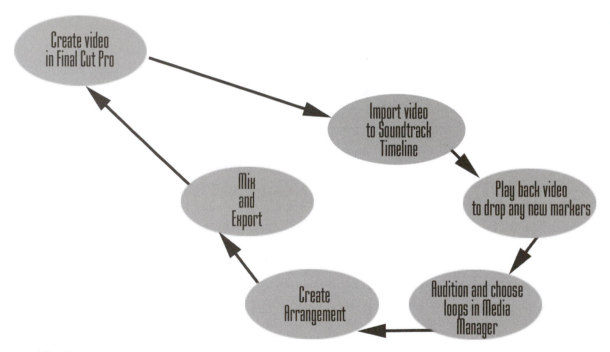

2.41 Workflow chart

ing specific scenes or cue locations. The composition may then be exported back and mixed to existing audio in FCP. This is known as the "round trip," when shuttling back and forth between the two applications.

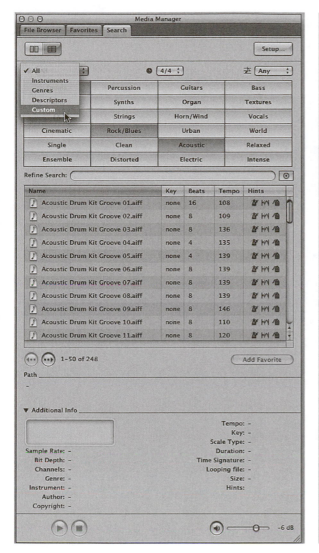

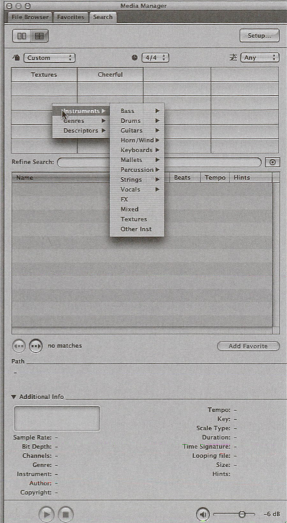

2.39   Select Custom from the dropdown menu to create custom search locators.

2.40   Choose custom search parameter tags by Right+clicking/Control+clicking on an empty box and choosing from the options Instruments, Genres, or Descriptors.

When working with Soundtrack and FCP, the two applications can work together in two ways.

1. Composing the music or video sequence

   a. Build the video project in FCP to be scored at a later time. If doing this, use some sort of tempo indicator in FCP that will be helpful for scoring later on.

 b. Create a simple musical score to be exported to FCP, providing a rough score for FCP for video cuts.

2. Import the media

 a. Create a score for near-finished video from Video to Soundtrack.

 b. Create a video sequence timed to the rough score from Audio to FCP. to.

3. Finish media

 a. Finish musical score/arrangement in Soundtrack, then export to FCP for final mixing and output.

 b. Finish video sequence in FCP timed to score created in Soundtrack.

4. Output media

 a. Output finished project from FCP containing score from Soundtrack.

 b. Export media from FCP back to Soundtrack for final tweaks to score, adding transitional audio elements, one-shots, and any other sweeteners to the mix. Project may be output at this point from either Soundtrack or FCP. Moving media back and forth between FCP and Soundtrack is known as a "Round-trip."

The applications can be used together by way of a couple of different methods. The most common method for video editors is to nearly complete the video, or video scenes in FCP, before moving into Soundtrack. Markers are dropped at key points in the video, denoting changes related to musical expressions or beds.

Drop markers in FCP by pressing the M-key. Pressing the M-key twice when dropping markers opens the Markers dialog, allowing the type of Marker to be noted. Choose Add Scoring Marker from the three-button menu. Give the marker a name and perhaps a comment, if that benefits your particular workflow. These Marker names/designations will show up in Soundtrack when the video is exported from FCP.

2.42 Pressing M twice inserts a marker and brings up the Marker dialog, allowing the Marker to be given a name and Scoring designator.

Typically, an editor and the director or music supervisor will sit in on a "spotting session," choosing locations for music and discussing what types of musical elements should accompany the scene. This involves playing back the video project in FCP, stopping to drop markers, taking notes/creating comments on individual scenes or sections, and having a discussion about the mood or emotional approach to the scene or section. Markers dropped for purposes of time location may be returned to and comments and marker types may be

2.43 Scoring Markers on the Timeline. Scoring markers exported with the file from FCP v4.0 appears as orange markers in Soundtrack, making it efficient and easy to hit musical cues in the video project. Notice that a Scoring Marker may also be inserted in the Viewer, during trimming/editing of a clip.

added at any point. Simply select the marker in the Timeline and press M to open the Marker dialog and select Scoring Marker, add comments or Marker name, and save the sequence.

After creating Scoring Markers on the Timeline in FCP, select File>Export>For Soundtrack and give the file a name and select a location for the file to be stored. The file will then be exported with markers intact to Soundtrack, where they will be seen on the Soundtrack Timeline with orange markers, named as they were named within the FCP application. Be certain that markers are exported from FCP, specified in the export dialog.

Open up Soundtrack to access QuickTime or MPEG files that may be imported for scoring.

Use the Media Manager to browse for the reference movie or section or other video file that you'd like to import to the project and compose for in the Soundtrack Timeline. Alternatively, the Finder may be used to search files and drag them to the Soundtrack Timeline.

Drag the file from the Media Manager to the Preview Window in Soundtrack and the Timeline will display the first frame of the video, along with any markers inserted in the FCP v4.0 Timeline.

Reference Movie

While Soundtrack can easily be used to create compositions for a full-length/long form video project, users starting out with Soundtrack will find it much easier to manage shorter segments or scenes from a video project. Sections to be exported as reference files may be defined in FCP, therefore making it easier to compose and create for segments rather than the entire project. In short, it's simply easier to manage smaller projects than larger projects, particularly when large projects may contain several tempo and dynamic changes.

To create a reference movie in QuickTime, mark in/out points on the Timeline in FCP v4.0. Use "I" for the In point of the reference movie, use "O" to mark the Out point of the reference movie. I recommend adding three seconds of pre-roll at the head and tail of the reference movie, providing Soundtrack pre/post roll time. Output the reference file to a location that you can easily find for import into Soundtrack. Bear in mind that uncompressed, or very large files may have a negative impact on the performance of Soundtrack. Soundtrack imports .mov and .m2v (mpeg 2) files as well as codecs supported by QuickTime. Both NTSC and PAL formats are importable.

Notice that when importing the movie, that the movie has its own audio track that may be effected, volume and pan controlled, and treated just as any other track in the project.

After the movie is imported, press the spacebar to start playback of the video file and associated audio in order to be certain that audio is in sync with the video. It should be, but it's a good idea to check this before starting the project. This assures you that you are composing to the correct audio moments/video time points.

Now place loops on the Timeline, lining up with markers inserted in the video. Once a rhythm is established with a loop or two in the project, it's time to let Soundtrack work its magic.

In the past, composers needed to know the exact length of a scene in order to score music to fit the in/out point of the scene. In some instances, measures would have to be offtime or of a different time signature in order to fit a score into a scene and fit the director's needs. With Soundtrack, the processor figures out the necessary number of bars and tempo for the scene for you, alleviating any math headaches and bar counting that would normally need to be done.

Place the Playhead at the end of a scene or on a marker and select/click on the marker from which Soundtrack will determine tempo. Now select Project>Score Marker to Playhead. Soundtrack will automatically calculate the time between the marker and the Playhead and determine the tempo required to fit into that span of time. Multiple tempos can be inserted. Viewing Master Envelopes displays the points in time that tempo changes and will display the actual tempo at a given point in time. This is called a "tempo map." Notice in the Master Tempo Envelope the tempo changes are marked in red on the handles and line between handles; this indicates that the tempo cannot be changed. These points may only be deleted, but not modified.

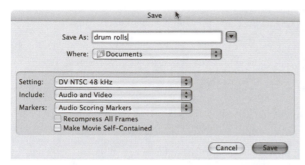

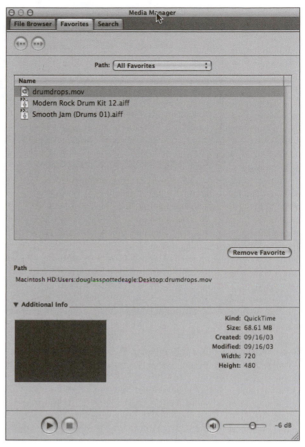

2.44 Be certain that the export dialog has the Markers option selected in order to see markers from the FCP v4.0 file in Soundtrack.

2.45 Browse for and locate the video file to be imported to the Soundtrack project. Import QuickTime or .m2v (mpeg) using the Soundtrack Media Manager. Once located, the file may be marked as a Favorite by selecting the Add Favorite button on the lower right side of the Media Manager. Files may also be dragged into Soundtrack via the Finder. *(right)*

2.46 Notice the markers from FCP v4.0 visible in the Soundtrack Timeline. If the file is not exported from FCP to Soundtrack, markers won't show up in Soundtrack; standard rendering of the file will not include Scoring Markers. *(below)*

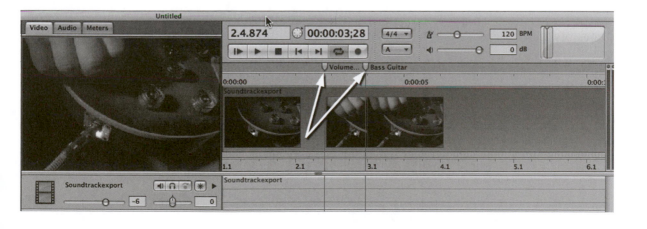

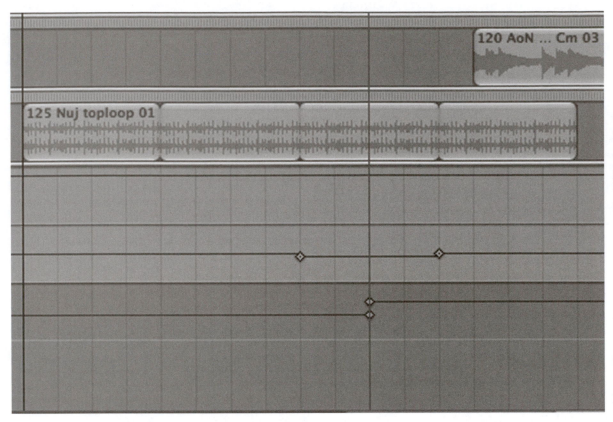

2.47 Tempo changes are automatically created when Score Markers to Playhead is used to calculate tempo over time. Notice the changes in tempo, mapped to markers.

This tool is most valuable in long-form projects, where multiple scenes require multiple tempos to properly match the length or attitude of scenes. Short-form projects also benefit from this by placing a marker at the end of a project, placing the Playhead at the front of a scene, and allowing Soundtrack to determine the best tempo to fit the composition to time.

Use Score Markers to Playhead before beginning the placement of loops on the Timeline. This will allow auditioning of loops at correct tempo. If loops are placed on the Timeline prior to setting tempo, it's possible that loops will develop artifacts when tempo is sped up or slowed down beyond reasonable values inherent to the loop. For example, a bass guitar originally recorded at 140BPM might sound poorly in a project of 90bpm. Scoring Markers to Playhead allows the bass line to be auditioned at the slower tempo prior to placing the loop on the Timeline, potentially saving time and effort. Shifting Clip speed may compensate for some tempo- or pitch-related artifacts induced from shifting tempo or pitch beyond a loop's capabilities.

Anywhere in the project that a FCP Scoring Marker is inserted, or anywhere on the Soundtrack Timeline where a Beat marker is inserted, the display of the movie thumbnail changes to the frame that falls under the inserted marker. This gives editors the ability to see the exact frame on which that the marker falls. Scoring markers may not be moved in the Soundtrack project; only Beat and Time markers may be moved or deleted.

EXPORTING FILES

After the composition is completed, the finished composition can be exported as a stereo audio track, multiple audio tracks, or a QuickTime movie containing video and audio.

To output to a stereo audio–only track, select File>Export Mix and choose the location where the file will be saved. This will blend all the separate tracks to a single file that may be now dropped into an NLE, DVD-authoring tool, or Flash. Be sure to check the Mute Audio from Video checkbox, or audio from the reference video will mix with the Soundtrack score and likely conflict with audio on the FCP Timeline.

After files are exported to FCP, audio may be "round-tripped" or sent back and forth between the two applications.

To perform a round trip from Soundtrack to Final Cut Pro:

1. Create a file in FCP. Place Scoring Markers in the project at desired points.

2. Choose File>Export>For Soundtrack, give the file a name, and save to location

3. Open Soundtrack

4. In the Media Manager File Browser, locate the file to be imported. Double-click to play thumbnail in Media Manager if desired.

5. Drag file to Soundtrack Preview window.

6. Place Playhead on orange markers that appear on Timeline and drag loops to the Timeline, creating a composition.

7. Choose File>Export Mix in Soundtrack

8. Open FCP and select File>Import Files and import the mix from Soundtrack. FCP will recognize the new audio files so long as they are saved in the same location with the same filename as the video file.

9. Edit and save.

10. Return to Soundtrack and reopen the file. Soundtrack will recognize all changes made to the video file.

11. When exporting subsequent edits/compositions from Soundtrack that are the same file, simply hold the Option key when selecting File>Export from the Soundtrack menu. The file will be automatically exported using the same name and may be automatically recognized by FCP.

No Previously Imported Audio: When performing a round trip between Final Cut Pro and Soundtrack, it's a good idea to not export audio from earlier Soundtrack mixes back to Soundtrack from Final Cut Pro. If previously exported audio is brought back in to Soundtrack, the same audio will be heard twice in the mix and potentially create some mix issues that could lead to errors in mixing or composing. No harm will come to the file or audio, however.

To prevent audio imported to FCP from Soundtrack from being exported from FCP back to Soundtrack during a round trip, simply deselect the previously selected files from the File>Export to Soundtrack dialog while in FCP.

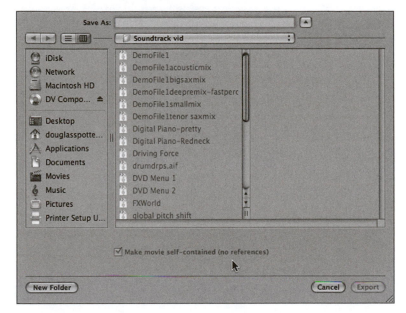

2.49 Files may be exported as individual stereo tracks or as individual mono tracks for import into an NLE or DAW for further processing, mixing, or editing.

2.50 Files may be exported as self-contained QuickTime files. This is a handy feature to export a reference file for a client without having to reopen the file in FCP or other NLE, or for sending a completed file to Compressor.

12. To re-export the file from FCP to Soundtrack, re-export by selecting File>Export for Soundtrack> and leave the original Soundtrack audio unchecked in the Select Which Soundtrack audio Files to Export setting. The Export dialog will not be seen, as the file is immediately saved with the same file name by this process.

EXPORTING MULTIPLE TRACKS FROM SOUNDTRACK

In the previous steps, audio is exported as a stereo AIFF file. Soundtrack also offers the means of exporting a stereo track for each track found on the Timeline. For example, a Soundtrack project that contains 12 tracks of audio may be exported as 12 separate tracks. This is very useful if a large mix is to be done in FCP or other NLE that contains good mixing tools. To export multiple tracks, select File>Export Tracks. Each track in the Soundtrack project will be exported as a stereo track with the same name as the first loop name on the track, or using the name of the track specified by the user. This is another motivation for naming tracks with specific names rather than leaving them named with the loop names. It will help tremendously when importing the audio tracks to an NLE or DAW.

Tracks may be exported as dual mono tracks as well. The process is the same as exporting files as individual stereo tracks, except that the Output Dual Mono files checkbox is checked prior to the export. In the previous example of a Soundtrack project exporting 12 stereo tracks, exporting

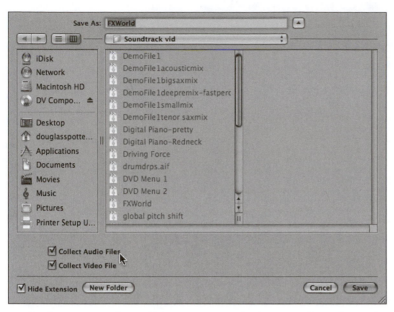

2.51   Audio files may be collected for burning to a CD or creating a portable copy of the project with by checking the Collect All Audio checkbox on the Save dialog.

as dual mono tracks will export a total of 24 tracks. This is best used in situations of exporting to a tool like Logic or ProTools where a surround mix or separate control of placement of audio might be demanded. It could become unwieldy to have so many tracks be exported, so individual stereo tracks or a stereo mix should be used for most purposes.

Finally, a complete project may be exported from Soundtrack as a QuickTime file containing video and audio and may even be exported as a self-contained movie. No compression or alteration of the video stream is performed; Soundtrack simply embeds the audio into the video stream, removing any references to separate audio tracks.

SAVING PROJECTS

Projects may be saved as very small loop files or may be saved with all media. After a project is started, save by choosing File>Save and giving the file a name. No audio is saved with the file, only pointers to loop file locations. Choosing File>Save occasionally through the project is a good idea, simply to update the save in the workflow in the unlikely event of a system error.

If files are saved to be shared with other users or to be archived, it's a simple matter of selecting File>Save or File>Save As and saving the project, this time checking the Collect Audio Files checkbox and locating the project to a folder. All audio loops, FX settings, and project settings are saved to this location. A CD may be burned, all media saved to a FireWire drive, or sent/saved to a network location for others to access by way of this feature. This is a perfect method for sharing projects with others.

Chapter 3

Recording

RECORDING TOOLS IN SOUNDTRACK

In addition to the millions of loops available from Soundtrack, PowerFX, Cakewalk, ACID, and other libraries, it's also possible to record and create your own loops using Soundtrack. These recordings are editable and can become part of your own customized loop library.

Recording requires more than just having the laptop and a microphone. Techniques for quality sound recording are laid out later in this chapter. However, with even a simple recording setup, quality-sounding loops may be recorded in Soundtrack to use in projects.

What sort of things might be recorded for a private loop library? How about trying one of the following

- Environmental sounds (industrial, natural, sounds specific to a particular video shoot)
- Common voice over sections
- Drumming fingers on knees, countertops, chairs
- Dog barks, other animal sounds
- Engine revs, exhaust, tires moving
- Train wheels moving at constant speed
- Rain at a fairly steady tempo
- Footsteps across various floor materials
- Humming/rhythmic mouth sounds

3.1   A typical recording studio control room.

You can also use any number of instruments for your own loops if you are musically inclined or have a friend or associate who has some musical talent.

To record in Soundtrack, you'll need at minimum a microphone and full-duplex soundcard. You can also input a guitar, synthesizer, or other device with electric output into the soundcard and record it directly to the Soundtrack timeline. The soundcard found in Apple systems is barely acceptable for serious recording, but adequate for recording a memo or limited-bandwidth voice. A high-quality soundcard such as those available from Echo Audio, M-Audio, Mark of the Unicorn, and other well-known card manufacturers is a tremendous benefit if much recording will be done. These high-end soundcards also open up much better audio monitoring experiences.

Connect the microphone to the soundcard, typically with an 1/8-inch connector, similar to a stereo headphone connec-

3.2   A typical connector (1/8-in.) for connecting a microphone to a computer soundcard.

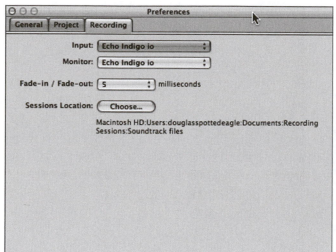

3.3 Determine hardware connections for recording your own loops in the Preferences>Recording dialog.

3.4 Meters are found underneath the Preview pane.

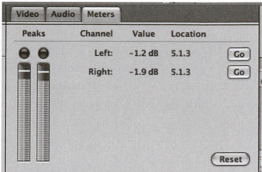

tor. Soundtrack will record stereo audio regardless of the input source, so if a stereo microphone is used, audio is recorded to both right and left channels. If a mono mic is used and the soundcard's mixer doesn't apply a mono signal to both channels, Soundtrack will record the audio only on one channel and nothing on the other.

SINGLE TAKE RECORDING

A Single Take Recording is an immediate method of recording audio used in Soundtrack. This might be a one-shot, such as a vocal embellishment, or a sound effect that is dropped in as an "exclamation point" to mark a transition or reinforce an exciting section in the video. Single Take Recording is also a good opportunity to drop in a unique sound on a title sequence.

1. Open Soundtrack and create a new project. Now is a good time to open the Soundtrack Preferences/Recording to determine the location of the recording. This is determined by the path shown in Soundtrack>Soundtrack Preferences>Recording>Sessions Location. Clicking the Choose button allows for a new location to be selected. If a second hard drive is available on the system, it's a good idea to route the audio to the second hard drive and to a folder that is identified as being a folder for Soundtrack projects. Preferences also determine which recording hardware will be chosen for recording audio.

2. In the input dropdown, select the hardware that the microphone is plugged into. This will route the audio from the microphone through the hardware and to the hard drive. Audio may be monitored through the hardware as well, allowing audio to be heard as it's being recorded.

3. Select the hardware through which the audio will be monitored, choosing Default, None, or any hardware that may be connected to the computer. This allows the recording artist or voice

Latency

Depending on the hardware, latency may be an issue. Latency is when there is a delay in the time between audio arriving at the input of the hardware and its routing through the hardware, hard drive, any processing or mixing before it's heard at the audio outputs or monitoring system. Hardware devices have differing latencies. Too much latency can be a difficult issue, particularly when monitoring against previously recorded tracks or loops in the project. Most higher-end hardware has a driver structure that allows for low-latency times. Some hardware systems have direct monitoring that bypasses processing all together. The Echo Indigo Cardbus card, for instance, has direct monitoring available so that previously recorded audio may be heard along with audio being recorded, with no resulting latency.

over artist to hear their own performance in real time via the monitoring system or headphones connected to the monitoring system. Close the Preferences dialog once these settings are satisfactory.

4. Open the Meters tab in the Preview pane. Metering in the Meter pane will not show recorded level, but does give a comparative level of any loops being played back from the Timeline.

5. Press the Record button found on the Master Control section. This opens up a dialog that asks for the name of the session and provides other pertinent information.

6. Give the recording session a name that is associated with the current project; If no name is given, then Soundtrack gives it a name based on the project name. Select the hardware to which the microphone or recording equipment is connected and select from where audio will be monitored, if at all, by using the dropdown menus available.

7. Check the session path by selecting the Settings button. This button offers no choices or changes in the path of recorded audio, since this is done in the Preferences dialog.

8. Input level is also determined in the Single Take recording dialog box. By default, this is set to 0dB (decibels). It's a good idea to set this level at a maximum of −.03 to prevent the audio from overdriving. While default on many recording systems is −3dB, if the audio source is not overly

3.5   The Single Take recording dialog offers choices of what hardware can be selected for recording and setting, as well as levels for recording.

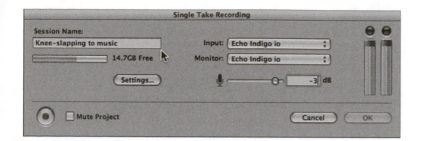

3.6   Settings dialog

dynamic and the maximum volume is known, the maximum level may be set higher, so long as the audio never reaches 0dB. If an external preamplifier is used to set the project, be sure its output is distortion-free by checking the levels from the preamplifier.

If the microphone is connected to the hardware and audio is correctly routed, the meters in the Single Take Recording dialog will move slightly, unless the audio is too weak to provide a signal causing the meters to move. This is addressed later in this chapter.

The best practice is to get audio as loud ("hot") as possible without clipping. Clipped audio will be displayed in the meter via the two red indicators at the top of the meters. Clipped audio cannot be reasonably repaired, therefore must be avoided.

Audio from the project is heard during the recording process, which provides a reference for where recording should be started/stopped. Project audio may also be muted by selecting the Mute Project checkbox.

3.7   Meters should peak at the very top of the meters during loud passages without lighting the Clip displays.

9. Pressing the Record button starts the recording process immediately. Note that there is no delay or pre-roll time. Audio is recorded to the hard drive location specified in Preferences. Clicking the Record button again stops the recording process.

10. After recording, press OK. The audio is now drawn on the Timeline.

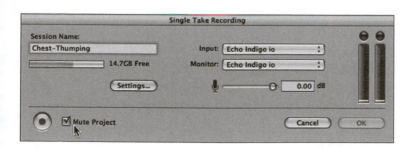

3.8   Mute Project checkbox

3.9 Drag a selection in the beat ruler to create a looped playback.

New recordings will create a new track for the new audio. This audio may be exported for editing, opened in the Loop Utility, or processed in Soundtrack, depending on the desired sound and use.

11. To select a different in/out point for the loop, drag in the selection bar using the zoom to fine-view the beginning and end of the loop point prior to saving the loop. This allows for the loop area to be cleaned up, removing any pre-roll or post-roll from the recorded audio.

12. Save the file by selecting File>Save. If the Add to Project When Saved checkbox is filled, the edited/completed loop is added to the Timeline as a finished loop and ready for mixing and processing.

 Monitoring: If Soundtrack is being monitored through speakers, it's a very good idea to turn the speakers off or at least significantly reduce their volume prior to pressing the record button. This step avoids audio bleeding from the speakers into the microphone and prevents feedback that can potentially damage the speakers and cause pain to the ear.

MULTIPLE TAKE RECORDING

Multiple Take Recording allows a series of recordings to take place based on a continually looping area in Soundtrack, looping over and over while the performance is perfected and recorded. Following recording, the various recordings are accessible as individual files and may be saved as loop takes or one-shots. This is a great way to "audition" a performance while recording all the "auditions." It's hard to know which performance is a keeper.

For purposes of recording loops to be used in future projects, this is the most efficient method of recording loops.

1. To record with multiple takes, drag a selection in the Beat Ruler to create a region for looped playback. This instructs Soundtrack to loop playback over this section, recording a new take for each pass over the loop selection.

 Monitoring: Selecting a few counts before and after the recording takes place will allow for a pre-roll and a post-roll, if this is necessary.

The In and Out points of the region determines where recording begins and ends.

2. Press the Record button in the Master Control. This opens the Multiple Takes dialog box.

3. Give the recording session a name, usually associated with the current project. If no name is given, then Soundtrack will give it a name based on the project name. In the same workflow as the Single Take dialog, select the hardware to which the microphone or recording equipment is connected and select from where audio will be monitored, if at all, by using the dropdown menus available.

4. Check the session path by selecting the Settings button. This button offers no choices or changes in the path of recorded audio, since this is done in the Preferences dialog.

5. Input level is also determined in the Single Take recording dialog box. By default, this is set to 0dB (decibels). It's a good idea to set this level at a maximum of −.03dB to prevent the audio from overdriving. If an external preamplifier is used to set the project, be sure its output is dis-tortion-free by checking the levels from the preamplifier.

If the microphone is connected to the hardware and audio is correctly routed, the meters in the Multiple Take Recording dialog will move slightly, unless the audio is too weak to provide a signal that causes the meters to move. Once you've started playing your instrument or speak-ing, the meters should indicate levels properly. (This is addressed later in this chapter.) As with the Single Take Recording process, the best practice is to get audio as "hot" as possible without clipping. Clipped audio will be displayed in the meter via the two red indicators at the top of the meters. Clipped audio cannot be reasonably repaired, therefore must be avoided.

Monitoring audio is possible from the Multiple Takes Recording session, just as with the Single Takes Recording session. Latency may be an issue, depending on hardware.

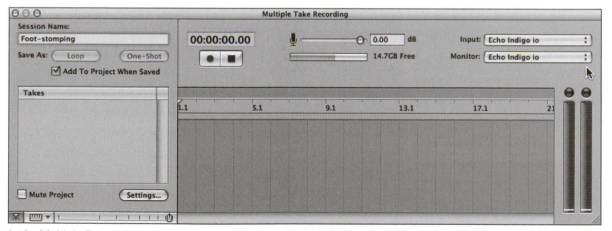

3.10 Multiple Takes allows continuous recording over a loop, enabling selection of the best take after recording is completed. Notice that the Multiple Takes window is different than the Single Takes window.

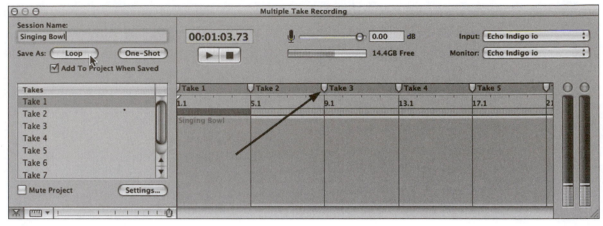

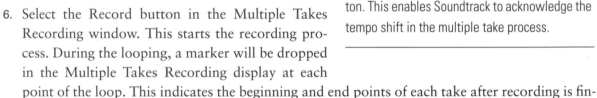

3.11   Markers in the Multiple Takes Record button

Audio from the project may be muted, just as in the Single Takes Recording window. Mute the audio if you'd prefer to record with no indication of time other than the Beat and Time indicators.

 **Tempo Change:** If the looped region covers a tempo change, hold Option while clicking the Record button. This enables Soundtrack to acknowledge the tempo shift in the multiple take process.

6. Select the Record button in the Multiple Takes Recording window. This starts the recording process. During the looping, a marker will be dropped in the Multiple Takes Recording display at each point of the loop. This indicates the beginning and end points of each take after recording is finished. These markers may not be moved as they are only indicators of the region-defined loop point.

7. Click the Stop button to stop the recording process. Once recording is finished, the audio waveform is drawn in the Multiple Takes Recording window with the markers indicating the in/out points of each take. The various takes are listed on the left side of the Multiple Takes Recording window and may be individually selected by take.

8. Audition or preview the takes by pressing Play in the Multiple Takes dialog window and the take will play repeatedly until the loop is stopped. Zooming in or out on a take may be accomplished by using the slider and scroll bar similar to the zoom in the timeline/workspace area.

9. Takes may be edited by dragging in the Selection bar, allowing the in/out points of the loop to be fine tuned to achieve the best loop. When dragging in the selection bar, the selected loop area is indicated in blue. Snapping is enabled by pressing the G-key, or by pressing the Enable/Disable Snapping button found in the lower left corner of the Multiple Takes dialog window (see Figure 3.13).

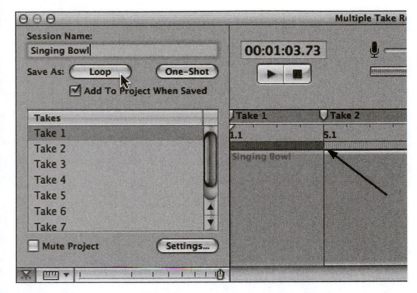

3.12 Dragging in the selection bar allows for fine tuning the in/out points of the loop placed on the Timeline.

10. Checking the Add to Project When Saved checkbox drops the saved loop area on the Timeline used in the current project.

TAGGING LOOPS IN THE LOOP UTILITY

After saving either Single Takes or Multiple Takes and adding them to the Timeline, the recorded audio may be opened in the Soundtrack Loop Utility to add metadata and metatags to the newly recorded loop. While this may be done at any time, it's most efficient to insert tags while still in the project that includes the loop. Otherwise, the tempo in which the loop was recorded must be referred to only by looking at the project. If the loop is in a musical scale, then the key of the project needs to be examined at a later point as well. By embedding tags during the creation of the project, all information about the project is close at hand.

Opening the loop in the Soundtrack Loop Utility also allows the file to be optimized for the best playback, particularly if the loop will be used in other projects. See Chapter 4 on page 147 for more information on using the Soundtrack Loop Utility.

GETTING THE BEST RECORDING

Understanding the recording process and environment will help in obtaining a good recording with any NLE or DAW application. FCP and most DAWs have good audio tools that can "repair" weak audio recordings, but it's best to have high-quality sound recordings in the first place.

Any microphone can be plugged into Soundtrack with nearly any Apple-compatible soundcard. To get a high-quality recording takes a little more effort.

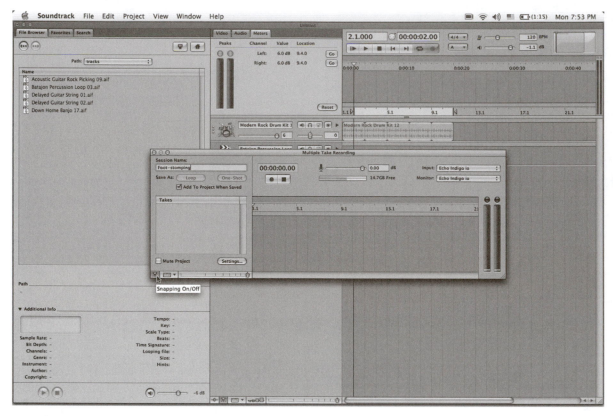

3.13 Snapping enabled.

Microphones (mic) and a good soundcard are only the beginnings of the recording process. Having a good room and good monitors are equally, if not more, important than having a good mic and soundcard. The recording area is critical; any noise from computer fans, air conditioning, fluorescent lighting, air movement, small reflections, transformer hum, and a myriad of other noise sources have a negative impact on the recording. While video engineers and multimedia composers certainly don't need a dedicated recording area, many tools can be employed to create a better recording and listening environment for any multimedia authoring area, making the composing/engineering space much more accurate and pleasant to work in. Setting up the room can be either complex or simple, depending on the needs involved. Most editing rooms are converted offices or, in some cases, bedrooms. It's safe to say that these rooms are typically around 12×12 in. size. Unfortunately, a small, square room is difficult to monitor in, not to mention record. Small rooms tend to reverberate and reflect higher frequencies, while not allowing bass frequencies to completely develop. However, if it's what you have, then it can be made to work without too much cost or difficulty, unless complete isolation is the goal. Just note that the quieter the room, the more accurate the mix and quality of a finished product.

Setting up the room

A room with a high ceiling is preferable, if only to reduce the compression of bass frequencies. However, at lower listening levels, standard-height ceilings do not present any obstacle. If monitoring at high volume is necessary, either a large room or sufficient room treatment are required.

Rooms that are too large or too small both present difficulties in the average recording/monitoring environment. A room that is too large may portray reverberations and time delay of unique frequencies, causing the ear to hear false colorations in the sound. A room that is too small will cause "bounce" and, even at nominal listening levels, sound will be reproduced inaccurately. Both large and small rooms benefit greatly from relatively- inexpensive absorption and/or reflective treatment.

Treating walls and ceilings is simple, relatively inexpensive, and supremely effective in reducing reflection in the average room. There are many myths surrounding reflection reduction; don't get caught up in what your brother the musician might have to offer. Using carpet and egg crate foam is not very effective in preventing any but extremely high frequencies from bouncing around a room. This is particularly true in commercial or public environments. In addition to the lack of effectiveness, egg-crate foam designed for use under mattresses or for packing is even illegal because it carries a high fire danger. A recent tragedy in a nightclub was attributed to blazing illegal materials installed for purposes of sound control.

Ceilings can be brought under control by using drop-in panels, which are available from most music or professional audio retailers. Heavy-density foam or fiberglass panel treatment will suffice, also. Gobos, another solution, are manufactured from frames of 2×2, filled with fiberglass insulation, and covered with any loose-weave fabric. Gobos effectively kill reflections, predominantly behind the listening space or sweet spot, and provide for a tighter, more accurate representation of what's taking place in the mix.

Also, don't ignore the windows in the room. If critical referencing is part of the production process (and it usually is for post-production and music composition), windows should have heavy coverings to prevent reflection and vibration. Some engineers use large pieces of foam mounted to plywood or foam core that fit snugly inside the window opening. The foam prevents the wood or foam core from actually making contact with the sill, sides, or top of the window enclosure. Heavy drapes made of a velvet or other thick fabric will do a good job of reducing reflections as well. Some absorptive product manufacturers have created product lines just for covering windows.

Corners can be treated effectively (saving both time and money) with round, concrete tube molds made from cardboard cut in half to fit the corner. To make these, drill large holes (approximately 1.5–2 in.) throughout the cardboard at numerous, random places. Then fill the concrete tube with R-11 insulation and cover the tube with a porous fabric, such as unpolished burlap, cotton, or another rough-weave fabric. There are many cost-effective possibilities for treating the room found on the web. Auralex and similar products do not cost much, but are extremely effective in most environments. Visit the Auralex or Auralex University website for more information.

3.14   The Hardy mic preamp is known as one of the best in the industry because each unit is handmade and hand-finished. It's also one of the most expensive.

The folks at Auralex will usually offer a number of ideas for your specific room at no cost (http:/ /www.auralex.com).   Of course, expense is important, though safety should always be the primary concern; make sure that you're using safe materials.

Soundcards

Any instrument, voice, device, or other means of producing sound within a room or other environment, produces vibration (sound energy). Vibrations carry a pure tone, plus a tremendous variety of harmonics, the number and order of which are determined by the instrument, voice, or source that generated the sound. This vibration generates movement of air. These same vibrations and pressures on the air are what the human ear senses and translates into information that the brain can comprehend. They may also be captured by a microphone. Microphones convert this air movement and vibration into electrical energy by means of a diaphragm, which moves when vibrations strike it. Varying qualities of microphones have different sizes and thicknesses of diaphragms and are made from a variety of materials.

The diaphragm converts acoustic energy into voltage. This voltage is sent down the microphone cable and into a preamplifier or amplifier. Most mixers have preamps for each built-in channel.

The preamplifier then makes the voltage greater, so that it reaches standard output levels for recording or input to a public address system. A preamplifier of some sort is required in all recording environments. They may sell for as little as $59 for a stereo unit, or as much as $2,500 for a

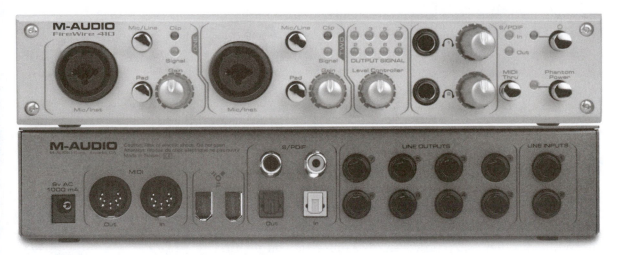

3.15   M-Audio makes great preamps for a very low cost.

single channel. Though, I cannot stress enough how valuable the preamp/microphone combination is in the recording environment. Having a good front end is critical to the quality of loop and voice over recording. While an expensive preamp and mic are not necessary for most recording situations, plan on spending around $400 for a minimum of good new equipment. Also, remember that there are many outlets for used gear as well.

In the computer/hard disk recording environment, the soundcard may have a built-in preamplifier. Most soundcards do. However, their quality is questionable and they are usually noisy if they are PCI soundcards. Professional cards use a PCI card, USB, or FireWire interface and a cable to a breakout box. In the case of a professional-quality breakout box, some boxes have preamplifiers built in, while others do not. If your breakout box doesn't have a preamplification circuit built into it, a preamplifier is required. (Devices such as the Echo Audio Layla, Indigo IO, or M-Audio Delta 1010 boxes do not have preamplifiers built into them.) The new FireWire card from Echo Audio has four excellent preamplifiers built in and a FireWire interface, as does the new M-Audio FireWire 410. I've tested most of these units with Soundtrack and they work great, not to mention their awesome sound with a good pair of studio monitors.

Analog audio that is input to the soundcard or breakout box is converted to bits that the computer can process. The conversion process is the most important part of any recording project, as converters, known as DACs (Digital Audio Converter), of poor quality will produce poor-quality audio that cannot be repaired or significantly improved.

Audio passes from the DAC to the processor and hard drive, where the media is stored until it's recalled for editing. The same soundcard or breakout box is usually used for monitoring audio during recording. DACs vary from two-channel to eight-channel devices, which permit up to eight inputs per breakout box at a time.

Soundtrack is also capable of recording/playback of audio at different sample rates. Rates of up to 24bit/96KHz may be selected by going to Soundtrack Preferences>Project and selecting the bit rate and sample rate desired. Be aware that not all soundcards can support all bit and sample rates. Check the documentation that came with the soundcard for more information.

Most of the newer sound cards support the 24/96 rate and some will even support sample rates up to 24bit/192KHz, known as High-Definition audio. Soundtrack currently does not support this high-definition rate. CD-quality audio requires that final output files be 44.1KHz and 16 bit for burning to a CD, however, audio may be recorded at any sample rate/bit depth. Be aware that audio at 24/96 consumes hard drive space at double the rate of a 44.1KHz/16bit recording, therefore 24bit/ 192KHz uses even greater disk space. Also, 24/96 audio files require faster hard drives with greater cache, as well as fast processors and adequate RAM to handle the file size and throughput/data rates.

For voiceovers, general recording, and dialog, 16bit/ 44.1KHz generally should be the preference. When working with highly detailed sounds, such as Foley work, musical instruments (particularly acoustic instruments), or sound design, the higher clarity of 16/48, 16/96 or 24/96 audio may be a better

3.16 The Echo Indigo IO card has a microphone input for laptops, but no preamplifier is built in.

choice, particularly when working with sounds that have higher frequency information. More "air" becomes apparent and the sound will be smoother. When the mixing is done in these frequencies for final output to CD-ROM, the information is truncated down to the lower sampling rate compatible with Redbook CDs. A small degree of information is lost in this dithering process where bits are thrown away. However, if a CD is the final destination for the media, there is no choice. Some Digital Audio Tape (DAT) machines accept the 24-bit files, allowing a duplicator or mastering house to keep files in their pristine state. At the time of this writing, 48KHz is the highest sample rate available to a standard DAT machine.

Audio is monitored from the computer via the soundcard or breakout box. An amplifier or amplified speakers are required for monitoring. Headphones allow for monitoring as well, but should never be used to create a mix because headphones don't present an accurate reference to what's really being presented in the recording. Mixes created through headphones tend to be bass light due to the headphone interaction with the skull/bone structure of the human head. Worse still is the body's insensitivity to the "power" of moving large amounts of air in a room. The ear canal

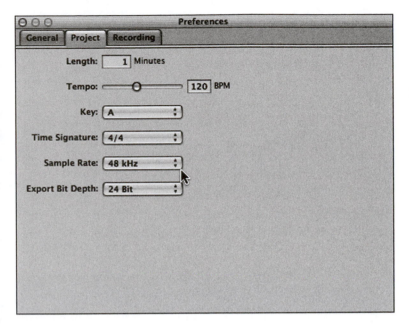

3.17 Set the desired sample rate in Soundtrack Preferences>Project.

is capable of perceiving higher frequencies more quickly than lower frequencies because of the proximity to the speaker/conductor in the earphone housing. All sounds are channeled straight into the ear, rather than having the benefit of reflecting around the mix room or listening environment, further creating a false sense of what's heard. There are diffusion-oriented headphones available at great cost that are designed to artificially simulate diffusion in a room. However, these are modeled after the shape of the human head and because no two heads are alike, sound will be perceived differently by different individuals. Use monitor speakers in nearly all instances for accurate representation of what the recording sounds like.

Audio Monitors

Often speakers/monitors are purchased too large for the average room. Smaller is typically better. In most instances, a monitor containing a four-inch bass driver, sometimes called a "woofer" is suitable. These types of monitors are called "near field" monitors because typically they are close to the editor's ears, usually not farther than four to six feet away. Far field, soffit mounted, or larger monitors are generally farther away, usually 10–18 feet from the listening point. Most video editing suites would not have good use for soffit mounted monitors, unless an exceptionally large room with a large viewing screen is available.

Large speakers that are too close don't accurately reproduce sound at the listening point or "sweet spot" because the sound waves have not had enough distance to properly develop. Speakers that have amplifiers built in are a great choice for many reasons. Most importantly, the amplifier is matched to the enclosure and components, reducing concerns about matching a system.

3.18 Soffit mounted monitors

Built-in amplifiers reduce the amount of cable found laying on the floor and reduce concerns for noise induction to the system.

Speaker monitors that are shielded for video use are available and should be used in most video previewing/editing rooms. Otherwise, the broadcast monitor may not operate to spec and video monitors can suffer in quality from the nearby magnets of the speaker monitor. Most near-field monitors are video ready. For program material that is musically intense or sound- design heavy, a subwoofer is necessary for small monitors. Even a standard video suite will benefit substantially from a small subwoofer of less than 10 inches in size.

While there may be a monitoring system designed as standard speakers, I've yet to hear them or hear of them. Anything smaller than a four inch one-way speaker is too small for almost any serious listening situation. Inexpensive speakers, such as those from Creative, JBL Home, Kensington, and others available at a computer store, are great for listening to CDs at a low level, though they are not suited for composing music or creating a mix for video. The other problems with inexpensive/low quality monitors is that they may exaggerate specific frequencies, making voices seem louder or softer than they actually are, or creating missed mix opportunities and mistakes due to the mix not being accurate.

When shopping for monitors, bring along a CD that is very familiar to your ear and has been heard in a number of environments. This will help you to choose monitors better. Also, make sure that if you're not shopping for a subwoofer, that one isn't connected during the monitor listening session. Choose monitors that make sounds pleasing to your ear. Staying with name brands such as JBL, MAudio, Genelec, KRK, Event, and Mackie assures only that the personal preferences matter. Because this equipment is of similar quality, with a few unique differences suited to personal consumer tastes, it's up to you to try it to find your preference. Some monitors have well-balanced response, while others are top or bottom-end heavy. Still others may be mid-range oriented. There

3.19 Mackie 626 THX® Certified monitor.

3.20 M-Audio speaker.

is no right or wrong in this part of choosing studio equipment; it's all about personal preferences. Any of the bigger brand monitors will suffice in a properly-treated room and none of them will sound their best in a nontreated or poorly-treated room, regardless of the primary goal of the editor.

Monitor speakers should be placed at a height that brings the high frequency drivers, sometimes called "tweeters," to the height of the ears when sitting at the mixing desk, editing desk, or listening environment. Otherwise, the speakers are what is known as "off-axis" and this is a critical point in the listening experience. Off-axis sound is colored differently than on-axis sound. So, when sitting in the sweet spot, the tweeters should be pointing towards the ear at ear height. It will look to you like the tweeter is staring you right in the eye. Having the monitors be on-axis also assures correct depth of field in the listening space. This is critical to evaluating placement of instruments or voices in the mix. In off-axis systems it is nearly impossible to correctly gage the relationship of right/left audio.

The distance between the monitors should be the same distance as it is to the listening position. In other words, an equidistant triangle should be formed between the listener and each monitor speaker. In the event of a surround sound system, such as a 5.1 surround system to author for DVD, similar rules apply. All speakers should be isolated as best as possible from the environment. Center speaker, front left, and front right should all be equal in distance to each other. This means that rear speakers may be closer than normally expected or planned for. Rear speakers may be set back from the standard distance to the sweet spot, while care must be taken to assure that the rear monitor speakers are on axis. The center channel should be at the same height as the front right

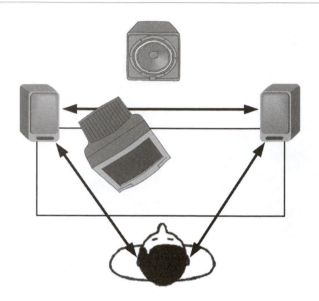

3.21 Correct monitor placement for near-field monitors. Maintain equal distance and have monitors at ear level for best monitoring experiences.

and front left speakers, but set back in space so that it is the same distance to the ear as the remaining four speakers. This is difficult to do in a small home studio/office environment because distances of at least 10 feet measuring front to back are required to create a spatially-accurate 5.1 mix. In the ideal situation, the center speaker will be equidistant from the front right and front left monitors. In reality, the room is rarely ideal and most home entertainment systems have the same depth of field for the center speaker as the front right and front left. When mixing for the average home listening environment, it is generally better to plan to mix for the environment in which the audio will be heard rather than planning for a theoretically perfect room.

Isolating the monitors from other surfaces is very beneficial in terms of reducing unwanted vibrations, preventing the monitor from acoustically coupling with the surface on which they are mounted and isolating the monitor enclosure itself. This can be done in a number of ways. Speaker stands are available from a wide variety of sources and are common choices. Often times these stands are filled with sand in order to make them acoustically "dead" or nonresonant.

Auralex manufactures a product called Mo-Pad that has been designed to dampen the acoustic coupling that takes place in all studios, as well as reduce vibrations. This is also accomplished by using dense foam cut to hold the speaker in place, providing at least an inch of isolation from the monitor bottom to the surface of the desktop.

Make sure all shelves, microphones, or anything else in the monitoring environment is battened down or foamed to prevent vibration. Most automotive and all recreational vehicle stores sell rolls of a rubberized fabric that computer monitors, pencil holders, and anything else that might be on your desktop area can be placed under to prevent them from vibrating. All things vibrate; it's just a matter of what frequency at which they vibrate. Minimizing these issues up front makes for much

3.22 Auralex MoPads™

better mixes in the end. While all of this is standard fare in a recording studio and may seem like overkill in a video editing suite, always remember that sound is the most important aspect of any production environment.

Connect the monitors to the sound card using either XLR or TRS cables. These cables are balanced, low impedance, and may be run great distances. If high impedance cables are used, such as a typical 1/8-inch connector found on all low-end sound cards, then short cable runs should be used, or hum and buzz may be induced. Balanced cables, properly connected, prevent hum and buzz from entering the cable path. Use balanced cable everywhere possible. Some sound cards will not accept a balanced input. In the event that your sound card does not allow for connection of a balanced line, obtain a direct box and a short (6–12 inch) patch cable with a male stereo mini plug on one end and a male 1/4-inch plug on the other. The microphone connects to the direct box via balanced cable, run as far as it needs to be run, and then the direct box is placed next to the computer with the quarter-inch plug plugged into the direct box and the male mini plug connected to the sound card input. This will eliminate hum and buzz normally induced by running long lengths of high impedance/unbalanced cables. At no time should speaker cables be used for microphone lines, also the reverse is true that line cable should never be used as speaker cable.

3.23 (1) balanced, (2) unbalanced
(3) XLR,
(4) Quarter inch, and
(5) mini plugs

3.24 AT 4033 Studio mic, AT Shotgun mic, Peavey EC2 Stick mic, and AT 831 Lavalier mic .

Run cables at a 90° angle over power cables. Running any cable parallel to a power cable is an invitation for trouble. Take care to assure that audio lines are far away from wall-wart/AC adapters that are very common in the studio. Also, keep cables tied in neatly, so that similar cables are running with each other. Power cables run in one tie system, speaker, microphone, line, patch, and other similar low voltage cables run in another. If the studio layout has not yet been decided, or equipment not yet installed, lay down the AC/electrical lines first. This helps keep things more organized in the end and assures the user that cables will not be laid over AC paths. AC hum presents itself as a 60Hz buzz that is constant, only by isolating the source of the hum can it be eliminated. Because this can be difficult, start by assuring that all equipment is properly grounded and connected with balanced cables. Never remove the grounding plug/tab from a power cable. While this will occasionally remove hum by removing the ground from the system, it is potentially lethal and masks where real problems may lie.

MICROPHONES

Microphones (mics) come in all shapes, sizes, prices, and qualities. A great mic doesn't have to carry a high price tag, however. For most loop recording, one or two mics will be sufficient depending on whether stereo separation is desired. Fortunately, many mics that might be used on a video shoot are also usable as a recording tool for loops. As an example, a shotgun mic is usually a terrific V/O mic as well. Many of the biggest names in the voice-over business use shotgun mics such as the Shoeps, Shure, or Audio Technica shotguns.

Shotgun mics come in a wide number of makes, models, patterns, and prices. These are the mics seen on the end of long booms, generally 8–16 inches in length, often covered over by fur windscreens or large acoustically-transparent housings known as a "blimp." Shotguns are great and usually necessary in video shots where a stick or lavalier microphone would be intrusive to the shot. Watch Jay Leno, Saturday Night Live, or David Letterman long enough and at some point you'll see the shotgun mic mounted on a boom drift into the picture at least once. (Here is a bit of trivia: the mic on the desktop of these late night talk show hosts is mostly for show, but in moments of system failure have saved the day.) Shotguns are also exceptionally good for voice over work and many V/O pros use shotgun mics in their work. Shotgun mics generally have a fairly narrow field in which they'll pick up audio. The further away the mic is from the source, the less audio is picked up with clarity. However, shotgun mics are electronically and physically tuned to work a narrow "corridor" to pick up audio from the source. This corridor is known as a pattern, which is often variable in a microphone. Some shotgun mics have a narrow pattern, others may be switched to be a wide field mic, and yet others may be

3.25   Shotgun mic pattern

switched from mono to stereo. The pattern is a characteristic of the mic's build. The long, narrow physical housing of a shotgun mic allows frequency filtering and phasing used to narrow the mic's pattern. The mic is pointed at a source and the primary audio is picked up, while sounds not relevant to the source are rejected. This doesn't mean that a shotgun mic may be taken into an exceptionally noisy environment and used to record a whispered interview. The mic gives priority to the source at which it's pointed, but cannot reject out-of-hand sounds that are coming from its sides (ambient sound); it also picks up the sounds with lesser volume. Many mics require phantom power, or power from a device such as a battery, or output from a camera or mixing device to supply voltage. This last type is known as a condenser mic. Phantom power typically raises the sensitivity level of a microphone, so that the mic can "hear" better. It also allows for the plates that make up the "ears" of the microphone to be more refined and to reproduce sounds more accurately. Shotgun mics fall into the category (usually) of unidirectional or stereo directional.

When looking for a shotgun mic, avoid mics made from plastic. Get a mic with a solid metal housing for the most satisfactory result. Plastic and cheap aluminum housings tend to resonate at mid-range frequencies making for a muddy and unclear recording.

Use the shotgun mic mounted on a stand, preferably with a shock mount that isolates the mic from receiving rumble from the studio floor or picking up transmitted noise via the mic stand.

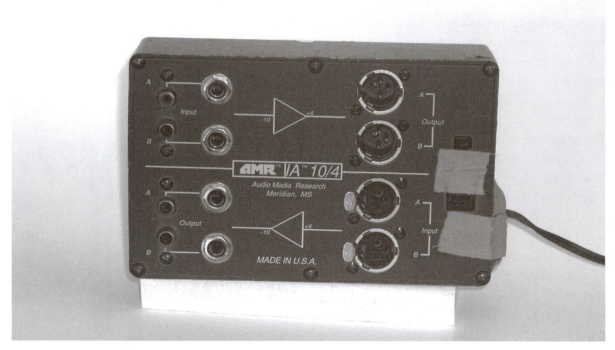

3.26 Peavey phantom power supply. Phantom power supplies may also be separate/stand alone.

Adding about 3dB of bass in the 120Hz region with most shotguns typically provides a powerful sound.

Another popular mic in the studio for voice over and general recording is the large diaphragm mic such as the Audio Technica 4055, the AKG 414, the EV RE20, and so forth. Large diaphragm mics are great for most purposes from voice over to recording many instruments. Large diaphragm mics tend to be fairly expensive and most use phantom power, a type of power that comes into the mic externally either from a power supply or via the microphone cable from a phantom power supply built into a mixer, soundcard, or sometimes a stand-alone box. Stand alone phantom power supplies sell for about $99.

Smaller diaphragm mics work very well in the NLE or multimedia authoring suite as well, albeit they are typically less sensitive than a large diaphragm mic. Even the very inexpensive Shure SM-58, a workhorse of a microphone, does great in most recording environments. SM-58s are a standard and may be purchased new for around $125 and purchased used for around $35 on Ebay and other outlets for used musical and stage equipment. The SM-58 is so durable that it is often known as a sledgehammer in the biz because it's literally possible to hammer nails with it.

Last, but not least, is the lavalier mic. Used for nearly every type of on-camera work, this type of small diaphragm mic is wonderful for many applications. Contrary to popular belief, lavs may be used to acquire great sound. The Audio Technica 830 series is a personal favorite. Not only have my Grammy Award-winning recordings been done with this small mic, but essentially they are bulletproof. As a low-budget mic, these definitely don't deliver low-budget sound if handled correctly. Mounted on a spring clip or affixed to a hard, nonvibrant surface, such as a heavy board covered with laminate, these mics are extremely versatile and may be used for recording guitar, voice, wind instruments, and sound effects. For a submarine movie, we took these small Audio Technica 831s and Sony ECM77 mics and put them in dry (nonlubricated) condoms in order to waterproof them while using them for recording in a large fish tank. The takes for a major picture sounded great and it was accomplished using very inexpensive mics. The Sony ECMs are available as used mics all over the web for a fairly low cost.

Mic Placement

Having the monitors, soundcard, and mic are all for naught if the sound being recorded isn't as present and full as it can be. Placement of the mic is as important to the quality of sound as anything else in the media-authoring chain. Most important of all is a critical ear. With even a low-quality microphone, proper placement can accommodate for some of the problems created by the mic itself.

Oftentimes, the inexperienced (and occasionally the experienced) user will place a microphone directly in front of the mouth. This might be great for radio and even look good on television, but it doesn't work in the studio. Depending on the type of mic, here are some placements that should provide a great voice over sound.

For instrumental recording, it's helpful to have two people working together: one to play the instrument and the other to move around the instrument with one ear towards the instrument, seeking the place that holds the fullest and most pleasing sound, known as a sweet spot. This isn't always the most obvious place. For instance, most non-brass wind instruments at first glance might seem to have the best sound near the end piece, when in fact, the sound is cleanest and richest near the mouthpiece, usually. Guitars are often best sounding just slightly ahead of or above and behind the sound hole. A quick hint with the piano is to remember that the piano has a wide and long sound board with unique frequencies across the distance. Placing a mic at each end of the soundboard, whether mixing to mono or stereo, is a great place to start the recording setup. Move the mics around while monitoring in order to identify the best location.

Use a pop filter for most vocal and wind instrument recording. These may be expensive from high-end mic manufacturers, mid-priced from the local recording store, or extremely low-cost by taking a pair of pantyhose and stretching them in an embroidery frame sized 6–8 inches. Use a separate mic stand for the pop filter. The pop filter will help prevent explosive sounds such as Ps and Ts from causing the mic to pop.

Use a script stand or clamp mounted on a stand that will allow voice over artists to read the script without having to handle the paper. Be sure the stand is capable of being raised fairly high to allow the artist to stand while reading the script. This helps prevent breath from reaching the

3.27 Pop filter

microphone while keeping the script in easy view. Also, standing puts less pressure on the diaphragm of the voice over artist and enables a more resonant, smooth voice. Another hint is to print type large so that the artist can read it with the stand at a fair distance away. This helps cut down on audible reflections bouncing from the copy stand or paper and hitting the microphone. Again, minimizing unwanted sounds from the recording area is always the goal.

Spending a few hours tuning or treating the room for the best possible audio in a given space manifests itself in due time. Ears, like eyes, can become fatigued and the better the listening room, the better the recording and monitoring experience will be. A project can only be as good as its weakest component, therefore, having the best recording environment is as important as any video monitor or computer system. Having high quality sound will actually make the video appear to be better as you preview scenes while scoring them.

Making your own loops is not only great for having your score sound just exactly the way you want to have it sound, it can be fun, and potentially profitable. Visit `http://www.soundtrack-lounge.com` to share files with others and have discussions on Soundtrack with other Soundtrack users.

Making a Voice Box

Using four squares of acoustic foam and some long pushpins or duct tape, a small voice box can be manufactured quickly. Typically the foam squares are 24-square inches and vary from 1–4 inches thick. Two inches thick is ideal. Using pushpins or duct tape, construct a box, leaving the bottom and one side open. Place the microphone on a stand inside the box, running the cable beneath the side the box. If the back of the box is left without permanent attachment, then the box may quickly be disassembled and stored in a closet, behind a desk, or underneath a bed. Sung or spoken, audio will be much better than if simply recorded in an untreated room.

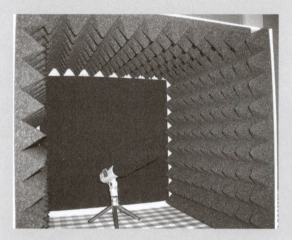

3.28 The recording box is a quick and easy method of getting great isolation without treating an entire room.

3.29 Auralex on the walls.

If it seems the box will be used a great deal, the back of the box may be treated with Foam Core or even 1/8-masonite, making for greater sturdiness. Velcro™ may also be used for this purpose. If the panels are backed with masonite and Velcro™, the box components may be used as wall treatment in a standard video editing room. Simply use industrial Velcro™ to mount the spiky side on the wall and the fuzzy side on the back of the foam panel. Mount the panels to the wall when they're not being used as a recording aid. Mounting them behind speaker monitors helps deal with reflection and resonance, tightening the sound coming from the monitor. This keeps them out of the way, providing a better sound/fewer reflections in the room, and looks great.

Chapter 4

Soundtrack's Loop Utility

THE HEART OF FINDING AND CREATING LOOPS

Although Soundtrack is a powerful creative tool for composition, it would be difficult to use without the Media Manager. Then, next in line of importance is the Loop Utility. This is where loops are managed so that Soundtrack can correctly interpret and include them in projects. The Loop Utility inserts metadata into the loop files. It is the metadata that provides Soundtrack with information necessary to speed up, slow down, and pitch shift the loops in the Soundtrack project without the loops sounding strange.

The Loop Utility can import .aif and .wav files and insert metadata into those files.

Loops that are imported to the Loop Utility will be saved as .aif files regardless of what format is imported.

The Loop Utility has two main windows: the Main window for defining and inserting metadata and the Transient window that shows the loop, which allows beats to be defined and marked.

Metadata is a file embedded in the audio file containing information about the file in which it is embedded. Metadata might include tempo, pitch, author, genre, instrument, and other descriptor information. It is what allows Soundtrack to intelligently manipulate loops. Metadata does not change the loop quality or data in the file; it merely acts as a tool for finding, manipulating, and referencing the file. The original audio is never changed.

147

4.1   Loop utility

Loops can be imported to the Loop Utility several different ways:

- Open the file via the Loop Utility File>New and search for the file to be opened via the browser.
- Select the Add File in the Loop Utility Assets drawer.
- Drag the files from the Finder to the Loop Utility.
- Drag the files from a CD, hard drive, or other device to the Assets drawer.

Any of these options import a loop to the Loop Utility.

The Loop Utility displays the file type, size, name, and any other information it can locate when it's opened.

While the main window Loop Utility is where most of the functionality and use take place, it is in the Transient window where the definitions of beat points are made. Without proper definitions of beats, the loop will not be in time in any project, no matter how it is used. So, we'll start with the Transient window.

 Locate the *Painted drum 2.wav* file found on the CD-ROM in this book. Drag it from the CD (or hard drive if loops have been copied to the hard drive) to the Assets window. It also may be opened by using the Loop Utility browser. If the Assets drawer is not open, select the Assets button in the lower left of the Loop Utility window. The drawer will open and files can be dragged directly into it. The drawer may be opened or closed during processing of the loop.

4.2   Assets Drawer. Files may be dragged directly to the Assets drawer to be converted or edited.

Click on the Transient tab. The waveform of the .wav file is drawn in the Transient window. Notice that these drumbeats are very defined and clear. Transients indicate where beats are in the loop file and are usually the loudest points in the file, indicating attack or initial beginning of a sound. This file is prelooped, but it may be modified in the loop utility. Notice the markers indicating the transient and beat division points in the file. These are indicated by the small blue markers and horizontal lines in the Transient window. Using the Up/Down arrows on the keyboard, zoom in on the loop and the specific points of the markers. The markers will line up with the attack points (where the drum is struck) indicating the various beats.

In the upper left of the Transient window is a pop-up menu offering choices for the Transient division that the Loop Utility will use to set transients and mark tempo. If the beat divisions are known, this should be set to the known value. However, if the beat division is not known, this should be set to 64th or 32nd notes for complex loops and to lower values for simple loops such as single percussive instruments. The Loop Utility determines the rest. For the purposes of understanding how beat division works with the *Painted drum 2.wav,* select whole notes from the pop-up menu. Notice that there are now only six markers in the Transient window. Change the beat value to half notes. Now there are 11 markers. Continue to change the various values to learn how the Loop Utility divides the beats. The more marker information in the loop, the more likely it is to be tempo-adjustable over time when placed on the Timeline in Soundtrack. The fewer the markers,

4.3 .Wav File in Browser. File information is displayed when possible during the import of loops.

4.4 Book loops/file window *(below)*

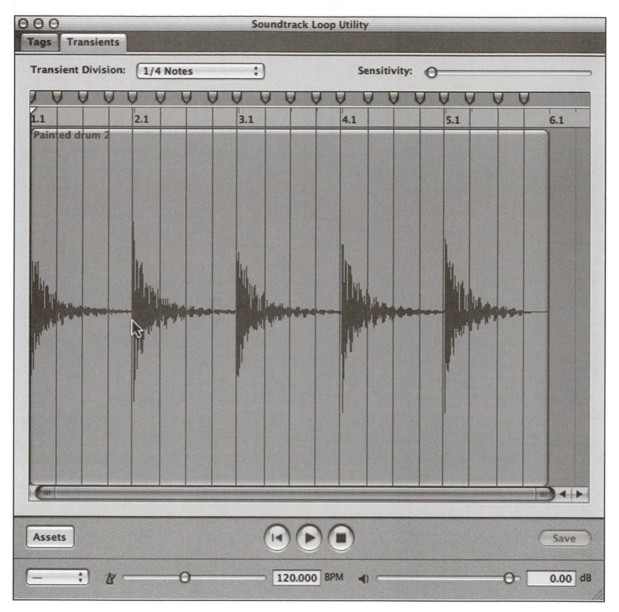

4.5   Notice that the marker is placed directly at the transient/attack point of the drum.

the more likely the loop will develop artifacts when shifted very far from its original pitch or tempo. The most important thing in the Loop Utility is that the markers match the transients.

Next to the beat division/note value pop-up menu is a slider that adjusts the sensitivity of the Loop Utility to the transients found in the file. This can easily be set too high or low. Normally,

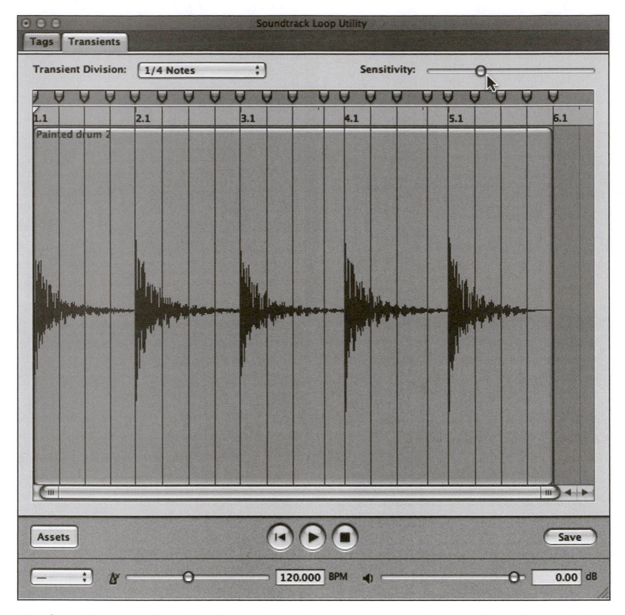

4.6 Correct Placement of Sensitivity. If you set this too high in a busy loop, it will create artifacts. Play back the loop at various sensitivities to find the best setting for that loop.

starting the loop creation process with this set to the low-mid point, or approximately 30%, is best. There are no hard or fast rules for setting this value, its usefulness is entirely based around the file loaded into the Loop Utility. A typical setting for loops is going to be the 64th note beat division and quarter sensitivity.

Play the loop by pressing the Play button found in the lower middle of the Loop Utility. It will loop until stopped by either pressing the Stop or Pause buttons or by pressing Save. While the loop is playing, click on the Tags tab and view the original file settings. The original tempo is 108 and is a mono file. The tempo and pitch information may be altered in the Tags or Transient windows and playback may be stopped, paused, or returned to the beginning of the loop in either window. This is a .wav file, therefore has no instrument, genre, or descriptor information embedded in the file. Such embedded information is unique to Soundtrack loops.

This particular loop does not have any pitch settings, just as a drum loop generally has no pitch or key information. If a loop that has key information is loaded, the Key menu can be used to hear the loop in various keys. The Key menu is found just below the Assets button in the lower left corner of the Loop Utility. When the *Painted drum 2.wav* is playing, adjust the tempo with the tempo slider. Notice that the loop speeds up and slows down without changing pitch. Extreme movements of the slider in either direction causes the loop to have artifacts; these may be adjusted somewhat by changing the transient division or the sensitivity while some anomalies are simply a byproduct of the loop being stretched beyond normal limits.

This is a simple loop used to illustrate the manner in which transients are detected and marked.

If the file is saved from the Loop Utility, it can only be saved as an .aif file unless preferences have been selected to keep .wav files as .wav files.

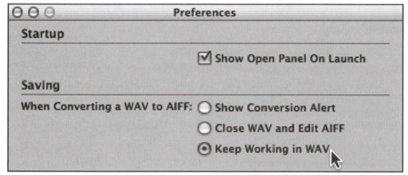

4.7   Preferences Window. Selecting Keep Working On WAV allows the metadata to be inserted to the wav file.

Locate the *echoflute9.5.wav* on the CD-ROM in this book, then drag and drop or open in the Loop Utility. Select the Tags tab to view the original properties of the loop. This loop is in the key of G-sharp or A-flat, has an original tempo of 66BPM, and is in the 4/4 time signature. Notice that although it's a minor key, the scale type is not indicated. This is because Soundtrack has many more levels of metadata insertion than the original *echoflute9.5 ACID®* loop has available.

Before inserting metadata, open the Transient window by clicking on the Transient tab. Notice the markers and settings. If the pop-up key menu is set at any setting other than – (no change/null), then the loop will be playing in a key other than the original. Set the key to the null point so that the loop is playing back at the original pitch.

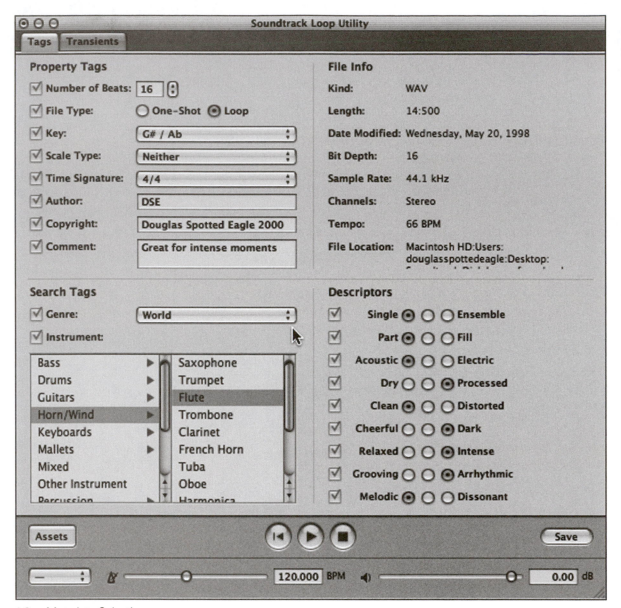

4.8 Metadata Selections.

If in this instance the tempo slider is at any position other than 66BPM, the loop will not play at original tempo. Generally, it's best to keep ACID loops or other library-obtained loops in their natural and default settings. However, if you find yourself constantly changing the settings of a loop to fit various projects, it might be more efficient to change it permanently in the Loop Utility.

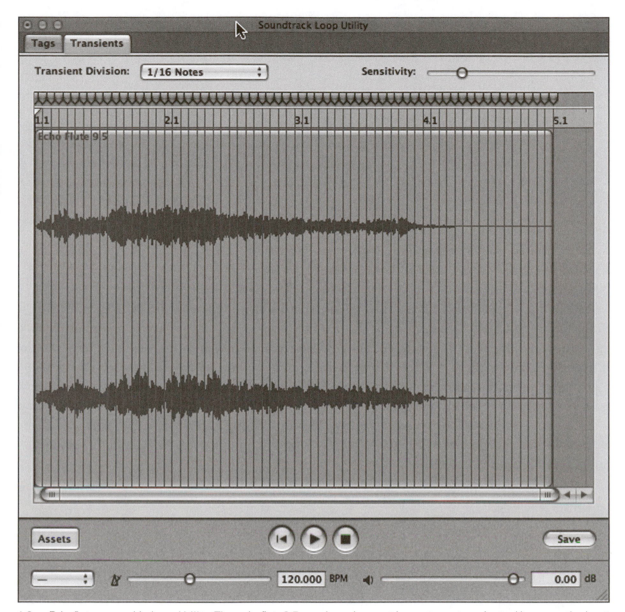

4.9   Echoflute opened in Loop Utility. The echoflute9.5.wav loop does not have strong transients. However, the beat information has already been inserted during the Acidizing of the loop library.

In the Transient window, increase the sensitivity to transients by moving the sensitivity slider all the way to the right. The Loop Utility will add more sliders to the file. Play the file back by pressing the spacebar to start playback or by pressing the Play button. Allow the file to loop.

Change the tempo of the file from 66BPM to 100BPM. The file will have some artifacts in the playback. While looping the file, reduce the sensitivity to about 30%. Notice that the markers become evenly spaced and the sound is smoother. Now, shift the pitch down to the key of D by using the pop-up menu. The loop should remain smooth and natural sounding even though it's been shifted far away from its natural pitch. Slide the sensitivity to its maximum setting again and notice the artifacts that creep in to the playback.

One of the primary goals in setting up a loop or editing an existing loop is to keep the beat divisions equal across the loop, otherwise it's likely that the loop will have playback issues. Use the sensitivity slider in combination with checking various key/pitches on the loop to preview loops, assuring that the loop is acceptable at all key settings.

> **Edit the Loop** by inserting metadata. Changing tempo or pitch information does not alter the original audio file. The original audio file remains unchanged.

Reset the key menu to the null point and set the sensitivity to zero. Then set the tempo back to 66BPM and select the Tags tab.

In the Tags window, select the Scale Type and set it to Minor. In the Search Tags, select World from the pop-up menu and click on the Horn/Wind in the Instrument window. Clicking this calls up additional specifiers in the Instrument window. Select Flute from the menu. This adds the Instrument information to the search information.

In the Descriptors radio button area all of the boxes are checked by default. Each descriptor doesn't need to be checked. Just remember that the more boxes checked, the more likely this loop is included or not included from searches in the Soundtrack Media Manager. For the *echoflute9.5.wav* loop, leave all boxes checked except for the Grooving/Arrythmic checkbox and select the following radio buttons

- Single
- Part
- Acoustic
- Processed
- Clean
- Dark (or Cheerful if it strikes you that way)
- Relaxed (or Intense if it strikes you)
- Melodic

After determining the Search attributes, once the file is saved, it contains metadata indicating the choices made.

Open the Assets drawer if it is not already open. Notice that next to the file name there is a small dot beneath the word Changes. This dot indicates that the file has been modified from its original properties. If a file indicates it's been changed when it hasn't, press the Minus symbol in

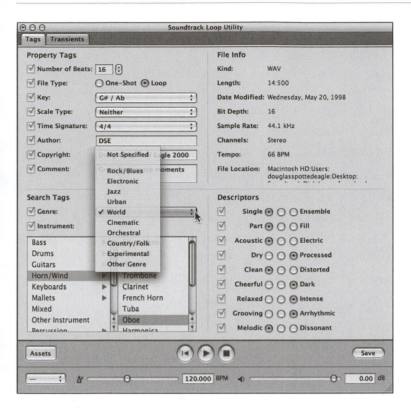

4.10 Setting metadata can be fast. Remember, you can be creative with the descriptors, genre, and instrument menus.

the drawer; this action removes the file and offers the choice to save or not save the changes. Regardless of original file format, the file saves as an .aif file.

There are several shortcut keys that may be used in the Loop Utility. See the printable PDF chart found on the CD-ROM in the back of this book.

PREFERENCES

The Loop Utility Preferences may be set to maximize workflow to individual liking. There are a few choices, though there is not much to set other than conversion and management preferences. Setting preferences to personal choice enables faster importing and loop saving.

4.11 The Loop Utility preferences can be set for the most efficient method of saving and editing loops.

Loop Utility as a Batch Converter

Soundtrack's **Loop Utility** is also a batch converter. Any ACIDized library may be dropped as an entire library into the Assets drawer directly from the hard drive or CD. Open the directory where loops are stored that need to be converted and select **Option+A**. This selects all loops in the directory. Now drag them to the **Assets** drawer in order to import the directory of loops to the Soundtrack **Asset** window. (The directory folder can be dragged as a single folder as well.) The name of the file(s) or folder becomes the name of the loop, then the **Loop Utility** will read as many pieces of metadata that it can. With an entire library in the **Assets** drawer, click on the topmost file and hold **Shift** while selecting the bottommost file. This selects all the files in the **Assets** drawer. Now all Genre, **Instrument**, and **Descriptor** data can be determined on a global basis for all loops from the imported library. After selecting metadata tags, select **Save All** from the bottom of the **Assets** drawer. The entire ACIDized file is saved in the .aif format containing all inserted metadata tags. This is an efficient method of converting loops and inserting the necessary metadata. Soundtrack's **Loop Utility** can insert tags and convert up to 2,000 loops in one session.

To convert ACID libraries to Soundtrack Loops/AIFFs:

1. Open the **Loop Utility**, then open the **Assets** drawer by clicking the lower left corner of the **Loop Utility** on the button marked **Assets**.

2. Insert the ACID disk into the CD drive.

3. Open the folder on the CD-ROM containing loops. (Sony libraries have a folder labeled Loops.) If multiple folders are available for different types of loops, don't open any of the folders, simply have all the folders visible.

Setting the Open Panel on Launch option opens a file browser/open dialog each time the Loop Utility is opened. Typically, this is best left checked as a default, but if the drag-and-drop is your favorite way of opening files, you may set this instead.

The Saving option is related to working with .wav files only. Selecting the Show Conversion Alert warns you any time you try to save a file as a .wav file.

Selecting Close Wav and Edit AIFF automatically converts a .wav file to an .aif file format. Close the .wav file and reopen the .aif file to be edited; this is the default setting and seems to function the most efficiently.

The Keep Working on Wav option keeps the .wav file open and allows the file to be edited. Selecting this option will limit the ability to disable Descriptors, even while the Descriptor data is selected.

4. If there is only one folder for loops, select **Command+A** to select all loops. Drag all loops to the **Asset** drawer. If multiple folders are available, drag the entire folder to the **Asset** drawer. (Folders might be named *Drums, Keyboards, Guitars, Percussion*, etc.)

5. When the loops appear in the **Assets** drawer, they can have metadata applied to the entire list of loops or applied individually. To apply metadata to the entire list, click the top loop and while holding the **Shift** key, click the last loop.

6. Make sure you are in the **Tags** pane, then check the **Descriptor** boxes and apply **Descriptor** tags. A genre may be specified by checking the **Genre** box and choosing a **Genre** from the dropdown menu. Instrument tags may be applied by checking the **Instrument** box, selecting an instrument class, and a specific instrument from the selector menus. Key information, such as beat information, is automatically read from the ACID metadata, so you won't need to worry about this. If individual folders have been dragged across from a library, the **Genre** and **Instrument** tags are usually automatically applied based on the information in the folder. This is the benefit of dragging individual folders if they are available.

7. After assigning all desired metadata/tags to the loop(s), the files need to be saved. (For best results, save to a hard drive other than the system drive.) To save all of the files, choose the **Save All** option in the **Assets** drawer. To save an individual file, choose the **Save** button in the lower left of the **Loop Utility** window.

8. If the loops are saved to a new folder/location other than the default Soundtrack location on the system drive, the folder will need to be indexed. Refer to Chapter 1 for information on indexing folders/files.

While the Soundtrack Loop Utility is a fairly simple and straightforward application/utility, indeed it is the key to efficient and effective search for loops that originate from outside any Apple loop library. ACID loops, loops from other parties, or loops recorded in Soundtrack or Peak, or any other tool for that matter, must be dropped in the Loop Utility to insert metadata so that Soundtrack can find it. Also, it can be dropped for the purpose of the Refine Search, key, or tempo parameters which can be applied in the Soundtrack Media Manager. As a batch-converter tool, the Loop Utility is fantastic and a great time saver. Of course, using it to convert full songs is possible as well, though difficulties may arise with full music files that have audio compression applied, thus limiting the transients. Be careful: if not properly understood and practiced, transients can be tricky. In the end, the Loop Utility is a necessary tool and worth spending an hour or so learning to use properly.

LOOP PROVIDERS

http://www.media62.com/trippyloops/
http://www.digitraxx.com/mainloopcd.html
http://www.smartloops.com/
http://www.powerfx.com
http://www.soundtracklounge.com
http://www.looplibrary.com/
http://www.loopsound.com/
http://www.sample-cds-online.com/
http://www.musicleads.net/loops.html
http://www.proloops.com/
http://www.peaceloveproductions.com
http://www.quparts.com

Chapter 5

Tips, Tricks, and Techniques for Working with Looping and Soundtrack

EDITING TECHNIQUES

Getting past the basics of music and workflow allows for the creative process to begin. That's what it's all about: being inspired by video, stills, Flash work, DVD menuing, or just plain music and then being creative. When scoring for video or film, you are painting a picture that helps the viewer know how to feel and how to react to the scene before them. A simple or a complex score can be thought of as the emotional quotient of the film. Interestingly enough, while all of us spend several hours a day watching film, television, or video media, very rarely do we really listen: We simply take the audio for granted. In the composing and authoring stages of a video or musical project, we can't take the passive view that the audio isn't that important. Audio is 70% of the visual experience and sometimes the best background or bed sound, underscore or effect is the one that goes unnoticed unless it's missing. If you don't believe that audio is everything, try watching anything without the audio turned on. You'll quickly become bored. Even in the early days of film, producers knew the importance of audio to the film. Silent films really weren't silent, as sheet music accompanied every reel. The person who fit the stereotype of the lonely librarian who played piano at church was often the theatre organist or piano player who performed music during the silent film. The music kept audience attention rapt and more importantly it helped the audience find the emotion contained in the scene, emotion that otherwise did not translate without audio. Populations in large cites were fortunate enough to have three or four-piece bands to accompany the silver screen presentations.

Compositions can be literal or abstract to the picture, providing movements that articulate themselves in sync with the action on the screen, such as a rising intensity as a scene builds to a climax. Conversely, the audio may enter the scene with great fervor and slow down as the climactic moment approaches, letting the visual and dialog carry the moment. A great soundtrack has the power to disguise poor camera work, assist in carrying a weak scene, or detract from great dialog, editing, and camera work.

This chapter provides some creative background that should help with mixes, loops, and compositions built out of smaller ideas. Most compositions start out as a "hook", or section that is memorable or repeatable. Sometimes this is as little as a sequence of a couple of notes, but can be as large as an entire chorus. While musical greatness is rarely a requisite in authoring for video, Flash, or DVD menus, the more musically appealing and creative the score, song, or soundtrack, the more energetic and exciting, compelling and interesting video or other multimedia becomes.

Loops are like words in a sentence, then these sentences form paragraphs, and paragraphs form a story. The better the choice and placement of words, the better the story. Isn't that what multimedia is—digital storytelling?

There are several elements to the musical story, but not all of them need to be used in scoring music for video. Elements of the composition might include

- Theme
- Rhythm
- Instrumentation
- Structure/Arrangement
- Melody (Rarely found in video scores)
- Lyrics (Rarely found in video scores)
- Harmonies (Rarely found in video scores)

Themes may be recurrent. Usually they are in feature films, corporate presentations, and other formats of long-form video. Short-form video on the other hand doesn't lend itself to any form of repetition, regardless of style.

The rhythm of the composition may be percussive, organic, or simply an acoustic instrument defining the way the piece moves and feels. Rhythm is the underpinning of the composition. Establishing the rhythm early on in the music is important in video work, as it helps move slower sections of video along and may be used to cut the video in time. Building a good rhythm section is the most challenging portion of creating a score or soundtrack. In a thematic score, where the theme may recur from time to time in the video or audio project, keeping an original melody and merely changing tempo and instrumentation is sometimes enough to create variety in the presentation. Most songs are driven by the rhythmic elements.

Instrumentation is the most easily varied part of the score, using a variety of loops to create the same emotion or movement in the score. With over 5 million loops available for ACID, Sonar, and Soundtrack, this is a fairly easy task.

Creative instrumentation with Soundtrack might include switching out a guitar for a mandolin, a drum loop for world percussion, or changing out a piano for a harpsichord or synthesizer loop. Loops can be built from other loops as well. This is discussed later in this chapter. In any event, there is no shortage of loops and loop styles available, and new loop libraries are coming out every month or so. In fact, Sony offers a loop subscription service, as does PowerFX, Sounds online, Soundtrack Lounge, and many other loop providers.

INTRODUCING THE STORY

Getting the attention of the viewer/listener is critical to getting eyes and ears on the scene quickly, whether it's a video scene, a multimedia piece, or a DVD menu. Otherwise, the viewer/listener may be focused on something else in the video, something in the room around them, or what they were doing prior to watching or listening to the piece of music.

Notice in most television commercials, something visual or aural happens at the head of the commercial to get the viewer's attention focused on the information being presented. Sometimes that attention grabber has nothing to do with the story and sometimes it has everything to do with it. Either way, whatever that attention grabber is, it's there to get attention focused on that moment and not on anything else that might take place. Even in daily speech, some folks do this by clearing their throat prior to speaking, or perhaps they'll say "listen up," or use a hand gesture. In the courtroom, the judge bangs his gavel or has the bailiff make an announcement. These are all attention grabbers. Musically, this may be done a number of ways.

Depending on the visual, if there is one, attention can be focused on the opening of a piece using a cymbal roll, boom, single drum hit, or introducing a drum loop early in the project for a few bars. A lot of rap music introduces the musical piece with scratching the record under the stylus. Sometimes taking a music loop, running it backwards just prior to the start of the composition, then launching into the composition is effective. Think of the introductory musical phrase as a transition in the video world, creating an element that transfers focus from one event into another.

What you hear absolutely impacts what you see. Put on a pair of headphones and watch TV while listening to Phish or Creed, then change the music to Bach, Air Supply, or Barry Manilow. I guarantee the perception of the picture will change too.

When approaching the scene, it's common to want to do a literal translation of the scene both with sound FX and score. However, watching the scene prior to scoring without considering the dialog helps. I often watch a scene without any audio prior to considering the score. This way I can ask myself, "What is the camera and edit really showing?" Oftentimes, the answer isn't the same as what it would be if I were concentrating on dialog.

SETTING UP THE COMPOSITION

As hinted at before, there are no hard and fast rules to create a composition properly. Composing is like writing: it can be done well or not. It is after all, a creative process. Generally, a video composition is short based on the length of a scene, a series of images, or a DVD menu. Musical compositions may be longer.

Before creating a composition, assuming the video has been spotted, ask yourself or the director some questions.

- What is the desired emotional portrayal? Excitement, fear, anticipation, insanity, sadness, violence, etc., are all emotions that might be expressive to the video sequence.

- Is the score pushing the storyline, or is it portraying/enhancing a mood?

- What is the genre of music that matches the imagery on the screen while appealing to the target audience?

- Does the score need to build to a climactic moment, or is it simply carrying the sequence?

- Should the music be cut to the tempo of the image cuts, or simply lay beneath the images without regard to the cut timing? (if this is the case, then the director needs to provide exact length of sequence, then cut the visuals after the music has been created.) How does the music interact with the dialog in the video? Does it have stinger elements taking place between dialogs? Does the music undercut or clash with the dialog?

- Should musical pauses occur to enhance a moment? Silence can be powerful at the right moments. Open the *Toubat.mov* for an example of how silence is used to enhance a powerful emotion.

If the composition will contain a melody, consider the melody to be akin to a conversation. One person speaks, another responds. Melodies are often like this: one instrument may "speak" a phrase and another responds. Simplicity is generally the key, particularly for those not familiar with the rules of music. It may be that the music underlying the dialog should repeat a phrase between dialog moments or setting tension. For example, a sentence is spoken in sadness, then the actor reflects in a tense moment. The music has been a basic drone beneath the argument as a long "pad" or single tone. A few moments after the tension is created with the dialog, a short melodic loop is quietly thrown in, perhaps to one side of the stereo spectrum or another, breaking the tension or enhancing it, depending on the loop chosen. Find the *Swedish Flute loop 02.aif* file. Place this on the Timeline, open an effect on the track by pressing the Effect button on the track. In the Effects menu, select the Platinum Reverb from the Emagic Category and either double-click the reverb or press the + key to add the effect to the effects chain.

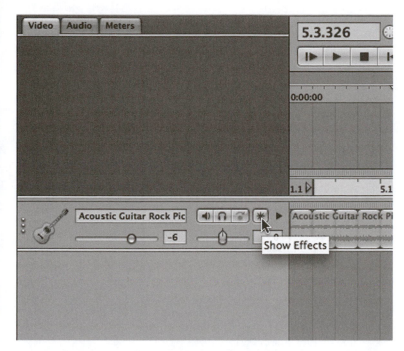

5.1 Insert screen shot of effect button in Soundtrack. Press the Effect button to open up the Effects menu.

Set the Mix on the reverb to 50% and set the reverb time to five seconds. Adjust the Initial Delay to a setting of 50 milliseconds (ms). Next, set the Stereo Base to 1.5m. This will add a fairly long reverb and slight delay to the track. Notice how this loop has a melancholy sound that could follow a sad dialog or scene. Consider using this sort of sound for "deep thought" or emotionally intense settings. Just as long visual transitions indicate romance, emotional moments, or contemplation, lengthy reverb acts much like a long transition, washing one sound to the next. Long reverbs mixed with delay, also known as DDL, rarely work on instruments that have sharp attacks and quick fades, such as when the delay is hit with a fast attack, a snare

Load: When working with the WAVES plugins, selecting the Load button loads factory-created presets, providing fantastic starting points for sounds. A demo version of the WAVES plugins is provided on the CD-ROM included with this book.

for example. The delay becomes too prevalent and the reverb will reverberate with each single repeat of the DDL, giving a strange effect sounding as artifacts. If reverb is applied to short attacking instruments such as a snare drum or percussive instrument, consider removing all delay, including predelay, and experimenting with the room size. Depending on the reverb used, whether it's the Apple, Emagic, or a third-party reverb, such as WAVES R-Verb or Trueverb, the settings vary greatly.

While creating the melody, remember that melody is dynamic: partially tension and partially a release of tension. Building up to a specific point with a melody, whether a loop or a recorded

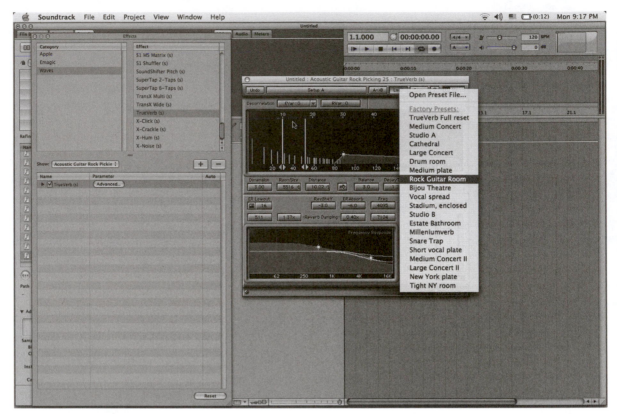

5.2   WAVES plugin presets

sound, then releasing the "power" behind that buildup is what creates a great piece of music. Most loop libraries have a variety of melodic structures from which to choose. If a more creative loop is needed, here is a method of creating your own melody:

1. Find a loop that is similar to the sound you wish to create in your own melody and put it on the Timeline of Soundtrack.

2. Enable snapping and set the Snap-to at a value of 1/32 or 1/64.

3. Zoom in on the Timeline using the zoom tools or the up/down arrows.

4. Play the loop, finding the notes that you'd like to use for the melody, and place the playhead just after the note or decay of the note. Press the S-key to split the loop.

5. Then break the loop up into slices.

Each note or sequence of notes may now be transposed, rearranged, or placed in other sequences, creating a new melody. If the Preferences have been set to fade the loop, the slices should play back cleanly and clearly. Depending on the content of the slices and the instrumenta-

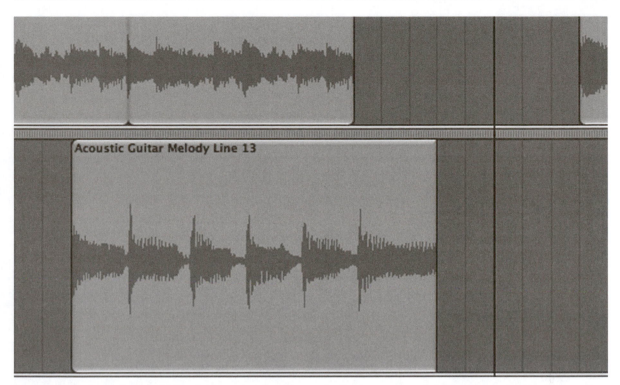

5.3   If a loop is cut in the middle of decay, then it may sound stilted or unnatural, depending on the instrumentation in the loop.

tion from which the slices were created, some loops may not slice and arrange as well as others. This is due to decay and the attack of various sounds.

By the same token, randomizing slices in a loop may also spark inspiration or create that ultimate lick that is needed to give the composition the right attitude and sound. Experiment with slicing the loops and you might be surprised. Most important is whether the music and audio post FX are "natural" to the picture, or if you find yourself fighting the aural images.

Compositions are 90% inspiration and 10% perspiration. Having a number of loops available to choose from and being familiar with them is the most helpful course of action to undertake. When buying a new loop library, take half an hour or so to listen to each loop. Not only will you possibly be inspired by a particular loop or series of loops, but also when composing music you'll know what's in the library on the hard disk or CD.

If you are new to creating compositions or new to the music world, start with simple tasks before tackling the bigger tasks. Start by creating music with percussion and drum loops, and build from there.

A step-by-step formula for building great music beds and soundtracks for video might be:

1. Two bars of a light percussive loop by itself, which continues throughout the project;

5.4   Notice how the transitional elements introduce new loops in the composition.

2. Drums that come in after two bars of light percussive loop and continue throughout the project.

3. At Bar 5, insert a drum roll, panned sound, or other transitional element that signals that the body of the song is beginning; this gets you into the song.

4. At Bar 7 or 9, inject the melody, if there is one.

The basic idea is to have some new element, or removal of element every four bars. Removing or adding clips any more often than every two bars becomes confusing, unless they are added as parts of the melody or alternating rhythm elements. Having more than eight bars pass with no new elements added or taken away causes the project to become repetitive and possibly boring.

Open the *Basic Song construction* Soundtrack file from the *Bookloops* folder in the accompanying CD-ROM. This follows the basic instructions noted earlier, but also adds some transitional elements and pitch shifts in the files. Notice that the open envelopes show volume changes and automated FX parameters.

The same is true with the *Driving Force* composition, also found on the CD. The kick and snare are one-shots and the melody doesn't kick in until after a break that ends at Bar 19. The melody is a simple loop, but it's really only an element in the composition. I've left this composition unfinished so that the pieces can be used to complete your own ideas in this piece. In fact, most of the Soundtrack projects on the CD are left unfinished so that users can finish or add to the songs to make them their own.

Compositions occasionally establish the melody early on, using the melody to introduce the song, rather than waiting to launch the melody later in the composition. Sometimes the melody itself is the hook, as mentioned earlier in this chapter, and the hook is established right from the start. Chuck Berry's "Johnny B. Goode" is a standard blues song, but the introduction itself becomes the hook and is repeated several times throughout the song. This is common with music releases, but not really relevant to the video editor, unless the score of the video is thematic.

Themes are terrific for video. Themes are the musical thread that pulls the whole score and video together. A theme might be related to a character. The fool, the hero, the damsel in distress, the assertive loudmouth, each may have their own small themes. If actors have appearances in the film that are not too repetitive in location or attitude, a theme might be used to indicate the approach or action of that character. The theme only needs to have underlying loops switched out in order to create a new sound around the thematic presentation.

A melody, percussion loop, or style may be introduced early on in the video, then repeated using different instruments, timings, or scales. A great example of this is James Horner's score of "Titanic." If you listen to the soundtrack of "Titanic," there are really only three melodies in the entire two-hour film. The main melody is repeated more than 20 times in the film, using different instruments from a pennywhistle, French horn, human voice, guitar, to strings in order to play versions of the same melodic theme. This is successful when done tastefully, as Horner did for the film. Used over and over with the same instrumentation, the score becomes boring and irritating and brings to the viewer's mind any previous scenes that used the theme. Open the Theme 1 and Theme 2 files from the CD. Notice how different the themes appear, but they are effectively the same composition with different backgrounds, rhythm section, and other elements that make the score different than what was heard previously.

Instruments alone can define a feeling or attitude in the theme. For example, often cellos and basses are used to indicate tension or danger, while acoustic guitars and mandolins indicate happiness. Pianos are easy to use with a touch of reverb to create a melancholic feeling. A solo violin will indicate happiness or loneliness depending on the key. (Minor keys tend to be more heartrending and less aggressive than major keys.)

When there is a budget for the project, it's a good idea to compose a rhythm track, select a key for a project, then (in the event that the melodies supplied by loop providers don't fill the bill) bring in a soloist who can play a guitar, flute, sax, harp, piano, or other melodic instrument over the project.

REMIXING

Remixing is an art form as well as a tool for bringing a popular sound to a video for a new feel. It is the art of taking an existing song and adding new elements, removing elements, and generally creating a new or derivative song from the original work. This is a great way to spice up a theme as well, supposing that the video or work has a specific composition written for it or music has been licensed for use. It's also a great tool for making stock music libraries breathe more easily and sound less canned.

Sometimes a director or editor will cut to temp music. Oftentimes, the director gets married to the temp music, yet doesn't want to keep it exactly as it is. Perhaps it doesn't build as much as it should, or perhaps it doesn't have the "moments" in the song that match up with the cuts in the picture or contain the correct transitional elements.

If the temp music has been recorded to a metronome (most contemporary songs and stock music libraries are) and has a consistent tempo, it can be dropped in the Loop Utility or Peak v4 and turned into a loop, even as a full-length song. Find the beat divisions in the song and save the file. Drop the file onto the Soundtrack Timeline and start adding additional elements to it. This is known as "remixing." If the song has accurate beat markers in it, loops may be added to the song as one-shots, loops, or transitional elements.

For doing remixes of current pop songs, the song may be cut up by splitting the individual sections out, adding loops as desired, and creating a new arrangement of original music pieces. Remixes are usually repetitive in nature; repeating elements of verses or choruses is common. Breaking up the repetitions of the elements is accomplished by using loops that underlie the original music with the original music as the main melodic element. Small sections of the song may be cut/pasted as consistent theme elements in the remix as well It's also common to take small loop sections of other music from the same artist and cut them into a song, creating one song out of two or three unique songs.

Another style of remixing is to mix two songs back and forth, allowing one to "drift" over the other, creating a mood element. Two songs of similar nature or two contrasting songs might be used to paint an aural picture or make a statement. As an example, Creed's "Lullaby" might float

Copyright: Here is a word of caution about using commercially released music for your Soundtrack compositions. If you didn't write the song and you don't have permission from the author of the original song, it is illegal to use the work. You could be subject to fines for this violation of copyright. Obtain permission. Fair Use and "de minimis" laws rarely cover illegally used music in commercial compositions, derivative works, or in syncing music to video. Creating a derivative work and syncing to video actually violates many copyright laws, visit http://www.loc.gov for more information on copyright laws and use of songs.

5.5   Pop/full length song cut to use in Soundtrack

very nicely into Metallica's "Enter Sandman," if a feeling of relaxed power ballad is desired. At the same time, "Lullaby" might float well into Train's "Drops of Jupiter" or Nickelback's "How You Remind Me," creating a feeling of confused angst.

Taking two copies of the same song in Soundtrack and cutting out sections of one copy, then creatively layering effects on the cut pieces and doing odd pans and slices of the song fitted over the "real" or original version, is a powerful way of spicing up a dull track, thus creating a unique emotional or power statement. For instance, cutting out a word from an ending phrase and split/copy/pasting that single word as the next verse comes into the song might drive home a particular point.

Try using the automated EQ to remove all bass and extreme high end from a song, then over time bring the bass and high end back into the song to introduce to the mix. Keep in mind, two songs could potentially be playing at the same time, with one EQd into total weirdness, while the other plays in musical time. Next, fade in the EQ on one track, while removing the EQ from the other as a tool to fade back and forth between the two compositions.

At the American Memory site of the Library of Congress (http://memory.loc.gov), there are many audio files of famous speeches and music that are wonderful for layering over the top of existing compositions. (Be sure to read the copyright notices.) Even the presidential speeches can be found and cut up to be used to create some funny and powerful political statements or dialog for a video project. A repeated or stuttered vocal phrase, created by slicing sections using the S-key in Soundtrack, allows you to create fun transitions or fills to go into the next musical phrase.

Build the remix around the common musical timings—eight measures, for example. Soundtrack grid indicators are on the measure, so this is easy to define. If you build the mix around shorter spacings, or use anything that is not common, you run the risk of losing viewer or listener attention, simply because of how our ear and bodies have become accustomed to responding to typical dance or pop music. Typically, eight bars define the length of a phrase. It's a good idea, if cutting on the eight-bar phrase, to have the incoming phrase be 10 measures/bars long. This allows the four beats of the first bar to act as a fade-in section and the last four beats of the phrase to act as a fade out just as the prior phrase is ending or the following phrase is beginning.

When selecting phrases for the remix, don't use beginning or ending sections of the song. Rather, find interesting phrases from the verse, chorus, or bridge of the song. If a phrase is less than eight bars/measures, don't be afraid of looping, slicing, or dicing to find a unique way to present the song.

Don't forget to throw in some scratching record sounds as well, if the music is intended to sound like the popular hip-hop styles. You'll find many record scratch-groove loops in the Media Manager. Just use the Refine Search tool with the key word "scratch."

CREATING CUSTOM LOOPS

Loops may be created from other existing loops. In fact, many loop libraries are made up of edited excerpts of existing loop libraries. Percussion and drum loops are the easiest loop forms to learn in this fun and creative process.

Open the *Custom Loop Slices 1* Soundtrack file from the CD. This is a four-bar, 9-track project consisting of individual hits/one-shots and additional under-support loops to give it some emotion. A chorus has been added to the hi-hat and a flanger added to the snare with a compressor on the kick drum and no other effects added to tracks. The master output has a light compressor on it that may be viewed by Control+clicking in a blank area of the track header and selecting Show Master Effects. This project should give you the basic concepts of building loops.

To start building a custom loop, set the Snap-To value at 1/8th or 1/16th notes. Find one-shot loops manually or click on the instrument that suits the desired loop attributes. The Refine Search tool is valuable here, as searches may be performed for kicks, snares, and other individual instruments.

Don't limit yourself to using instruments that match a preconceived notion of what an instrument should sound like. In other words, notice in the *Custom Loop Slices 1* project, the main snare sound is an air wrench. The underlying hi-hat sound is chorused to give more of a "fat" feel to the overall loop, and the temple blocks are mixed very low in the mix, almost not audible at all. They are there to give the mix an offset when the mix is soloed in other projects, and to provide a filler sound. Track 4 is half of another loop, adding a floor tom-type sound, but is much larger than a

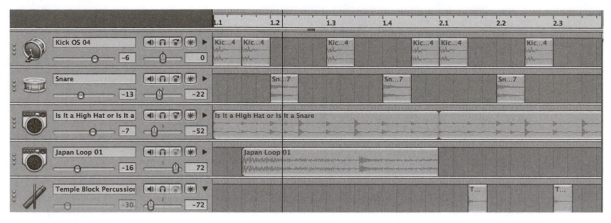

5.6   Custom Loop Slices 1

floor tom, giving a sense of unstated power to the loop. Track 9, the SubmPulse Tablas from PowerFX, keep an undulating beat happening beneath the overall loop components. A busy drum loop, EQd to remove the majority of the bass and high frequency information, might be another good alternative. Any number of sounds can be used to create a foundation beneath a loop.

Another great method for learning how to create custom loops is to locate a loop that is similar to what you'd like to create. You can find one-shots that sound similar and lay the one-shots so that they correspond with the original track, though on new tracks. Once the various tracks are approximately the same timing and sound as the original track, remove the original. Listen to the new loop and start to create other variations by moving snares, kick drums, and other sounds around in time. Be sure to have snapping enabled.

Volume and pan envelopes can be part of the new loop, also. Put a pad or other instrument that has drone-like qualities on the Timeline and use envelopes to pull the volume in and out at loop points. If snapping is enabled, it pulls the volume at grid or beat points, making the changes tight with the timing of the loop. Pans may be used in the same way. Pan the sound from side to side to give the mix a feeling of movement. Panning may become part of the instrument sound as well. When using pans and volume envelopes to create part of the new loop, it's a good practice to do the panning first, as volume changes or "power perception" of sound happens as a result of panning and may create silent or overly-loud parts of the mix. This potentially results in distortion of the loop. Setting up panning first helps you to avoid this issue.

WORKFLOW SHORTCUTS IN SOUNDTRACK

Soundtrack is filled with simple options that aren't easily found in the owner's manual/help files. Oftentimes, the lack of information can make it seem harder to use the application than it really is. These tips should get you working through Soundtrack more quickly and efficiently.

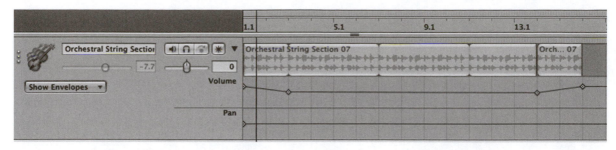

5.7   Pan/volumes used to create looping.

Locating Lost Files

Soundtrack doesn't actually store files, unless instructed to gather all files when saving a project. Instead, Soundtrack merely saves location information or file references when the loop file is saved. When working with external hard drives, CDs, or perhaps a DVD containing thousands of loops, it's easy to lose file links. If the files have been moved, the drive has been removed from the FireWire bus, the network isn't active, or the CD isn't in the drive and the project is opened in Soundtrack, a Can't Find Files dialog box opens that offers three choices. The file may be

•**Skipped** The Soundtrack project opens without referencing missing files. If the project is saved, the missing files are saved as such unless they are reconnected in the Audio pane of the Viewer.

•**Canceled** Soundtrack cancels the Open File command.

•**Find File** Soundtrack allows you to search for the file manually, locating it by plugging in a drive, CD, network cable/Airport card, or new location.

If you select Skip File from the choices, you can then go into the Audio pane found beneath the Video pane. Control+click or right-click the missing file in the pane and choose Reconnect. This also allows Soundtrack to open a dialog that permits manual location of the file. Once the file is located, click OK, and the file will be reconnected to the project. The same process works for video files if the video file associated with the Soundtrack project is missing. Simply Control+click the video file in the Video pane and select Reconnect Offline Source. Locate the video file and select Open from the dialog to open and reconnect the missing file. If you have stored your Soundtrack files in any location other than the default *Macintosh HD:Documents:Sountrack Loops:*, it's highly likely that you've already become familiar with this particular feature.

Selecting Multiple Files/Tracks

When working on a project, it's common to realize that additional time needs to be inserted to a project, but perhaps not all tracks should shift backwards in time; maybe there are tracks that should remain in their current position with no movement. There are several methods to move multiple files, but it isn't as clear as it could be. This workflow should help make this task simpler.

First, take any tracks that don't contain tracks and move them to the bottom or top of the Timeline, effectively grouping all tracks that should remain static.

Second, click on the uppermost and first loop that should be shifted in time. Next, while holding the Shift key, select the bottommost and last loop that should be shifted in time, covering all tracks. In Figure 5.8, the first and last loops have been selected across many tracks. This selects all loops in between the first and last loops regardless of how many tracks have been covered. By Click+dragging on the selected files, they may be moved forward or backward in time as a group.

Multiple tracks that are contiguous, or next to each other, may be Shift+clicked as well. This allows the various files to be moved or copied. Files that are not contiguous can be Option+clicked to select multiple tracks. This is a good way to select several tracks that should be grouped together, moving them to the lowest part of the Timeline to create a group.

Viewing Multiple Tracks

Soundtrack's preview area may be split, enabling a dual view of tracks. This is accomplished by clicking and dragging the divider bar between the video preview timeline and the loop timeline.

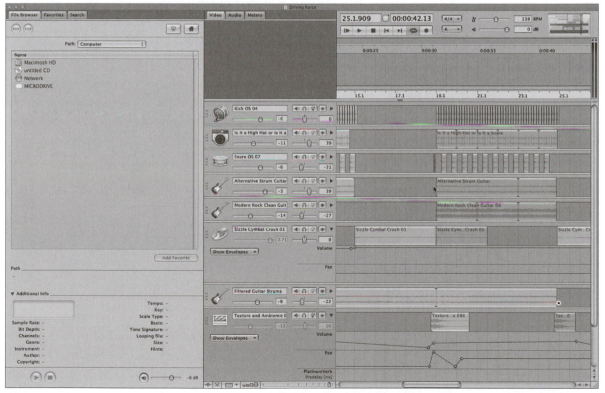

5.8   Driving Force. Notice that the entire project is selected except for the lowest two tracks, so that all audio may be shifted down without effecting the location of the bottom two tracks.

5.9   Clicking and dragging this divider bar splits the preview screen into upper and lower sections. This is useful for viewing large projects with more than 10 tracks.

Splitting the preview screen is not worth the effort if 10 or fewer tracks are in the project depending on the size of the track as determined in the track-size selector. Splitting is most valuable when, for example, Tracks 1–4 and Tracks 20–24 need to be viewed simultaneously. For long-form projects this may be exceptionally valuable, but for small projects that don't contain large

> **TIP!!**
>
> ***For Unedited Video:*** If a score is going to be written for a video project, but the video has not been edited, open the Fingersnap.aif file in Soundtrack. Work with the director or editor to find the correct tempo and length of time for the video piece. Next, set the tempo in Soundtrack. Then, drag the Finger-snaps file out to the expected length of the video scene or project and export the mix. This can then be dropped into FCP or another NLE for a timing template, making it significantly easier to score in Soundtrack because the video sequence is cut to tempo.

numbers of tracks, this feature may appear to be confusing because it shows duplicates of tracks appearing on the Timeline when insufficient numbers of tracks exist to fill the entire workspace.

Cutting a Loop on an Offbeat

Sometimes, it's desirable to end a loop on an offbeat or create an ending to a song on a kick drum or other percussive note. Snapping may make it difficult to do this on some loops. To end the loop cleanly on an offbeat, disable Snapping by pressing the G-key. Place the play head roughly at the point that the offbeat/cut point will occur. Zoom into the loop with the Up Arrow key. Then place the playhead precisely where the cut should occur. (Unfortunately, Soundtrack doesn't have a scrub option, although holding down the L-key offers some marginal forward scrubbing options and the K-key pauses the forward playback, approximating part of the J,K,L functionality found in most NLE/DAW systems.)

Now press the S-key to split the file at the exact point. With snapping disabled, getting an exact cut point for an offbeat is easy and fast. Don't forget to re-enable snapping by pressing the G-key once again.

Creating a Metronome in Soundtrack

Soundtrack does not offer a metronome for timing the recording of loops. However, this really isn't necessary because Soundtrack provides loops that work wonderfully as a metronome.

Locate the *Finger Snaps* file in the *HD:Documents:SoundtrackLoops:Soundtrack Loops:PowerFX Loops:Percussion:Finger Snaps.aif* location.

Drag this to the Timeline, and use this file as a metronome for your recording. This can be monitored via studio monitors or headphones. Be careful not to allow the metronome, also known as a click-track, to bleed into the microphone while recording, otherwise it may be difficult or impossible to remove.

Getting FX to Play Past the Project File's End

When Soundtrack sees the end of a project on the Timeline, it naturally assumes that the project is over. This can be a pain in the neck when the project ends and a delay or reverb is supposed to continue its natural sound decay and Soundtrack clips it off. Soundtrack FX sends are post-fade. This means that if the volume of a track is automated to mute or fade audio, then the send to the FX processor is also muted or faded. This will kill the decay of an effect in progress. However, Soundtrack can be fooled into thinking that the project isn't over.

On the Timeline, Click+drag over a selection in time, starting at the beginning of the composition and going past the end of the composition by at least four bars. With or without a volume fade, this allows Soundtrack to continue to allow the decay of a file. Without the loop selection in the Timeline, the file will autoloop at the end of the last loop. If the delay or reverberation continues longer than you'd like, simply use a volume fade on the instrument or master envelope to fade out that track at the point that the delay or reverb should fade. Make sure that the time selection in the beat timeline is equal to or longer than the time of the last volume point.

Ending Compositions

I'm often asked, "How do you end a song?" There are a few methods to achieve this. Probably the most common method of ending a song or composition is to repeat the ending phrase several times and fade the song out over time. In Soundtrack, this is an exceptionally easy method because it's a simple matter to copy the last few bars of a song and paste them repeatedly. Copy all tracks using the Select/Shift+click method described previously. Make sure the top track is selected and Paste Repeat (Option+Command+V) the files up to six times. Then create a fade out using a volume envelope. If you'd like the track to have a sense of movement, a slight and slow pan to one side or the other gives the mix a sense of moving off the screen. Slow and slight is the key, it's rare that a mix should pan entirely to one side or the other in a fade out.

Another method is to use the "big boom" or punctuation mark at the end to signal the end of the song. In other words, the song simply ends, say, at Bar 20, Count 4, so a big boom is placed at Bar 21, Count 1. This is another easy method of ending a song, but can be disruptive to certain moods. It's also a great attention getter when transitioning from one scene to another, but I prefer to use aural transitions in the editing stage of the video file rather than attempting to get it tight in Soundtrack. Of course, if the video is complete and the entire project is being scored in Soundtrack, then this is the place to add the big boom. A few ending file examples for this process might be

- Sizzle Cymbal Crash 01
- DJ Scratching one-shots (several)
- Conga Percussion (several)

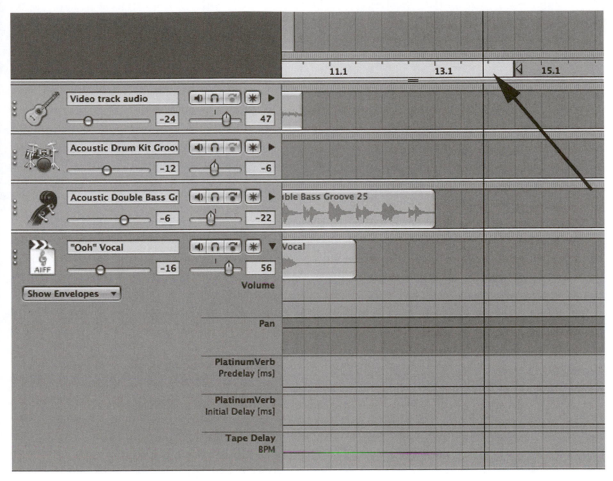

5.10 Click+drag of Timeline

- Rain Stick Percussion 01
- Soundtrack Tambourine Loop 05
- Vibraslap Rattle (several)
- Texture and Atmosphere 018 (there are several Textures that may work, play the Driving Force project for an example
- DAF Frame Drum 07 (Cut after 3rd beat)
- Djembe Groove 03 (cut very last hit from loop)
- Ceramic Drum Percussion Loop 01 (cut all but first bar)
- Timpani Loop (Several)
- Synthetic Designer FX

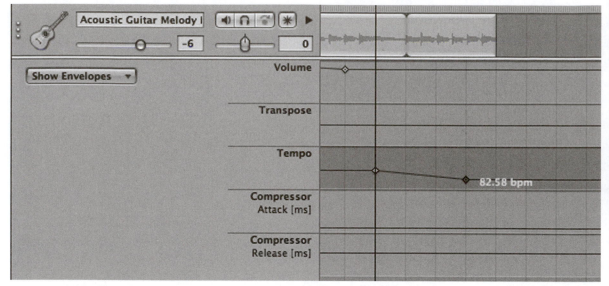

5.11   Reducing the tempo over a short period of time at the end of the composition can give a sense of ending. Be cautious of too much reduction over too long a time, as many loops will not tolerate being slowed too much.

Of course, using one of these ending style loops and one-shots may be easily enhanced by adding the Emagic Tape Delay, Platinumverb, Modulation Delay, Stereo Delay, Apple's Soundtrack Reverb, Matrix Reverb, or Delay, and allowing the file to tail out.

Still another method of ending a file is to slow down the Timeline near the end of the file. This shouldn't be a significant tempo change, unless a significant change feels good for the composition. Reducing tempo by anything greater than 20BPM may create issues for some loops. Typically reducing a file by 10BPM clearly signifies the end of the song. Also, this can be done in conjunction with a fade, a big boom, or simply allowing the file to slow down. Unlike tape, the pitch of the music will not shift downwards during a tempo or speed shift. However, the pitch may be shifted down during the slow down, resulting in some interesting and potentially intriguing sounds at the end. Some loops will perform better than others with this method of pitch and tempo shifting to create the end of a composition. To create a pitch bend over time, you'll need to use a third-party application like Peak™ to slow down the audio.

Another unique method of finishing off a composition is to take the end of a composition or a featured audio loop, open it in a third-party editor, such as Peak™, and reverse that specific section of the composition or loop. Try using a volume ramp to silence the initial attack of the reversed section; also, this can be done in Soundtrack using volume envelope points. Save the audio as a separate one-shot file, then drop the reversed section of the loop into the Soundtrack project at the end at a point just prior to the end of the loop project. There is a reversed drum hit in the *Book-loops:Bad Loop 1-reverse.aif* for your experimentation.

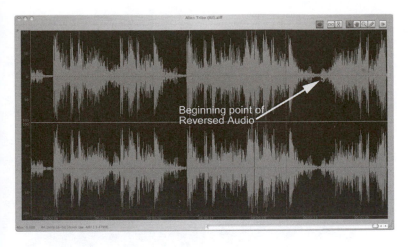

5.12 Reversing the end portion of the project may be inserted on the Timeline, giving the sound a rushed quality that makes for a unique end quality and sense of finality.

Locking to an External Device

If by chance you are fortunate enough to have a scorist working on your film for specific scenes, or if you are using an external video device, Soundtrack can sync to incoming time code. Figure 5.13 displays the connections required to chase or receive MTC if using an external video deck. Connect the T/C output of the video deck to a SMPTE to MTC converter such as the Midiman 8 × 8 as illustrated in Figure 5.13. The MTC output then is connected to the Appletalk connection or hardware card of your G4/5 or cardbus card. Soundtrack will read this incoming timecode and sync to it. Soundtrack may also be used as a master control for other hardware or software devices, as Soundtrack will send T/C as well. Figure 5.14 demonstrates how to set these options in the Soundtrack Preferences dialog.

Use the Offset to mark where playback in Sountrack should begin. If for example, your external video plays through several Soundtrack projects and you only wish to work on one project at a time, locate where in the video the Soundtrack project should start. Roll back at least 2 seconds (5 is recommended) and look at the time code displayed on the external deck. This is the offset time for Soundtrack to start at. This will allow for pre-roll. If set to the exact time the scene is to begin, Soundtrack may not be given enough time to sense the incoming timecode and it may hiccup for a moment.

External video or audio decks *must* have a Timecode output, or must have SMPTE recorded on an audio track that can be discreetly input to a converter box in order to have external T/C control.

Using Option+Drag

Rather than always dragging a loop out over the Timeline, drop a loop for the full length of the Timeline. Enable snapping if it's not already enabled, then holding Option, click on the loop and

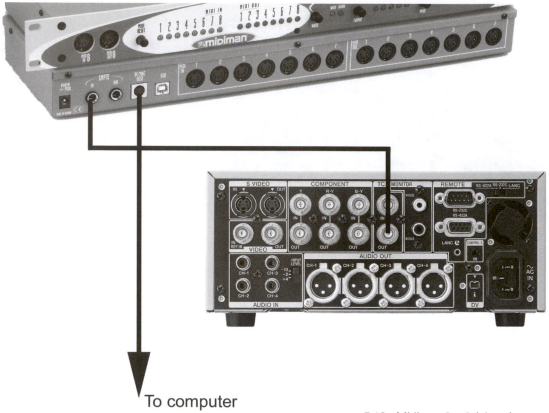

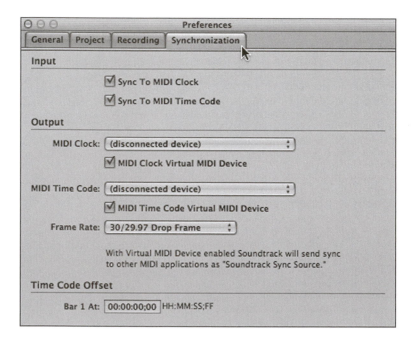

To computer

5.13   Midiman 8 × 8 *(above)*

5.14   Soundtrack set as Master Control *(left)*

drag to the right, making a copy of the loop. Next, drop the second loop next to the first loop. This second loop can be transposed and copied later to another location if necessary. A progression may be established in a few copies of the original loop by using this method, Once a progression is established, all the loops can be selected and click-dragged to continue the progression. This is much easier than repeatedly transposing each loop. Even if progressions are not established, once a loop has been transposed, it's very easy to Option+drag the transposed version to a new location, alleviating the need to continually transpose.

Progressions are a series of loops that have chord, note, or other changes that uniquely identify one bar from another. Open the Progression 1 file on the CD to get an indication of how a progression works. (Progression formats are discussed in Chapter 2.) Notice that the markers in the file demonstrate the changes in the chords used in the progression. In many cases, a section of a loop has been cut out to continue the progression through a repeated section without sounding like the loop has repeated. In any event, using the Option+drag is a smooth method of making copies of the audial sentences that make up the paragraphs of the composition.

Phattening Loops

Loops can be made "phat" or supercool and thick by doubling the loop. Although this is mentioned in passing in Chapter 2, it's a technique worth revisiting. To add a loop to a track, add a new track (Command+T) and Option+Drag the loop to the new track so that it sits directly above or below the original. Set snapping to a value of 64th notes. Then shift the new loop copy to the right or left by a 64th and play back the file. This gives the file a phatter sound. Sometimes the file needs to be shifted by less than a 64th, so snapping should be disabled (G) and the loop manually placed to create the best sound. Pan one track heavily left or right and pan the duplicate track slightly left or right. Listen to how thick the sound is and how much of the spectrum it occupies without feeling louder. This technique works particularly well with nonpercussive sounds such as pads or sound FX, but it can be applied to many loops that are percussive, providing that great care is used to offset the copied loop from the original loop.

Never be afraid to have two copies of the same loop happening on two tracks. Shift one, then use a flanger or chorus applied deep and thick and use volume envelopes to shift the audio in/out of the mix, while panning at the same time. The copied track may even have moments of being louder than the original track. This can create some powerful emotional elements in an otherwise static scene.

Shifting Keys

Use the Transpose Envelope or shift the project key using the project key slider to audition/preview the composition in a different key. While this may sometimes have a negative effect on the overall project, it also may provide a new feel to the composition, particularly when placed as an underscore or bed to video. Returning to the original pitch/key on which the project was built is a simple

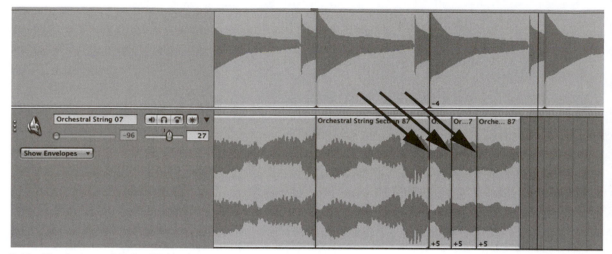

5.15 The Orchestral String 07 has been stretched to create the illusion of a six-bar sustain by using a combination of split/copied segments and Clip Speed settings. Reverb and volume changes have been applied to mask the joint between the outgoing and incoming sustain segment points.

matter of pressing Command+X. You'll be surprised how much a slight change to the key of a project creates a totally new sound or feel in the project, perhaps stretching some instruments and shrinking others. Don't be afraid to experiment with the key signature.

Shifting Tempo

Similar to shifting a key up or down on a project, shifting tempo can incur a drastic difference in a composition. Faster tempos may encourage movement in the picture, while slower tempos may feel more relaxed. In any event, shifting tempos will nearly always shift the feel of a composition. While this may not always be beneficial once the project has been nearly completed, it's a tool that shouldn't be forgotten.

Maintaining, Sustaining

Wouldn't it be great to be able to hold the tension of a moment, just to let it dissolve in time and fade into silence?

Some loops contain a sustained note that would be perfect for the end of a song or phrase. Unfortunately, the end of the loop comes before the desired point and loses the power of a drawn-out phrase. There are a couple of methods that may be used to create the illusion of this phrase. The first method is to disable snapping and find the point at which the loop's amplitude is highest, possibly near the point to sustain. Split the loop at this point, then click the right side of the split loop to select it as you deselect the left half of the loop. Now Control+click/right click the right half of the loop and select Clip Speed. Set this value to half. With some loops, this provides the illusion of a sustain. This is tricky though and requires some practice. Notice in the Progression 1 project that the string loop in the middle of the bridge has a sustained note. Typically this also requires some fancy volume control work and possibly a reverb or delay if the amplitude point isn't exactly correct. If the amplitude hasn't been correctly selected and split, there is likely to be a pop or strange volume anomaly at that particular point. A small amount of reverb or delay often hides this noise if it's not too noticeable. Remember that it's difficult to get away with this technique while working with solo instrumentation.

This technique is much more easily accomplished in a dedicated audio editor such as Peak. Peak™ allows the sustained note to be selected in the middle of the sustained portion, stretched out over time and blended with itself. Peak has the tools for this very process.

Creating Loops in Peak

Soundtrack is a powerful music composition tool for the video, DVD authoring, Flash project, and sketch pad/conceptualization user. However, Soundtrack is not an audio editing tool and has limited audio editing features. However, FCP ships with a product called Peak Express, which is a light version of the audio editing tool Peak v4.0 from the Bias software company. Peak is the standard two-track audio editor for the Mac platform and is a powerful tool used by professional audio editors in all industries. Trial versions of several Bias applications are found on the CD in this book.

Peak (all versions except Express) allows several file types to be brought into the editor, converted to aiff, and saved for import into Soundtrack. Peak also contains loop creation tools that allow for off-time audio files to be accurately looped, complete with full file preview and loop tuning. If burning Redbook-compliant CDs is a necessity, Peak also burns audio CDs complete with indexing information and ISRC codes.

Bias offers several versions of Peak, including Peak DV, a lower-cost, pared-down version of Peak v4.0. Peak DV is perfect for the video editor that doesn't need the full version, which is oriented towards mastering, full-time audio editing, and the professional music industry. Also, Peak's LE version is great for the video editor. Only the full version of Peak has the Loop Surfer and provides crossfades and guesses tempo. Though the DV and LE versions are definitely worth the small

---

 Loops by themselves may be placed in FCP without the benefit of Soundtrack scoring. Loops need to be placed end to end specifically in order to function properly. Short compositions consisting of loops of the same key and pitch (and very few tracks) may be built directly in FCP, potentially saving some time, However, there are extreme limitations in what might be done with those same loops in Soundtrack. Of course, sometimes all a scene needs is a simple, single line of audio beneath it to bring it to perfection. For these instances, these loop may be dropped on the FCP Timeline.

investment of $99 for LE and $499 for the full version. (These prices are based on suggested retail prices at the time of this writing, though many webstores offered lower prices.)

For this section, all versions of Peak except for the Express versions perform these functions. The basic functions are also available in Peak Express, which all FCP users have bundled with FCP.

Oftentimes, loop libraries that aren't Acidized or prelooped have an extra beat in them, providing editors the ability to precisely choose looping points whether working with a DAW or a hardware-based sampling tool such as an Akai or Roland sampler; this is more common than not. Importing these audio loops directly into Soundtrack won't work correctly with most time signatures, and Soundtrack does not offer the ability to edit the loops.

1. Open the *Bad Loop 1.aif* file in Peak Express in the CD-ROM.

   Notice that the attack of the loop comes after the beginning point of the file and that the Out point of the file comes before the end of the third drum hit. This file will not loop properly in Soundtrack no matter what is done to it in Soundtrack. It could be edited using splits on the Timeline and careful placement, then copy/pasting to the loop, but this is generally inaccurate and terribly slow.

2. In Peak Express, zoom in on the beginning of the file and select all audio from the beginning to the very first movement of the waveform indicator.

3. Press Command+X to delete all audio in the selection.

4. Go to the end of the file and select the very first transient in the attack of the third (last) drum hit, then highlight remaining audio to the end of the file. Again, select Command+X to delete all highlighted audio.

   Only the two drum hits should remain at this point.

In Peak Express, this is about all that can be done with the file, but it's plenty to prepare the file for use in the Loop Utility. At this point, save the file as an uncompressed .aif file. Next, open this loop in the Soundtrack Loop Utility and it is seen with its two beats and is loopable with metadatainserted. I've already saved a correct version of this file named *Bad Loop 1 edit.aif* for you to drop into the Loop Utility, compare, and work with. No metadata has been added.

If any other version aside from Peak Express is loaded on the computer, a great deal more can be done with the file. For example, this file could stand some compression, EQ, and potentially a touch of reverb to smooth out the fluctuations in the drum head. (This is a 36-inch drum with a leather head, so it has a lot of movement.)

If you are fortunate enough to have the full Peak v4.0, you can also use the Loop Surfer, Loop Tuner, Guess Tempo and many other tools (see Figure 5.18).

With any version of Peak other than the Express version, the audio can be reversed, creating a unique sound to introduce or mark the ending of a project. I've saved a reverse version of this loop

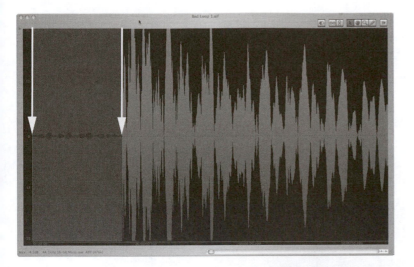

5.16 The selected area is audio that must be removed in order to start the audio on the attack of the drum.

5.17 After editing the Bad Loop 1 file, only two drum hits should remain of approximate equal length.

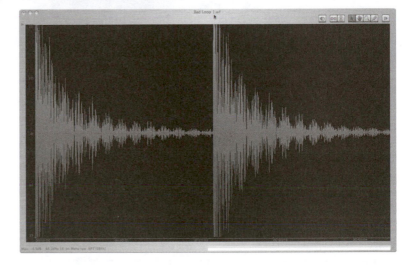

for your own use, named *Bad Loop 1-reverse.aif*. This single-hit loop is ready for your own use in Soundtrack.

One of the primary benefits of upgraded versions of Peak is the ability to import mp3 files from the hundreds of loop sites on the web. Many websites offer mp3 files as free loops, providing incentive for users to purchase higher-quality loops in wav or aiff format. However, converting these mp3 files cannot be accomplished in very many tools. Peak provides these conversion services and allows loops to be created with all versions of Peak except in the Express version.

Creating a loop of length in Peak is very simple.

1. Open any audio file in Peak, regardless of whether it's a loop or not.

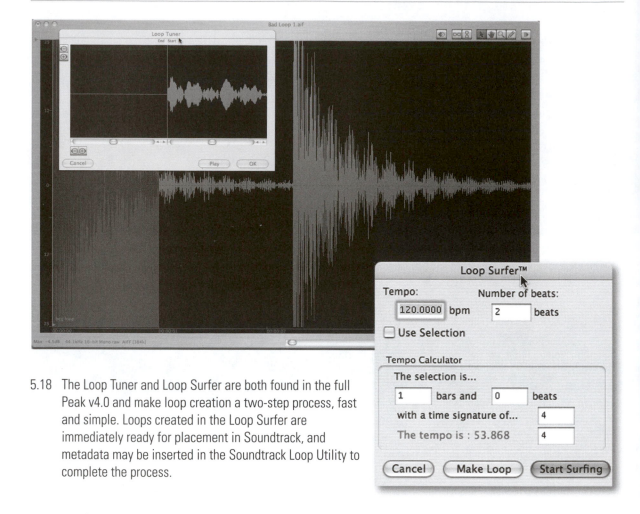

5.18 The Loop Tuner and Loop Surfer are both found in the full Peak v4.0 and make loop creation a two-step process, fast and simple. Loops created in the Loop Surfer are immediately ready for placement in Soundtrack, and metadata may be inserted in the Soundtrack Loop Utility to complete the process.

It could be a spoken word from your stock library, a sample from a record, a third party audio file, or it might be rain falling outside your window. Regardless, nearly any audio file can become a loop.

2. In the workspace window, click where you'd like the loop to begin and drag it to the point where the loop should end.

3. Press Command+L (Command+L) to enable looping in Peak.

Markers showing the Start/End point of the loop will be shown.

4. Click the Loop button in the transport window to begin playback.

The selected area between the Start and End points will play in a looped format.

If the file is correctly looping, seamlessly ending and beginning, then congratulate yourself. This is rarely accomplished in the first selection, which is why these looping tools are provided.

5.19   Press this button to loop playback of the file.

5.20   The looping Start and End points can be adjusted during real-time playback in Peak. *(below)*

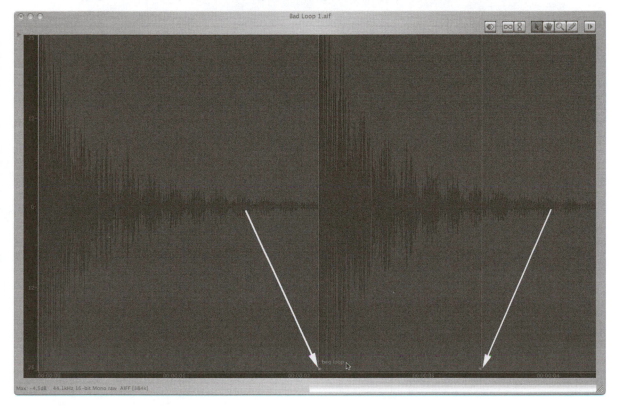

Fine tune the loop by moving the Start or End points backward or forward in time while the loop is playing back. These can be moved in real time, providing the ability to hear the loop points being edited as they occur in the file. Find a point where the loop ends and begins seamlessly. A hint is that if the loop is a spoken work file or another nonrhythmic file, leave a space at the end of the loop to allow the loop to end with a moment of separation, then the word or other audio begins again. If you have the full version of Peak, you can also call up the Loop Tuner to assist in the Start/End selection process, which will help find the best points for the loop points. This tool visually provides information surrounding the End/Start point that allows for easier looping.

Peak also allows for recording directly into the application. This provides some easier editing tools than Soundtrack, although it is at additional expense. To do true audio editing, this tool is indispensable.

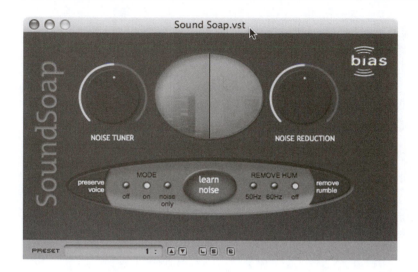

5.21   Bias Sound Soap plug in/
standalone application.

Peak also has created a tool known as Sound Soap. Sound Soap is a noise-reduction application that is fantastic for getting rid of room noise, camera motor noise, AC hum, hissing due to a poor preamp or noisy mic cables, and other noise sources from the audio file. It does this without affecting the original audio when it is used correctly.

Open the original *Finger Snaps.aif* file from the *Soundtrack Loops:Soundtrack Loops:PowerFX Loops:Percussion:Finger Snaps.aif* location. In the Bookloops folder on the CD in this book you'll find a *Finger Snaps-denoised.aif* file. Load them both on the Timeline. Listen to them side by side and note a fair amount of room noise. In a mix, this noise is acceptable, but solo this noise may prove to be distracting. The denoised version of the file has had all the room noise taken out. At first preview, it may seem that the Finger Snaps have had some of the high end taken out. When room noise is removed, some of the frequency response of a sound may be removed. In some files, there is a balance between noise and the relativity of noise and the actual audio content. Any time a sound is played in an open, live room, there is bound to be room noise, but the room noise interacts with the instrument or voice that's heard. Removing too much noise removes some of the interaction between room and instrumentation. In other words, expect some degradation of sound when a loop is denoised.

Removing constant, noninteractive noise, such as AC Hum, camera motor noise, or an air conditioner, is a little easier because it's not part of the original sound. This is exactly what Sound Soap was designed to do.

To use the plug in, load the audio file into the NLE or editor. Peak is great for this, but Sound Soap works well with FCP, some other NLEs and DAWs do as well.

After loading the audio, select an area that is noise-concentrated. Smaller selections are better than large selections. Open the Sound Soap application. Select Learn Noise from the Sound Soap

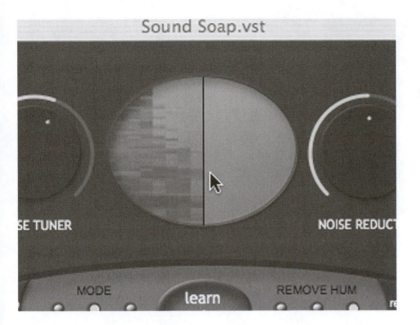

5.22 This graphic waterfall-type display helps to visualize the noise as it's being tuned and removed with the dials on the application.

dialog. Loop the playback of the file in the NLE/DAW if possible and use the Noise Tuner, then locate the sweet spot of the noise. The graphic display in the middle of the Sound Soap application shows the noise being "tuned" in real time. Once the noise has been dialed in, reduce the noise by using the Noise Reduction dial. This allows you to control the amount of noise removed. Consider it a volume control for the noise that can only turn the noise down.

Selecting the Noise Only radio button filters out the original sound and allows you to hear the actual noise being processed, so that the amount of original audio effected can be monitored. The Remove Hum radio buttons are tuned to various locations around the world. If you are using a 120 volt electrical system, such as in the USA, Canada, most of Mexico, select the 60Hz radio button. If you are in an area that is 220 volts, such as Europe, Australia, Africa, then use the 50Hz setting. This will automatically kill AC hum.

Many times, the Remove Rumble button alone is all that's needed for working with noise, particularly rumble generated from vibrating floors, low wind noise, or mic stand noise.

If most of the work in Soundtrack is to be done using loops and little to no recording is being done for custom loops, voice overs, or CD ripping, then the Express version of Peak may be enough for you. If recording loops, recording voiceovers, or downloading MP3 loops from the various websites is more your forte, then the LE, DV, or full version of Peak is valuable.

Finally, at the time of this writing, Bias had announced the release of Sound Soap Pro containing Hum & Rumble, Click & Crackle, Broadband, and Noise Gate filters arranged in specific order that allow users to remove all sorts of noise for mastering audio or high-level noise reduction in one step and with one tool (see Figure 5.23). This is set up so that there is no question or difficulty working with the applications that are often separate applications. When you process the

5.23   Hum & Rumble, Click & Crackle, Broadband, and Noise Gate are all part of the new Bias Sound Soap Pro application, which ships soon.

audio in separate applications, you can run into any number of problems. While I've not heard Sound Soap Pro as of yet, if it meets the quality of the other Bias tools, it's something to look at for the recording, video editing, or voice over environment.

While I don't often endorse specific products for general functions, I do recommend that regardless of the level of video or audio editing and composition work, the Sound Soap application provides tools that nobody recording or video editing should be without.

Sound Design

Sound design is an ambiguous term, usually dealing with creating sound for picture that isn't tied directly to Foley or canned sound. Sound design may involve any number of edited sounds. As a great example of sound design, the sound of a robot moving through steel bars in a science fiction film was created with the sound of dog food slowly falling out of a can. BB guns fired under water become torpedo tubes firing, and a marble inside a plastic bowl becomes a monstrous rolling stone. Soundtrack is not designed for creating these sorts of sounds, but many loops available from loop libraries are wonderfully suited for sound design in a sequential sense. While the loops cannot be edited in Soundtrack necessarily, FX can be added along with volume changes, pans, and automation of various FX processors in order to build designer sound and bring a great presentation of emotional stimulation to a shot. As an example, open the Tense Liftoff project from the CD in the book. A simple helicopter liftoff that contains no dialog becomes fairly tense when the background loops are used against the sound of the helicopter. Soundtrack can be used to output a transitional audio element that also contains emotion-inspiring pieces of music, sound elements, and designed effects to extract or inspire a feeling from the viewer and deepen the visual experience.

It was said earlier that sound is 70% of the visual experience. I often get looks as though I'm crazy when I say this, and although some video editors or shooters may think I'm nuts, try the following experiment.

Have a friend blindfold you for an hour. Just try an hour of no visual stimuli. Try walking down a street or go through the mall. You might look goofy, but you'll learn a lot about how many sounds are really happening around you and that there is truly no such thing as silence. Notice how the sounds blend together and how no single sound truly stands out unless you are in a specific area. Notice the placement of the sounds around you, right to left, foreground to background, bright tones closer than dull tones, which are in the distance. When a sound does reach out and grab your ear, it is often louder or unique to the environment. Use this discovery in your sound placement in the mix of score and sound design. While most directors will tell you picture is primary, that isn't as true today as it was years ago; viewers today have come to expect that if there is action on the screen, then there is audio to accompany it. Silence is as much a sound design tool as the DAW.

Color: Look at the colors in the image. Do they inspire emotions? For example, dark colors and dim lighting call for darker, more bass-oriented music in most situations, while bright colors, whites or near-whites call for higher end, "tinkly" sounds. Color washes might imbue a fast-moving composition, while slow, less-saturated colors might call for slower dynamics in the music. Red is a passionate, intense color, while blue and green hues are friendlier. Grays and blacks that dominate the screen often inspire ominous expressions in the composition.

Consider adding sounds totally unrelated to a scene. For instance, an opening door that leads to an intense or scary scene might call for a moaning voice to be mixed with the creaking of the door's hinges. In a film that I worked on, I was trying to paint the villain as an animal. So each time his motorcycle started and drove away, I added a lion's roar to the back of the exhaust. It fit perfectly with the throttle sound. The sound of cannons may be mixed with that of flashbulbs, or the sound of a rocket engine might accompany that of a beefy car. Golf swings create wonderful punches being thrown, or a toilet plunger or wallet striking a flat surface make for a great body impact sound, particularly with some bass/bottom end added for depth.

Sound design may be taken too far in terms of being too obvious or inappropriate for the scene. Many sound designers have said, "If you can hear what I've done, I've missed the goal." In other words, if the design and placement don't complement and enhance the visual, it can only detract from the scene, and this is not desirable.

Creating Audio for DVD Menus

DVD menus typically loop the audio in various menus structures, providing a seamless transition from the end of the menu video to the beginning of the menu. Properly done, this allows viewers of the DVD to see the menu repeatedly without jarring changes between the end of the menu and the beginning of the same menu when looped.

Soundtrack is ideal for creating these sorts of looped menu beds or underscores. The video portion of the menu may be created in FCP or another NLE, then imported to Soundtrack, and the score is created to match the exact length of the DVD menu. Soundtrack will provide a looped preview of the file with the video, giving a real-time preview of exactly what the menu will look and sound like once output from DVD Studio Pro or another authoring application.

In Soundtrack, import the m2v or .mov file that will be the menu. This sets the length of the project. If you'd like this to be totally foolproof for timing, drop a time marker at the end of the project, place the playhead at the beginning of the project, and select Project>Score Marker to Playhead. This creates an automatic tempo based on the project length.

The key to looping audio is to be sure that the audio starting the menu audio is the same as the audio finishing the menu. This does not mean that audio needs to be boring and contain no movement, it simply means that care must be taken to ensure that the end and beginning points of audio are the same file. It also helps to use a split loop if the beginning points of the audio move into another sound partway through the loop and the ending loop finishes at the same point.

To demonstrate this we'll set up a loop sequence that is 30 seconds in length. This is a common menu length, so it should realistically help you to understand future menu creation/looping sequences.

1. Locate your starting loop, any loop will do. For this exercise, we'll select the *Orchestral String Section 07* loop. Drop it on a new project, starting at Bar 1. Place the playhead in the middle of the loop, which should be at 3.1.000 on the Beat Time window. Split the file using the S-key.

2. Move the right half of the file to the end of the project, so that the end of the second half ends on the 30-second mark, which should read 16.1.000 in the Beat Time window, assuming that the project tempo has been left at the default of 120. After the split, Bars 3 through 13 are now empty (see Figure 5.24).

3. For this exercise, drag the right edge of the first half of the `Orchestral String Section 07` loop to the right until it meets the left edge of the last half of the original loop, thus filling the empty space between the loops in the Timeline. Now play the Timeline. Notice that the beginning and end of the loops on the Timeline are perfect and indistinguishable from each other.

   The reason for splitting the loop is that in some loops the beginnings and middle sections may not be the same, or you may wish to offset the incoming or outgoing portions of a loop. If the loop is to be used straight with no offset in the beginning or end of the loop, splitting the loop is not necessary, assuming that the loop is permitted to completely end at the end of the project.

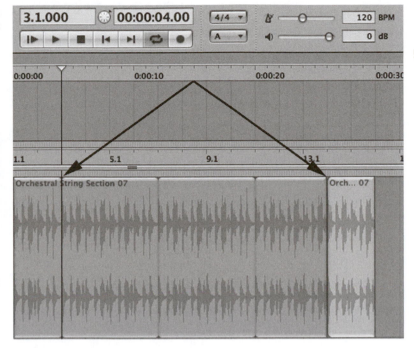

5.24 After splitting the Orchestral String Section 07 file, Bars 3 through 13 are empty to be filled later with other audio files, or the Orchestral String Section 07 loop may be dragged out to fill the empty space.

However, if a loop is not permitted to end at the end of the project, the starting point of the loop at the start of the Timeline must be the remaining portion of the last loop on the Timeline that was not permitted to end. Splitting loops like this makes it much easier to assure perfect looping.

4. Open the *DVD Menu 1* file from the CD in this book. This loop has been created with a variety of loops for a DVD menu, using the splitting technique described previously. Notice that various points have been placed in the project that may be used as punctuation points in the DVD menu, such as an image moving on the screen and the syncing sound movement with motion in the menu, etc. With the menu video in the Preview window, identify moments of movement and lay subtle or not-so-subtle audio files at those moments in time. Punctuation, or files enhancing a particular movement or action on the screen, does not need to be in time with the musical aspects of the project, so it may be off-time. The most efficient method of placing punctuation points is to disable snapping by pressing the G-key.

5. Use volume and pan points to create fades to bring sounds in and out; this helps keep the sense of movement in the loop without the menu appearing to be a loop. In fact, if sounds are not sudden in the menu, often viewers can watch a looped menu many times before realizing they are hearing a loop!

1. Open the *DVD Menu 2* project. This is a simple menu project, 30 seconds in length. This is an ethereal loop with some moments of tension, release, and intensity. The driving drumbeats pro-

vide a background for the play off of other sounds. In the case of the Electric Guitar Clangy loop, it uses heavy delay to cause the decay to carry over into the next transitional loop. Notice in the Electric Guitar Clangy loop that the last note of the loop has been removed. This is to prevent the loop from resolving, or leaving the door open for another sound to be introduced.

2. Drag the right edge of the Electric Guitar Clangy to the right, completing the loop and listening to what the resolution does to the project. It causes the next loop coming in to be out of place and grating on the ear because there is a sense of closure in the Electric Guitar Clangy loop.

3. Undo the drag by pressing Command+Z, then press the sideways triangle on the track header for the Electric Guitar Clangy track. This opens the Envelopes view. Notice the Stereo Delay Right/Left mix sends. This is what fades in the delay line used to fatten up and sustain the decay of the loop, keeping it echoing with the last notes of the loop. If the echo is left on for the entire loop, the guitar would become muddy and confusing to the ear. Tastefully bringing in a delay or verb on the end point of a loop gives the loop a sense of departing the soundstage, particularly if it's panned to the right or left as it's decaying. In Track 4, the Texture and Ambience loop, pan, delay, and volume are all used to give the loop a sense of movement through time and space.

4. If the envelopes are not visible, open the envelope view of Track 4 to view the automation taking place.

Finally, on Track 1 notice that the loop in place is the same loop for all 16 bars, but the loop has been split into four separate segments. Each segment has been transposed, creating a sense of musical arrangement even though nothing specific is actually taking place. The pad in the loop shifts in pitch, yet the drums in the loop appear to hold pitch as the movements are too small to have a dramatic effect on the drums.

5. To understand what happens to a mixed loop containing pitched and nonpitched instruments, Control+Click/Right-Click the last Looping Texture on Track 1.

6. Transpose the loop from –2 semitones to +5 semitones.

Oftentimes, DVD Menus are set loudly in the Hollywood menus, particularly the lesser budget films. I'm of the opinion that most of them are obnoxious in their mix and/or EQ. I suspect this phenomenon is due to monitoring menus on small speakers in sound-poor rooms, monitoring at quiet levels, or perhaps a mixture of both. Many menus in Hollywood are not created in audio facilities, but rather created by graphic designers that have little knowledge of audio. (I may easily be wrong on this, but I can't find any other explanation.) Check your mix on a good set of monitors at both loud and quiet settings. You might want to check the mix on a set of cheap monitors too, but if it sounds good on a decent set of monitors, it should sound great on a television. See Chapter 4 for more information on setting up a monitoring system.

7. Then play the project back while paying close attention to the drums in the Looping Texture. Notice that the drums start to "flam" or sound like they have artifacts. This is due to the instruments contained in the loop not being able to stretch to new pitches. The pad contained under the drums can shift pitch with no difficulty. The alternative is to build a new drum loop similar to the drums in the Looping Texture, creating a separate pad/drone track, and mixing the two together. Such a process allows a substantial amount of transposition to take place, providing greater flexibility of sound. It also requires many more tracks and a great deal of time, but if a particular key is required or called for to match a recorded instrument or vocal, it may well be worth the additional time to record.

8. After completing the project, export the mix by selecting File>Export Mix.

9. Save the file as an uncompressed QuickTime mix to a location that you'll be able to find when working with the DVD authoring application.

10. The mix can also be exported to FCP or another NLE application for combining the audio/video stream, or for further editing, so long as the length of the video does not change. Of course, the video and audio may be saved as a QuickTime file to be imported into a DVD authoring tool as well, potentially saving a step. If you save the audio file with the same name as the video menu file that you've been working with, most DVD authoring applications will import the audio file when the video file is imported.

Importing Menu Loops to DVD Studio Pro 2.0

DVD Studio v2.0 is capable of importing various audio file types including .aif, AC3, and .wav files. This means that even straight loops from a looping library may be added to DVD Studio Pro, even if they are Acidized .wav files. They will be converted once the DVD is assembled, compressed, and burned.

1. Adding audio as an asset in DVD Studio Pro v2.0 is accomplished by opening the Assets Palette, clicking on the Audio tab, and selecting the + or Add folder. Browse to the folder containing the finished audio file.

2. Then, holding the Command key, select the Main Menu Assets, the Main Movie Assets, and Slide Show Assets. Next, click the Add button.

   The folder/files selected now show up in the Audio tab listings of the Palette.

3. Select the Main Movie Assets window (see Figure 5.25).

   You'll now see your audio file loaded into the Main Movie Assets Audio list. Audio may also be kept in the Palettes menu.

4. Drag the file to the Menu Editor while holding the mouse button until the Set Audio pop-up menu appears (see Figure 5.26). The orange button indicates the audio may be dropped on the Menu Editor, setting the background audio for the DVD Menu.

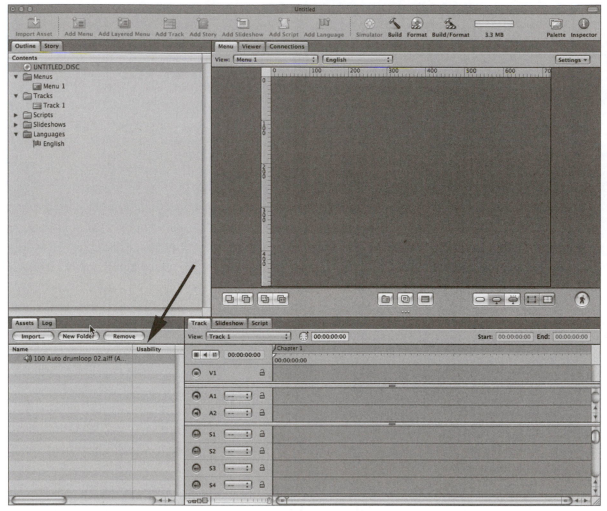

5.25 Find the Assets window in the lower left corner of the application.

By using hidden menus attached to an active button, DVD Studio Pro is even capable of providing an audio cue as each menu item is moused or buttoned over in a DVD menu. While this gets into a tutorial for another book, it's essentially an auto action hidden in buttons overlaid on the visible menu. One-shots found in the Soundtrack library are wonderful for this, but you can also record a single word or effect in Soundtrack, process the sound with the processing tools, and export it as a small QuickTime file from Soundtrack to import to DVD Studio Pro v2. *(Tip courtesy of Linda Dee, Indigenous Pictures)*

Don't forget that with the multiple audio tracks found in DVD Studio Pro v2, you can also create alternate musical scores in the place of language tracks. By placing a one-shot at the head of a chapter point, you can also introduce chapters in a unique and interesting manner.

5.26 Holding the mouse button, drag audio from the Palettes window to the Menu Editor workspace until this indicator appears.

Adding Audio to Flash

Flash animations can carry audio with the animation. Often, these animations loop and Soundtrack provides tools for adding audio loops. It's valuable to know the length of the Flash animation prior to creating the loop, otherwise the Soundtrack score may need to be revised once the Flash animation is made. Of course, if the audio is created first in Soundtrack, then the Flash animation may be synchronized to sound in the Flash application. If the general length of the Flash project is known, it's a simple matter to shift the tempo of the Soundtrack project up or down to match the length of the Flash animation exactly once it's completed. Flash is capable of importing a .wav, aiff, .mov, or MP3 file, however, Soundtrack can only export an aiff file. Soundtrack cannot import a .swf file, so there is no direct interaction between the Flash application and Soundtrack. Also, Flash may output QuickTime files that open in Soundtrack. This seems to be the easiest way of managing the Flash score. However, if the Flash project is not completed and requires creating the Flash project to sync with audio, the audio must be mapped out and potentially finished before the Flash project may be completed.

In Flash, audio may either be a streaming sound or an event sound, in addition to a start or stop instruction. Streaming sounds are synchronized to the animation and don't begin until sufficient data has downloaded to a browser. Event sounds will not play until completely downloaded.

For a file to be most efficient in the Flash animation, the sound should be compressed from its native setting of 44.1K/16bits to a compressed format that usually entails using a lower sample rate/bit rate. This enables both streaming and event sounds to download more efficiently. Flash can compress these sounds on its own or it can import pre-compressed sounds. Instruct Flash by selecting the sound in the library, then selecting Option>Properties. Setting files to 22KHz and mono is the standard in Flash, but smaller sampling rates may be used.

Insert audio by selecting Insert>Layer to create a new audio channel.

Most Flash designers tend to create a second Flash file to play on the Timeline, allowing the audio to be stopped/started at will. To import an aiff file to Flash:

1. Select File> Import

2. Select File, Click OK

3. Add a Sound to a Movie from library:

4. Select Insert> Layer

5. Select Insert> Keyframe

6. Select Modify> Frame

7. Select Sound Tab

8. Select Sound from Dropdown box

9. Access Sound Properties Dialog Box

10. Select File> Publish Settings, Select Flash tab

11. Modify the Sound Attributes in Frame Properties

12. Choose the number of times the audio file should loop from the loop box located on the sound palette.

13. View your Flash movie; reedit as needed.

At the end of the day, it all comes down to being creative, doesn't it? Tools and work techniques are all important, but the bottom line really comes down to every editor creatively generating a message, emotional experience, explanation or expose, singular masterpiece of the moment, a major life's work or a 30-second spot for commercial use. We each wish to provide the best possible product that we can create for the client's satisfaction and our own.

These tips and tricks are all a means of moving the technology aside and accessing the creative element within ourselves. Soundtrack finally allows nonmusicians to be musically expressive without spending a lifetime learning about Neapolitan sixth, odd meters, theory, harmony, contrapuntals, or even an instrument.

Soundtrack opens new doors for DVD authors, video editors, producers, directors, Flash animators, musicians, and anyone else who needs a sketchpad or musical finishing tool. Nonmusicians frequently surprise me with the compositions that they are able to create because they don't feel hindered by the rules of music. Rich Harrington, a highly regarded writer, editor, teacher, and friend, recently played a television commercial for me that he'd done with Soundtrack. I was astounded simply because of the brilliance in the composition. While a traditional musical concept would prevent a classical flute from appearing in the same composition as a banjo or mandolin, or an upright bass in a rock n' roll sound, the unconventional thought process of a nonmusician coupled with clever layering of instruments made for a wonderful sound. Don't feel like any rules need to be observed other than the technical rules related to output levels. Approach Soundtrack with the blind enthusiasm of a child with a new found talent or toy, and perhaps you'll find yourself composing a magnum opus.

Glossary

Some of these audio terms are relevant to Soundtrack specifically and other terms are related to the audio and video industry generally. Some of the terms are newly adapted from the analog world from which many features of Soundtrack and FCP are derived.

A/D Converter Analog to Digital Converter. Many A/Ds are also D/As, which convert Digital back to Analog for monitoring.

ACM Audio Compression Manager, developed by Microsoft as the standard interface for signal processing of audio data in the Windows environment, particularly geared towards the wav file format. Some tools allow custom ACM processes.

ADC Another name for Analog to Digital Converter.

ADR Automated Dialog Replacement. Also known as "looping" the dialog. Soundtrack may be used for this function, setting up a Multiple Take recording, having talent watch the preview screen, and speaking in time with previously recorded dialog. ADR is typically used to replace a poor field recording of dialog in a video or film project.

AIFF Audio Interchange File Format. Can be used for storing audio in high or low resolution formats and sharing them between computer systems. Format used by Soundtrack for loops and metadata information contained in the loops.

Amplitude The height of a waveform measured from the middle, where silence would be indicated. If no waveform is drawn, then the audio section is silent. The measurement from center to the highest point in the graphical drawing is the value of the amplitude.

Acoustic amplitude is measured in dB *(See decibels)*. The louder the signal, the higher the amplitude, regardless of the measurement format. (peak, RMS, Instant, etc.)

Asset Any digital file that is part of the library is considered an asset. The Soundtrack loop library contains over 4,000 assets.

Attack The first part of a sound heard, measured by the amount of time that the sound goes from silence to its loudest point. Attack time varies by instrument. For instance, a snare drum has a fast attack, but a cello pad has a slow attack.

Attenuate An analog term, referring to decreasing the audio level. Usually described in decibels.

AU Audio Units, Apple's interface for plug ins and software instruments. Provides real time scaling and adjustment to plug in parameters.

Audio File Audio stored in any digital format is an audio file. Not to be confused with audiophile, an audio aficionado.

Audio Meter A tool used to measure the volume level of audio in a DAW or NLE. Soundtrack provides two unique audio meters, one in the preview pane and the other on the far right of the workspace that is always visible.

Auto Pan Panning audio left to right, managed by inserted envelope points, moving automatically over time.

Automated Mix Mixing with envelope points, similar to keyframes, that control the volume of audio over time, removing the need to manually change volume of a track while audio is playing back. An automated mix function can manage several tracks of audio levels simultaneously.

Balance The difference in level or apparent loudness between right and left in a stereo audio signal. See *Pan*.

Balanced Cable A cable that contains two conductors carrying audio, plus a shield for the ground that carries no audio. Professional mic cables are always balanced.

Bandwidth The range of frequencies in an audio file, EQ, or other signal or device that passes a signal. This term also refers to the data rate of a streaming file.

Bass Low frequencies in the overall spectrum of sound. Bass is approximated in the 0–300Hz region of the frequency spectrum.

Batch Tags Soundtrack can batch process files and add tags while processing grouped files. Batch tags are tags inserted to a group of files, as opposed to being added to an individual file.

Beat A rhythmic recurrence in a piece of music. May be counted in a variety of note values.

Bed Background music or sound effect laid under a voice over. Typical term in television and radio.

Bit Depth The number of bits in a sample. The greater the number of bits, the greater the resolution of the audio file, and therefore the more accurate the digital file will reproduce the original audio image.

Boost Raising the volume of an audio signal

BPM Beats Per Minute

Brickwall When digital audio hits the 0dB threshold, bits are truncated and lost. This is known as "hitting the brickwall" because there is no recovery from lost bits. Digital form of distortion.

Bridge A bridge is a middle section or contrasting section of a song. Most songs contain a verse, chorus, and a bridge. The bridge is often referred to as the "middle eight", meaning middle eight bars.

Bright Descriptive term to describe high frequencies. If a sound is "bright," then it contains a number of high frequencies. If the sound is not bright, it may be considered dull and contain few high frequencies. Sibilance is typically bright, allowing breath and Ss, Ps, Ts, and other sibilant sounds to be heard.

Bumper Stock audio identifying the television, radio, or cable station, or perhaps designating a corporate audio identity, such as the famous Intel sound.

Bypass To disable a processor, such as a compressor or reverb. To bypass means that the processor/effect is left in place, but merely disabled.

Cardiod A microphone that has a heart shaped pickup pattern is referred to as a cardiod mic. Also referred to as a unidirectional mic.

Chain Multiple FX in a line are referred to as a chain of FX. Soundtrack allows FX to be chained.

Chorus (FX) A series of short, modulated delays with slight shifts in pitch to create the effect of multiple voices stemming from one voice. This effect allows a solo instrument to have the sound of an ensemble due to the slight differences in timing and pitch.

Chorus (music) A portion of a musical composition, often appearing as the "hook" or repetitive section, occasionally referred to as the refrain. More commonly known as a B section in the composition. Typically, a song contains the A section (verse) the B section or chorus, and C section (the bridge).

Circle of Fifths The circle consists of all 12 pitches, which are arranged in such a way that any pair of adjacent pitches represents the interval of a perfect fifth.

Click Track An audio track that serves as a metronome, typically recorded to tape or generated by the DAW or recording tool being used to record a performance. Provides a permanent and portable record of the timing used in the composition, and also aids performers in their performance precision, marking accurate beats.

Clipping Distortion, given its name from when audio is clipped off after exceeding maximum levels, can be caused at input, output or processing stages. In the digital realm, clipping becomes brickwalling.

Comp Track In professional recordings, multiple recordings are made of similar performances. The best portion of each performance is then extracted and assembled to a single track. This final track is a compilation of the bits and pieces extracted from performances, creating a final track that is the sum of all the best performances.

Compress (dynamic range) To reduce the amount of dynamic range of an audio signal, making the overall output more consistent. A compressor acts like an automated fader, bringing loud portions of an audio signal to a more quiet point, and raising the level of quiet sections to match louder transient peaks.

Compress (file size) Resampling, reducing a file size for streaming or sharing over the internet or intranet. Usually a lossy process, causing some loss of audio quality. REAL Media, MPEG, MJPEG, Microsoft wmv/wma are all examples of compressed media. Use Apple's Compressor to compress media.

Condenser Mic A mic that uses power for an electrostatic device rather than using inert magnets as an electromagnetic device. Power is supplied via a battery inside the microphone or via phantom power delivered to the microphone down the microphone cable, supplied from a mixer, soundcard, or specialized phantom power box.

Copyright Just as the word implies, the right to copy. Any composition is copyrighted as it's completed. No one has the right to copy the composition, video, or other art forms without the permission of the author of the work.

Cue A specific piece of music composed to play at a specific moment in time. The moment the composition is to play is called a Cue Point. A list of Cue Points is called a Cue List, generally determined in the Spotting Session. See *Spotting*.

Cue also refers to set up a piece of media (audio or video) to play at a specific trigger, such as a DJ cueing up music or video to play at the press of a button.

Cut To remove, delete a section from a digital event. Also refers to a composition, typically in album form, with the composition being a cut of an overall album. Also refers to reducing frequencies in an equalizer, as in "cutting the bass" from a mix, which means to reduce the amount of bass in a mix.

Cutoff Frequency The frequency that audio is deeply attenuated or reduced. Low pass and High pass filters both center around a cutoff frequency. The higher the cutoff, the less original audio is allowed to be heard.

DAW Digital Audio Workstation

DDL Digital Delay Line

Decay All sounds have a point at which they diminish. This is referred to as decay. Opposite of *Attack*.

Decibel (dB) A device of measurement. Describes electrical power referenced to one milliwatt so 0dBm is equal to one milliwatt, or 1m. dB may refer to dBu, dBv, dBm. To a listener, audio must be 6dB louder to appear to be twice as loud, while electronically only 3dB of voltage difference are required for the same result. This is why a 200-watt amplifier is not twice as loud as a 100-watt amplifier.

Descriptor Feature in Soundtrack that allows information about a file to be embedded in a file. See *Metadata*.

Destructive/Nondestructive Soundtrack and its Loop Utility are nondestructive editing processes in which the original files are not damaged during editing. Destructive editing alters the original file and cannot be recovered. In the DAW and NLE worlds, destructive editing is often used to save disk space. With the cost of hard drives coming down, destructive editing is less prevalent than it was not too long ago.

Detune A small amount of pitch shifting used to create a fatter, thicker sound. Detuning is not actually possible in Soundtrack, but the effect of detuning may be created by using octaves and half/double speed combinations of duplicated tracks. Chorus FX do a slight detune of the original audio signal.

Digitize Converting analog to digital audio. The moment analog audio is stored on a hard drive, by whatever means, it arrives there and becomes digitized.

Distortion The point at which audio no longer maintains its original integrity, intentionally or not. Audio that exceeds physical or electronic limitations becomes distorted. Also used as an effect, particularly on guitars, violins, and other stringed instruments. See *Clipping*.

Downbeat/Upbeat The first beat of a bar is the downbeat. This is marked as the "one" when counting music. The upbeat would be counted as the "four" in a count, or beat just prior to the downbeat. The term comes from the maestro's hand movements when conducting an orchestra.

Dry Audio signal containing no processing. Opposite of *Wet*.

Ducking A device that uses one audio signal to lower another one. If a music bed is playing and a narration comes in over top, the narration track would force the music bed to reduce volume so that the narration track can be heard. In Soundtrack, volume envelopes are used to "duck" primary audio beneath other audio elements.

Dull Opposite of *Bright*. Sound that is dull lacks high frequencies. May be perceived as unexciting.

DV Digital Video

Dynamic Range The difference between loud and quiet passages in an audio performance. Sometimes referred to in terms of how loud audio is permitted to go without distortion or how quiet audio may go before noise is heard.

Dynamics Varying levels of amplitude that audio demonstrates throughout the project.

Early Reflection Direct reflections of audio occurring within the first 20–100ms. Sometimes referred to as "small wall" reflections. Soundtrack's reverb tools simulate these small wall reflections. Also, sometimes referred to as PreDelay, or a delay before a delay.

Echo Sound reflecting off of surfaces displaced from the original source, such as a canyon wall, distant walls. Any audio delayed by more than 50ms (milliseconds) is considered an echo.

EDL Edit Decision List

Effects (FX) Signal processors are referred to as Effects or FX. Reverbs, choruses, delays, phasers, flangers, are all referred to as FX.

Envelope A graphic display of a volume, pan, or FX control, allowing automated control over the behavior of specific parameters in the mixing of sounds. Also referred to as the acoustical contour of a sound, its Attack, Decay, Sustain, and Release. (ADSR)

Envelope Point A handle or node inserted on an envelope in Soundtrack, used to control various parameters of volume, pan, and automated FX functions.

Equalizer (EQ) A plugin that allows specific frequencies to be manipulated and controlled. Bass, mid range, treble frequencies are all broken down into specific bands and are controllable via sliders or dials, to cut or boost specific frequencies. This is one of the most important tools found in any DAW or NLE tool, as it allows specific contouring and shaping of audio events to help it fit more easily with other audio events.

Export Sending media from one application to another, such as exchanging audio from Soundtrack to Final Cut Pro v4 is an export process. See *Import*.

Fade A gradual decrease or increase of video or audio. Audio fades from audible to silent, video fades from visible to black. A fade may also be used to transition from one event to another. (crossfade)

Favorites Soundtrack allows commonly accessed audio files to be added to a favorites folder, allowing quick access to these files.

Feedback Live audio feeding a microphone feeding a speaker, which in turn regenerates itself from speaker to microphone, creating a loop, increasing in volume, and potentially damaging speakers, microphones, or ears. Mic/headphone feedback is common in a recording studio. Reducing speaker volume solves this problem.

File Browser Soundtrack's file browser allows users to browse through the computer files, locating specific video or audio files to be used in a project.

Final Cut Pro Apple's professional video editing application. Final Cut Pro v4.0 comes with Soundtrack, Compressor, and LiveType.

FireWire An IEEE1394 High bandwidth/high speed interface created by Apple as an industry standard for file I/O, not limited to, but commonly related to video and audio. Also used as a hard drive interface.

Flanger From the recording reel flanges being held during the process of recording. Modulation, delay, and phase cancellation combine to create the effect of flanging. Similar to chorusing, with a slower delay and speed of modulation.

Foley The art of creating ambient sound for film, synchronized with action on the screen. A Foley room used to record audio for film contains various surfaces and equipment to simulate or imitate sounds heard in the field recorded audio for film/video.

Frame Film moves at 24 frames per second, meaning that 24 individual pictures or "frames" are required for each second of film/video. An extracted still image, as well as the place where the playhead parks in Soundtrack, is referred to as a frame. NTSC video moves at 29.97 frames per second, and PAL video moves at 25 frames per second.

Frequency In audio, this refers to how fast a waveform or audio signal repeats itself. Measured in Hertz. Low frequencies are 20Hz–250Hz, midrange frequencies are 250Hz–2000Hz or 2KHz, and high frequencies are 2KHz–20KHz.

Fundamental The base tone, key, or frequency of an audio signal. This is usually referred to as a base pitch. Usually the lowest tone in a particular musical scale. Soundtrack sets the fundamental key with the dropdown menu. The default fundamental key in Soundtrack is the key of A.

Gain The amount that a sound is amplified from its original value; the change in its power point. See *Amplitude*.

Gate A process by which a threshold is set and audio not as loud as the threshold point is unable to pass via a "gate" opening and closing. Used for preventing noise to enter a mix in a live session, to quiet noise in recording sessions, and, in Soundtrack, to eliminate background noise or shut off a reverb for effect. Phil Collins/Hugh Padgham made this effect very popular on snare drums and tom toms back in the mid 70s.

Genre A hint or musical descriptor that may be used in Soundtrack's Loop Utility or Media Manager's search function.

Hints One of the forms of metadata that may be inserted in the Soundtrack Loop Utility or used to search/sort loops in the Media Manager.

Hz Abbreviation for Hertz. KiloHertz is abbreviated KHz and Megahertz is abbreviated with MHz.

I/O Abbreviation for In/Out. Relating to Soundtrack, generally referring to hardware used to get audio in or out of a computer. See *AD Converter*.

Import To open a file in an application that originated in another application. Soundtrack can import .wav, aiff, mov, and m2v files.

Key One of 12 possible keys, specified for musical foundation of a composition. The default key in Soundtrack is A-major.

Keyword A word or words embedded in the name of a file to aid in the search of files using Soundtrack's Media Manager.

KHz KiloHertz, (Hz) abbreviated KHz.

Latency The processing time between audio's origin or trigger point and when the signal is actually heard. Latency above 10 milliseconds (ms) is unacceptable in a recording situation, as there is no way to properly match recorded audio with audio being recorded, resulting in out of time files.

Lavalier A small microphone, also referred to as a lapel or clip microphone. Usually "lavs" are condenser microphones, requiring outside power to function.

Layback Importing, matching, and dubbing a finished score or soundtrack back to the video master. Exporting audio from Soundtrack and importing to FCP for final rendering, for instance, can be considered a layback.

Layover Recording audio from an analog source to a multitrack, DAW, or audio portion of an NLE.

Layout The manner in which a workspace or surface is defined and viewed. Soundtrack permits single or split window layouts.

Limiter A limiter is a processor that specifies a maximum output level to either create a specific sounding effect, or to prevent output above a specified level, allowing the user to avoid constantly adjusting loud passages downward in volume. A limiter is actually just a hard compression processor.

Loop A segment or slice of audio that repeats without any indication of the end of the segment adjoining the beginning of the segment. Loops are the foundation of the Soundtrack application. Loops may be in the aiff or wav format in Soundtrack.

M&E Industry term for Music and Effects.

Marker An indicator of time, beat, or cue in Soundtrack or FCP. FCP allows the insert of scoring markers that export to Soundtrack.

Master The finished product after a final mix has been created and the final mix components have been finalized with all EQ, compression, and volume settings. The final product on hard disk, tapes, or authored DVD is referred to as The Master.

Measure   A specific length of music containing the number of beats in the project's time signature. A 4/4 time signature contains four beats per measure. Indicated by grid lines in Soundtrack.

Media Another term for a file, related to audio, video, graphic, etc. in the digital environment.

Media Manager Soundtrack's tool to locate all media importable to Soundtrack. Contains a File Browser, Search Utility, and Favorites tabs.

Metronome A software or hardware device that indicates precise tempo, allowing time to be measured for performance purposes. See *Click track*.

Mic Abbreviation for microphone.

MIDI Abbreviation for Musical Instrument Digital Interface.

Midrange Audio found in the frequency bandwidths of 250Hz–2000Hz (2KHz).

Monitor Any device that allows audio or video to be seen or heard. Audio monitors are in the form of speakers or headphones; video monitors are in the form of a television, CRT, or LCD.

Mono A single channel of audio information as opposed to stereo audio containing two channels.

MOTU Abbreviation for Mark of the Unicorn.

MP3 MPEG Audio Layer 3 compression format. Used to compress files for delivery over the internet or for playback on portable hardware devices to save space and bandwidth.

MPEG Abbreviation for Motion Picture Experts Group, a group that defined a standard for compression of video or audio media.

Multimedia Media/files that contain audio, video, graphics, MIDI, animation, or text in any combination. Broadly used term to describe nearly any form of media.

Mute A software or hardware switch that prevents audio from being heard on a channel or channels. Soundtrack has a mute switch/button on every channel.

Near Field Monitors Small reference monitors/speakers within close proximity of the engineer/editor. Used in small rooms or for monitoring at low volume levels in larger rooms. Generally less fatiguing to the ear.

Needle Drop Separated use of a copyrighted composition. Needle drops require a royalty to be paid to the publisher each time the musical composition is played.

NLE Nonlinear editor.

Normalize A digital process for increasing the level of an entire audio files to a preset level without clipping.

NTSC National Television Standards Committee. (Sometimes humorously referred to as Never The Same Color.)

Nudge Slightly moving a handle, node, or loop in Soundtrack using arrow keys.

Octave The interval between two notes, six whole tones, or twelve half steps apart that bear the same name; thus, C natural to C natural. An augmented octave is C natural to C sharp; a diminished octave, C natural to C flat.

Omnidirectional The pick up pattern of a microphone that "hears" or picks up sound in 360 degrees. Usually used in a recording situation, rarely used in live audio.

One shot An audio file in Soundtrack that does not contain looping information, but is intended to play once, not necessarily in time.

Output Getting audio out of the computer to an analog speaker, digital output via SPDIF, AES/EBU, or other file format external to the computer.

Pad Attenuation of the original audio level. See *Attenuation*.

PAL Phase Alternation Line. Most all countries use PAL outside of the US and Japan. (Sometimes jokingly referred to as Picture At Last.)

Pan Abbreviation for Panorama, or moving audio across the audio spectrum left to right, front to back, or a combination of both. Each channel in Soundtrack contains a pan control that may be automated.

Peak Audio level's maximum point in a file. Also the name of two channel audio editing software from Bias, Inc.

Pitch Relative note to a key, also relative to a frequency. How high or low it sounds relative to key.

Playback Listening/monitoring the recording after it's been laid to hard drive or tape. Reviewing the audio file as it's being composed. Also referred to as "Previewing", which makes no sense because you are not viewing the video or audio prior to any edit, instead listening or watching video post edit.

Playback region A defined region on the Timeline of Soundtrack that plays only within that region, looping repeatedly.

Playhead Where the cursor lies within the DAW or NLE application. Cursor and playhead are generally interchangeable.

Plug-in DAW or NLE term referring to audio or video processors that may be used to supplement the application's audio or video editing tools. Reverbs, compressors, EQs, etc., are all plugins to the Soundtrack application.

Post Fade Audio that is allowed to be heard after the track fader has been lowered to its lowest point, usually through an FX bus or control. Processing level controlled by channel fader level.

Post Roll Audio or video that continues to playback after its out point. The opposite of Pre roll.

Pre Fade Audio that is allowed to be processed regardless of fader position. Fader may be set to all off, yet audio is heard via processing or bussing.

Pre Roll Audio playback that begins before a specified In point.

Preset Predetermined parameters of a plug-in, template, or other predetermined setting for an application.

Preview Viewing or listening to media from an application. In Soundtrack, preview is defined by watching video associated with a project and listening to audio loops/compositions assigned to the video, or listening to playback of a musical composition with or without video. See *Playback*.

Project A collection of audio files, video files to be assembled for a final product.

QuickTime Apple's multimedia player application.

RAM Abbreviation for Random Access Memory

Region A predetermined space/time on the Timeline in any DAW or NLE application, controlling playback area/time. A segment of audio or video that may be separately managed for editing.

Release The time it takes for an audio event to drop from its sustained level to zero. The last stage in ADSR. See *Attack, Decay, Sustain*.

Render To blend all multimedia files together in one master file format. Akin to baking a cake from all its individual ingredients.

Reverb Reflected sound waves in a given environment of various angles and surfaces. Simulated reverb may be accomplished with springs or digital devices, including software modeled after physical spaces. Soundtrack contains reverb processing to simulate a sound being reproduced in large or small physical spaces.

RGB Abbreviation for Red, Green, Blue.

Roll Off The point at which frequencies are filtered out. A low frequency rolloff will rapidly diminish frequencies beginning at the specified point. See *Attenuation*.

Room Tone The practice of recording the ambience of a room pre or post recording for purposes of dropping into edited "silent spots" to mask edit points. Room tone may be simulated with wind, hiss, hum, traffic noise, atmospheric sounds, etc., at low volume levels to hide edit points. The personality of a particular room or environment. May be pleasant or not.

Root Note The base or lowest note in a given scale.

Ruler A linear measurement in a Timeline as related to Soundtrack.

Rumble Low frequencies too low to actually be clearly heard but taking up audio information space. Footsteps, vibrations, motors all create rumble. Many mixing/recording consoles incorporate rumble filters, set to approximately 60–75Hz, rolling low frequencies off at that point to clean up audio. See *Roll off*.

Sample A "photograph" or capture of audio at a fixed time interval, converting analog to digital information. Sample level is the lowest form at which audio may be viewed and edited. Soundtrack does not provide sample level accuracy while Peak does.

Sample Rate The interval and resolution at which audio is "photographed" or measured. Audio CDs are sampled at a rate of 44.1K and 16bits. Soundtrack is capable of much higher resolutions and sample rates.

Scale Series of notes differing in pitch in a given range. Scales are predominantly major or minor, but there are other, less common scale types. Soundtrack recognizes major and minor scales.

Scratch Vocal A temporary vocal recorded to mark time or make compositional decisions to be replaced at a later time when arrangement and composition are closer to a finished stage. Often used as a reference for composers, editors, and musicians.

Search Asking Soundtrack's Media Manager to locate files based around specified parameters is known as a Search.

Segment One of several parts or pieces that fit with other parts to constitute a whole audio file.

Semitone A half-step in a musical scale. An octave contains 12 semitones.

Sensitivity The level at which the Soundtrack Loop Utility looks for and recognizes transients within an audio file or segment.

Session A space of time dedicated to recording audio. Each time a new recorded file is created, it may be referred to as a session. Digidesign's ProTools uses this term for their basic document of assembled elements.

SFX Abbreviation for Sound Effects.

Sibilance The hissing sounds of the human voice, most noticed in Ss, Ps, and Ts. High frequencies, sometimes challenging to control. Use a DeEsser plugin or an EQ to control this phenomenon.

SMPTE Society of Motion Picture and Television Engineers. Also used as a timecode reference. Soundtrack has no SMPTE capabilities.

Snapping Value The point at which Soundtrack snaps audio or cursor to a moment in time. Definable as accurate as 1/64th in Soundtrack.

Snap To The snapping value at which Soundtrack is set. See *Snapping Value*.

Solo A button or switch that allows a single channel to be monitored. Mutes all other audio during playback when engaged. Soundtrack offers a solo button on all tracks.

Source Audio Audio from the original program media. In a video file, this is on location sound or audio related to the original source and is often replaced or enhanced.

Spot Announcement for broadcast, a commercial for example.

Spotting Identifying and documenting cues for music, effects, sound design, or other audio information should occur. See *Cue*.

Stereo Two channel audio, consisting of similar or dissimilar audio spread across the left/right spectrum. Two separate mono channels separated to one left and one right, would not be considered stereo, but rather dual mono. Stereo mixes in Soundtrack consist of placing elements on the multi track timeline in representations of their occurrence across the left/right spectrum, and then mixed to a two channel/stereo mix reflecting the positioning of audio elements.

Streamer Slug or graphic overlay on video playback, marking exact points that a cue is to take place. Functions as a visual hit point or Cue. See *Cue*.

Subwoofer Speaker enclosure optimized to reproduce sounds from 20Hz–125Hz.

Sustain The points after an audio elements Attack has taken place, and Decay has begun. The length of time the sound maintains existence. The S in ADSR. See *Attack, Decay, Release*.

Sweet Spot The prime listening area between two speakers in a stereo environment or a 5.1 listening environment. This is the point that all audio channels are most precise, arriving at the same location at the same time. A relatively small area in most any listening environment.

Sweeten Polishing or improving an existing recording through adding other parts to the composition or audio elements. Processing of sound is also considered sweetening. Anything done to original audio in order to enhance it's quality.

Sync Abbreviation for synchronize. A means of ensuring events consistently occur at the same time. Time Code is generally a common source to assure events being in sync.

T/C Abbreviation for Time Code.

Tags 1. Another term for metadata found within Soundtrack's loop files. Also a term for an empty space at the end of a commercial or advertisement for a local business might insert their own recorded information. In a 30 second commercial, 23 seconds might be recorded for a national ad, with seven seconds left blank for local information to be added. Sometimes referred to as a "doughnut." 2. A musical term related to repeating an ending phrase; an outro.

Tempo The speed at which music is played back. Counted in Beats Per Minute. Length of a song equals tempo x time. See *Glossary Chart*.

Time Signature Indicates time/meter of a composition. Soundtrack recognizes several time signatures.

Timeline The main workspace in Soundtrack, a linear depiction of time.

Timeslice Selection of all time in the Soundtrack interface. Also carries different meanings outside the Soundtrack realm.

Tonic The base note of a scale. See *Fundamental*.

Track An individual line containing audio loop elements. Soundtrack may have up to 126 individual tracks.

Track Controls Parameters controllable in a track header. Soundtrack allows FX, Pan, Volume, Mute, Solo, and automation envelopes to be controlled at the track level.

Transfer rate How fast a disk drive or CD drive can transfer information to the CPU. May be a burst rate or sustained rate. High cache levels (8 meg) or larger assist in providing information to the CPU at fast rates, important when running several tracks of loops in Soundtrack.

Transient The difference between the lowest point of decay and highest point of attack in an audio file. Soundtrack uses transients to detect beats.

Transport Play, record, stop, rewind, fast forward, record are all functions of the Transport in Soundtrack. The Transport tools control position of playback and the playhead.

Transpose The act of moving the relative pitch of a composition or loop.

Treble The high end of the audio frequency spectrum, generally 2KHz and above.

TRS Tip, Ring, Sleeve audio connector.

Underscore Background music, not necessarily musically composed, to create an emotional atmosphere or environment. Similar to, and often called a music bed. See Bed.

USB Abbreviation for Universal Serial Bus.

Video File In Soundtrack, this is relevant to QuickTime or m2v files, data files that contain video information.

Viewer The Preview window in Soundtrack, containing the video preview, Audio library, and Meter views.

Volume The indicator for overall level of a loop, track, or master project output level.

Walla A sound effect term. In the early days of radio, it was found that background voices best were created by several actors repeating the word "walla" over and over, as it has no hard consonants to interfere with primary dialog.

Wave (.wav) The Microsoft designator for audio file formats, a common file type. Used by ACID® and many other libraries as a file format.

Waveform A graphical representation of audio on a timeline in a DAW, NLE, or music tool like Soundtrack. Drawn to indicate amplitude of an audio file.

WAVES A software plug in company, makers of some of the finest audio plugins in the world. Only AU shelled plug ins will work in Final Cut Pro and Soundtrack.

Wet The ratio of processed versus unprocessed sound from an effect plug in. A totally wet sound contains no original audio. See *Dry*.

Workspace The primary work surface in Soundtrack, main window where most of the work is performed.

Index

Updates

Want to receive email news updates for *Using Soundtrack*?
Send a blank email to soundtrack@news.cmpbooks.com. We will
do our best to keep you informed of software updates and
enhancements, new tips, and other Soundtrack-related
resources.

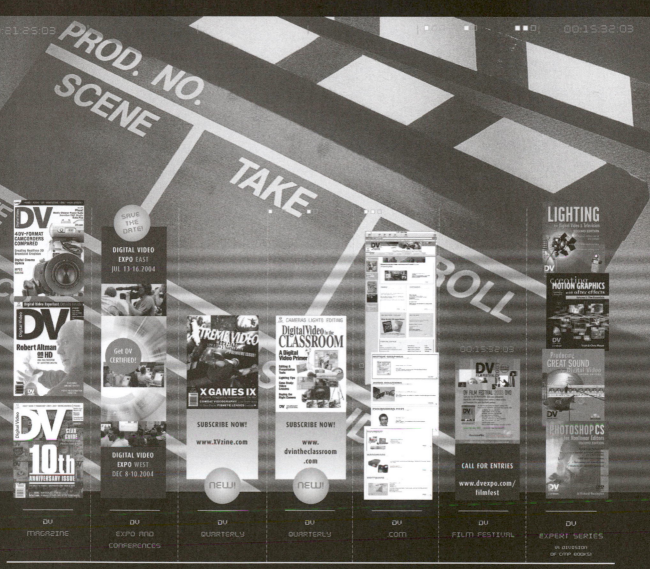

Producing Great Sound for Digital Video, 2nd Edition

by Jay Rose

"A careful reading of Producing Great Sound *will help any film-maker avoid huge disappointments in the edit room."*
—S.D Katz, *millimeter* magazine

Produce compelling audio with this arsenal of real-world techniques to use from pre-production through mix. You get step-by-step tutorials, tips, and tricks so you can make great tracks with any computer or software. Features expanded sections on microphones: boom, lav, and wireless techniques. The companion audio CD contains sample tracks, demos, and diagnostic tools.

$44.95, Softcover with Audio CD, 428pp, ISBN 1-57820-208-6

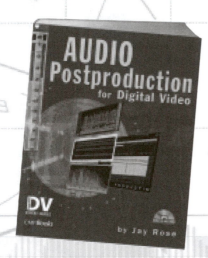

Audio Postproduction for Digital Video

by Jay Rose

"The best audio text on the practical and technical aspects of audio for digital video postproduction." — Bob Turner's *The Cut* e-newsletter

Perform professional audio editing, sound effects work, processing, and mixing on your desktop. You'll save time and solve common problems using these "cookbook recipes" and platform-independent tutorials. Discover the basics of audio theory, set up your post studio, and walk through every aspect of postproduction. The companion audio CD features tutorial tracks, demos, and diagnostics.

$44.95, Softcover with audio CD, 429pp, ISBN 1-57820-116-0

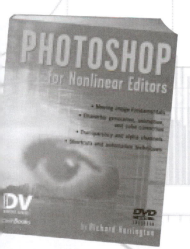

Final Cut Pro 4 Editing Essentials

by Tom Wolsky

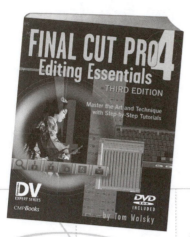

Master the craft of editing with Final Cut Pro 4. This editing workshop gives you firsthand experience with the art and technique of editing using eight tutorial lessons that cover the essentials: capturing your material, organizing it, editing, adding transitions, employing basic titling and sound techniques, and outputting from the application. The companion DVD contains tutorial media and plug-ins

$29.95, Softcover with DVD, 284pp, ISBN 1-57820-227-2

Final Cut Pro 4 On the Spot

by Richard Harrington & Abba Shapiro

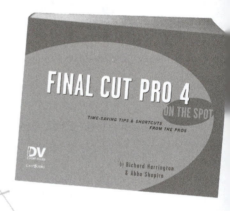

Learn what you need to know—when you need to know it. Packed with more than 350 expert techniques, this book clearly illustrates all the essential methods that pros use to get the job done. Experienced editors and novices alike will discover an invaluable reference filled with techniques to improve efficiency and creativity.

$27.95, Softcover, 236pp, ISBN 1-57820-231-0

Creative Titling with Final Cut Pro

by Diannah Morgan

Create compelling title sequences using Final Cut Pro and LiveType. Packed with four-color illustrations, explanations, instructions, and step-by-step tutorials, this book teaches and inspires editors to produce work that is a cut above the rest. Covers conceptualization, design, methodology, and the mechanics of successful title sequences.

$44.95, 4-color, Softcover, 192pp, ISBN 1-57820-225-6

Available in North America only

MULTIMEDIA / DIGITAL VIDEO / DIGITAL AUDIO

CD-ROM INCLUDE

"Ideally we'd all learn Soundtrack from someone who is a skilled musician and understands the structure of music ... I can't think of a better person to unlock its power for the rest of us than the very talented Douglas Spotted Eagle."
— Philip Hodgetts, *DV Guy* and president of Intelligent Assistance, Inc

Douglas Spotted Eagle is a virtuoso performer, pre-eminent music producer, and noted videographer. The recipient of the first-ever Grammy award for Native American music in 2001, he also has received Emmy, Peabody, Dupont, and Telly awards. Currently under contract with Virgin/Higher Octave, he has recorded 14 solo albums and collaborated on more than 300 CD, film, and television projects. Widely recognized as an authority in the ACID product knowledgebase, he has created music loops for Sony Pictures Digital ACID—loops that work well in Soundtrack.

Finish your video and multimedia projects with compelling audio tracks. All it takes i Soundtrack, the ability to count to four, and a measure of musicianship. More than guide to the software, this fully-illustrated guide to Soundtrack delivers the work knowledge you need to master the aural aspects of your project. Music and aud concepts are presented on a need-to-know basis. Practical examples and tutorials demonstrate how to use the tools to create audio that meets the s high standards as your video.

Music composition—the practice of assembling various pieces of medi create an exciting musical message—is analogous to video editing. A like video editing, there are principles and techniques that help to en quality production. As a renowned musician, video editor, and teach author Douglas Spotted Eagle is eminently qualified to help you to realize your musicianship.

Edit, mix, record sound, and use loops and effects to create trac with the confidence that you have practical training. All the whi use the Soundtrack shortcuts and workflow-integration techniq that audio pros use to speed production.

The companion CD includes tutorial materials, plug-ins, and hundreds of dollars worth of royalty-free loops.

User Level: Novice to Advanced

Includes original loops worth hundreds

$34.95 / CAN $48.95 / UK £25.99
ISBN 1-57820-229-9

DV
Digital Video
®
EXPERT SERIES

CMP Books

CMP
United Business Media